When Father Kills Mother

Guiding children through trauma and grief

Second edition

Jean Harris-Hendriks,
Dora Black and Tony Kaplan

London and Philadelphia

First edition published in 1993
Second edition first published 2000 by Routledge
11 New Fetter Lane, London EC4P 4EE

Simultaneously published in the USA and Canada
by Taylor & Francis Inc
325 Chestnut Street, Philadelphia PA 19106

Routledge is an imprint of the Taylor & Francis Group

© 1993, 2000 Jean Harris-Hendriks, Dora Black and Tony Kaplan

Typeset in Times by Keystroke, Jacaranda Lodge, Wolverhampton
Printed and bound in Great Britain by Biddles Ltd, Guildford and King's Lynn

British Library Cataloguing in Publication Data
A catalogue record for this book is available from the British Library

Library of Congress Cataloging in Publication Data
A catalogue record for this book has been requested

ISBN 0–415–19627–2 (hbk)
ISBN 0–415–19628–0 (pbk)

When Father Kills Mother

Children bereaved by the death of one parent at the hands of the other, almost always the father, in effect lose both parents, and are often forgotten in the midst of such dramatic situations.

Reflecting the increased interest in child protection and child law systems, this second edition of *When Father Kills Mother* brings to public knowledge, in amplified form, information about the effects of psychological trauma and bereavement on children. By combining knowledge about bereavement with that of post-traumatic stress disorder, the book remains informative and essential reading for all those involved in the field, both professionally and personally.

Jean Harris-Hendriks is Honorary Consultant to the Traumatic Stress Clinic, Camden and Islington Community Health Services NHS Trust, London, and Honorary Senior Lecturer, Royal Free Hospital and University College Medical Schools, London. **Dora Black** is Honorary Consultant Child and Adolescent Psychiatrist, lately, Director, Traumatic Stress Clinic, Camden and Islington Community Health Services NHS Trust, London, Honorary Consultant to the Royal Free Hospital, Great Ormond Street Hospital for Children and the Tavistock Clinic, and Honorary Senior Lecturer, Royal Free Hospital and University College Medical Schools, London. **Tony Kaplan** is Consultant Child and Adolescent Psychiatrist in the Enfield Child Guidance Service, and Honorary Consultant and Senior Lecturer, Traumatic Stress Clinic, Camden and Islington Community Health Services NHS Trust, London.

To our parents

Contents

Preface
Confidentiality

Each child bereaved by family violence has a story which is unique, yet these stories have common patterns too. We wish to bring alive these tragedies, so personal yet so universal, in ways which will alert all those who read them to the common themes of loss, trauma and dislocation.

What we have done, therefore, is to create and illustrate new stories, none of which is based on an individual child but which all cast light upon the common tragedy. The recurrent dilemmas faced by parents, carers, other relations and the professionals are illustrated in the same way.

We have chosen first names for the children in each story, adding invented surnames where there is need to refer to a parent or other relative. Any resemblance to real-life family names or circumstances is coincidental.

Acknowledgements

We are grateful for advice, consultation and help with the creation of clinical stories to: Gordana Batinica, Judith Bevan, Anita Colloms, Andy Cotgrove, Ricky Emanuel, Steven Isaacs, Deborah Lee, Annette Mendelsohn, Joanne Morris-Smith, Margarita Wood and Linda Zirinsky; to Bob Blizard and Amanda King for statistical advice; and to Ann Shearer for helping us to make the book more readable.

Our grateful thanks are due to Christine Fuller, Stephanie Hamer, Sandra Kalabza, Fred Morris and Catherine White for their work on preparation of the manuscript.

Second edition

Michael Grosvenor-Meyer advised on the Introduction; Martin Newman collaborated in the revision of Chapters 1 and 2; Judith Bevan and Annette Mendelsohn with the revisions of Chapters 5 and 8. Kirsten Huitfeld contributed to the stories in Chapter 8; Philippa Hyman, Jill Knox, Lisa Strickland-Clark and Tracy Thorns contributed to Study II, Chapter 12.

Esther Levy and Donna Shears have given permission for their stories to be included in Chapter 10.

We thank Diana Hendriks for sub-editing and preparing the manuscript for this edition.

We also acknowledge permission to quote from the following sources:

Chapter 1 Isaac Rosenberg (1937) *Collected Works*, edited by G. Bottomley and G.W. Harding (eds), Chatto & Windus, London.

Chapter 2 Donald Atkinson (1991) 'A sleep of drowned fathers'. Permission of the author. Peterloo Poets, Cornwall.

Chapter 3 A.L. Hendriks (1987) 'The feathers'. Permission of the author's estate.

Chapter 4 Roland John (1992) 'Celebrants'. Permission of the author. Headland Press, Merseyside and Spacex Literature, Devon.

Chapter 5 Peter Dale (1992) 'The Old Path'. Permission of the author. Hippopotamus Press, Somerset.

Chapter 6 John Cotton (1992) 'Clearing the house'. Permission of the author. Headland Press, Merseyside.

Chapter 8 Alan Harris (1992) 'Trapdoor'. Permission of the author's estate. Headland Press, Merseyside.

Chapter 9 Robert Louis Stevenson (1912) *Poems*. Chatto & Windus, London.

Chapter 10 R. Gabriele S. Silten (1991) 'High tower crumbling'. Permission of the author. Fithian Press, California.

Chapter 13 William Wordsworth. 'To a child: written in her album' (1835) *Wordsworth: Poetical Works* (1904). Oxford University Press, Oxford.

The first court report first appeared in *Child Psychiatry and the Law*, edited by D. Black, S. Wolkind and J. Harris-Hendriks, 2nd edition, 1991 and is reprinted by permission of the publishers, Gaskell Press and The Royal College of Psychiatrists.

How we came to the work

'Are you sure you want to see it? I can only draw sad faces'
(Harry, aged 6, when asked to draw what he saw when his mother was
shot by father who later killed himself)

Jealousy, passion, hatred and anger are intense human emotions which fascinate us all. Our literary heritage abounds with accounts, both true and fictional, of such feelings between kindred which result in tragedy, beginning with the story of Cain and Abel, continuing with the richness of Greek myths, Nordic tales of the gods, Shakespeare's plays and contemporary novels and operas. We can identify with the adults whose passions may lead them to kill, or be killed by, those they love most. But what happens to the children – often the innocent witnesses of adult passion and inevitable victims?

Over the years, because of our interest in children who had lost a parent through death, we found ourselves being asked to help with more and more complex problems, the most difficult of which related to children where one parent had killed the other. Realising that we had a unique group of children, we searched for guidance from other workers. What had our colleagues written about these children? The world's scientific literature contained little to help us, so we turned to the world's story-tellers for help.

How had the children in these tales fared? What we found was that, as in the academic literature, so it was in fiction – few stories mention the children. Even if the writer notes that the couple had children, their fate following the killing is ignored. Indeed we found few stories of one parent (as opposed to spouse) killing the other. Perdita in *The Winter's Tale* is a notable exception, although the tale barely qualifies since we find in the end that the mother was not really dead at all. Most writers, absorbed as they (and we) are with the violent emotions of the adults, spare not a thought for the plight of any children left behind. *Wozzeck*, the play by Buchner which Berg made into a powerful opera, is one of few literary works which even mention the existence of a child; yet we learn nothing of her fate following the death of her mother at her father's hands.

Rebecca West (who wrote in the 1950s a novel published in 1987 after her death) in an uncompleted sequence describes a family of young people abandoned by their father, who afterwards kills himself. In the years before 1914 they survive through mutual affection, talent, study, and a perceptive mother. In contrast, their friend Nancy loses both parents when her mother poisons her father and is imprisoned.

Nancy lives with her father's family, who cannot bear that she should see former friends, let alone her mother's relatives. She is given a new surname, visits her former friends as a young adult and speaks of 'a silly made-up name. It is not mine.' Her friend's thoughts are:

> Nancy was without employment, she had had her own name taken away from her, she had nothing.
>
> 'And it was quite useless too,' she continued. 'Everybody in Nottingham realised who we were as soon as we were brought there, and of course no one wants to marry me.'

Nancy adds, 'And I would not care, either, to marry anybody who thought it was nothing that my mother murdered my father.'

There is some indication, in the uncompleted sequence, that friendship, and a belated opportunity to speak of what she has felt and experienced, will create possibilities for enrichment of Nancy's life.[241]

In Greek mythology, Electra, the daughter of Clytemnestra and Agamemnon, was brought up by her mother during the first ten years of her life while her father was at the Trojan Wars. When Agamemnon got home he fell under the sword of Aegisthus, Clytemnestra's lover. Thus Electra lost her father at the behest of her mother. In adult life, Electra, who had been treated as a kind of slave by her mother and Aegisthus, encouraged her brother Orestes, whom she had protected as a child and who had taken flight at her instigation, but returned, both children killed Clytemnestra and her lover. Orestes, pursued by the fates, became mad after this deed and was cared for by his loving sister Electra.

Orestes, Electra and Hyacinth – the son of a woman who killed her husband (described by Henry James in *The Princess Casamassima* (1885)[112] and whose story is outlined in Chapter 10) – are unusual in world literature in that their stories are recounted from childhood through into tragic adult life (Hyacinth commits suicide).

Perhaps we should not be surprised at the virtual absence of children from the pages of history and fiction and indeed, until we began our study, from the criminological, psychological and social evaluation of parental killings.

As our interest in the children of families where one partner has killed the other became more widely known, we were asked more often to see them and to see them sooner after the tragedy had occurred. Initially those caring for these children, often maternal relatives, themselves bereft of a daughter or sister by the same act that had orphaned the children of their mother, had been reluctant to look at the children's distress for fear they would not be able to cope with it. The children too strove to suppress their disturbance, fearful that they would overburden their new carers and lose them also. Many carers, social workers, and relatives have been shocked to learn about the long-term existence of troubling nightmares in their charges, symptoms that were only revealed when the children were able to tell us about them during the course of our assessment, months or years later.

Our interviews enable the children, often for the first time, to tell what they had heard or seen on the day of the killing or in the weeks and months before. Young children, or those who fear to tell what they have experienced, often can only approach the subject indirectly by means of play, or by drawing and modelling in clay or by story-telling. Very often they give messages in code, hoping that someone will understand, but fearing to be direct.

There are many reasons for this. Sometimes they pick up subtle communications from those with whom they now live that it is dangerous or unwelcome to talk about what they know. Sometimes they believe that they were to blame, or that they should have been able to stop the killing, and guilt prevents them from discussing their feelings. Often they do not understand the full import of their experiences or their troubling nightmares and it needs a skilled interviewer to help them both to express what they have witnessed and to make sense of it. When this does occur it can bring dramatic relief.

> Jody was 5 when her father killed her mother in her presence. She developed a severe wheeze soon after which was treated with anti-asthma remedies by her doctor. During the course of psychotherapy, begun when she was 7, Jody tried on several occasions to paint a rainbow but could only complete a red arc. Eventually, she produced a picture of her mother, painting an ugly red semi-circular gash round her neck. She immediately began to wheeze. Jody's wheezing ceased only when her therapist could link the red 'rainbow' with the wheezing noise Jody heard her mother make in her death agony as she attempted to breathe through a windpipe lacerated by father when he cut her throat.

At the time we started our search, in 1987, we could find only two papers, each describing only one or two cases like ours, in the world scientific literature.[143, 175] And yet we had calculated that in England and Wales alone every year at least fifty children were orphaned by the death of one parent at the hands of the other.[26]

Finding that there was so little written about such children, we looked carefully at the characteristics of those we had seen and a few that colleagues had seen, and described them in a series of papers and chapters, making recommendations about their needs.[23, 26–29, 31, 32, 123] These needs included treatment, but went far beyond that. Many of the children had suffered multiple losses; they had lost not only their mother, but their father, other relations, home, possessions, school, friends and community. They had to live with their shame at being the children of a killer, and with their guilt that they had not been able to prevent the killing. In many cases they had been witnesses to the killing and some had been left alone with the dead body of their mother all night.

After the death they might have been the only source of information for the police or social worker about what had happened and who their relatives were and where they lived. Occasionally their own lives may have been in danger, especially if they had witnessed the killing. They may have had to give evidence at the trial of their father or mother (although this was rare, usually there was no doubt who committed the crime).

Traumatised and bereaved, they have then had to adjust to life with a new family who might be strangers to them or, even if related, not well known. Relatives might themselves be grief-stricken or ashamed of the part their kin played in the death and therefore not fully available to the children to care for them in their need. They might be parted from their brothers and sisters, blamed for the tragedy, and certainly have had to cope with the curiosity of their peers as well as the adjustment to a new school and neighbourhood.

Most of the children have had several homes after the killing. They may be placed with temporary foster parents in the middle of the night; when their relatives are found, they may go to them, only to become the objects of a battle between maternal and paternal relatives that at times seems to mirror the fatal battle between their parents. They may have to move again and again. Many of the children we have seen have had four or five moves.

Battles over where they will live, about possessions, about contact with the parent who committed the crime, both during a prison sentence and after release, may continue unabated over many years. Mourning and anger reach renewed heights at the time when the perpetrator is discharged from prison. In a small number of cases, children have moved back to live with that parent after sentence is completed and, as will be described in Chapter 12, follow-up, always difficult, becomes almost impossible under such circumstances.

What chance have such children of growing up straight? Other than in times of war or civil conflict, they must be among the most deprived and uprooted children in the developed world. Most of the children, whose tales we tell in the accounts that follow, have not yet grown up. But we have two accounts of the experiences of survivors who contacted us when our work became more widely known and these appear in Chapter 10, with our thanks.

We have now seen more than 400 children who have been affected by one parent's violent death at the hands of the other and the stories we tell are based on these experiences. We are grateful to the many children and their families who have helped us learn about such tragic events. All the experiences we describe are true but we have disguised identifying features, as indicated in our preface on confidentiality, to protect the privacy of the children involved. In general, we refer to the father as the killer because that is the majority experience. Chapter 12 (Study I) refers to details of the first 100 children seen in our study, from 62 families, 56 devastated by father's killing of mother and 6 by mother's killing of father. We have updated this chapter to describe the longer-term outcome (Study II).

This particular group of children had a ratio of nine killings by men to one killing by a woman; our later studies show a higher ratio of male to female killers.

We have written this book to help those people who may find themselves for the first time having to care for such children and who share the common experience of feeling shocked, horrified, suddenly deskilled and all at sea. Most experienced social workers, child psychiatrists, lawyers and guardians *ad litem* may only have to deal with one or two such families in a professional lifetime and, if they are to do the job well, and keep faith with their charges, they may find our experiences helpful.

For ordinary carers, especially if they are related to the dead parent, coping with the sudden addition to their families of traumatised and bereaved children, who may have lived for years with warring parents, requires skills of an exceptional nature, and yet they may also be traumatised and bereaved themselves. Even experienced carers are unlikely to have had to look after doubly orphaned children before and they may find guidance and illumination within these pages. This book may be helpful too to adults who went through similar traumatising experiences when they were children. Some of them have told us how isolated they felt, believing that they were alone in suffering a shameful and horrifying past.

Part I outlines what is known about the general effects of trauma, violence and grief on children and adolescents. The interaction of trauma and grief is considered in Chapter 3. Chapter 4 by Art O'Connor outlines what we know about why people kill their partners and the response of the criminal justice system to such killings.

Part II deals specifically with the results for children of the experience of one parent killing another. In Chapter 5 we tell the children's stories, and Chapter 6 deals with the first impact and immediate aftermath and discusses ways of intervening to minimise the trauma and prevent avoidable psychological injury. Chapter 7 considers the killing of fathers by mothers. Chapter 8 contains some accounts of therapists' work with individual children. Chapter 9 considers the implications of caring for children of families broken in this way, and Chapter 10 looks at what we know of the impact of the trauma on adult life. Chapter 11 discusses legal issues.

Part III summarises the findings from our researches and makes recommendations about how to plan services for all children and adolescents affected by either loss or trauma or by both. Two anonymous court reports may be of help to social workers or child psychiatrists who have to prepare one.

There are five appendices. The first sets out a framework for interviewing a child who has just lost a parent, followed by the detailed schedule which we aim to use for more systematic evaluation. Appendix 2 outlines the principles which informed the thinking of legislators responsible for the most recent revision of child law in the UK – principles that apply equally in any society which attempts to offer justice to children. Similarly, we discuss guidelines for those situations where children are unable to live with their original families and require legally secure alternative homes.

Appendix 3 discusses the clinical concept of post-traumatic stress disorder, with particular reference to the American Psychiatric Association classification, and is updated to take account of new knowledge concerning under-fives, including children not yet able to speak.

Appendix 4 offers relevant addresses of professional and voluntary associations.

Appendix 5 outlines and summarises our principles for practice in offering services to all children traumatised and bereaved by family violence.

Part I

Violence and loss in childhood

Chapter 1

Children and trauma

> Sombre the night is
> And, though we live our lives, we
> Know what sinister threat lurks there.
> (Isaac Rosenberg, 'Returning, we hear the larks')

SUMMARY

The concept of post-traumatic stress disorder is discussed historically and with reference to recent research. Disaster caused deliberately by fellow-humans is sometimes more difficult to comprehend than natural catastrophe. Adults who wish to protect children may have difficulty in recognising traumatic stress in children. Its effects are described and discussed so that children's suffering may be brought to light. This chapter may be read in conjunction with Appendix 3.

Historical overview

Two Czech writers outlined the history of childhood experience of traumatic and destructive events, dividing this history into four periods:[130]

1 **The empirical period: 1850–1930.** Doctors who worked with children drew attention to the high incidence of both death and the slowing down of intellectual and physical development in children housed in institutions, particularly orphanages and hospitals. Writers at this time focused in the main on the need to improve the physical environment, particularly sanitary conditions.

2 **The alarm period: this did not begin until the 1930s and 1940s.** Large numbers of children were wandering through Europe, deserted by or separated from those who cared for them, dislocated and rootless. Writers began to express concern about their emotional, mental and physical development and the effects upon children of imprisonment, malnutrition, concentration

camp experiences and loss of family, community and education. During this period there was also worry about working women, poor housing and the high incidence of breakdown in wartime marriages. Studies of infants in institutions indicated that children who survived this kind of upbringing were under-stimulated, with difficulty in learning and in developing trusting relationships.[209]

3   **During the third period** were the beginnings of evaluating what was known and drawing conclusions from it, characterised by the work of Bowlby, which he overviewed in 1979.[37-39]

4   **During the fourth period, the 1960s and early 1970s**, there were advances in systematic research on the effects upon children of separation and dislocation. All of this preceded and, with hindsight, has provided a framework for, work specifically on the effects of trauma upon children.

The problem for all of us who study the effects of dreadful events on children is that both historical accounts, as indicated above, and recent research tend to blur together negative effects (loss, hunger, neglect) with the results of positively dreadful experiences such as assault, torture, threat to life, seeing loved ones going through such experiences, or witnessing homicide. Today, when we try to understand the effects upon children of traumatic events, a pool of knowledge exists which ranges from the study of deprivation and neglect in the context of war, civil unrest or institutional care, to neglect within families.[61] We know a lot about what is needed to enable children to become securely and safely attached to those who care for them, and about how horrifying events affect both mind and body from childhood onwards. We develop these themes in future chapters.

Until as recently as 1985 there was considerable scepticism expressed within the psychiatric establishment that children reacted even to overwhelming stresses with anything other than mild and transient emotional and behavioural changes. In the second edition of the standard British textbook on child and adolescent psychiatry, *Child and Adolescent Psychiatry: Modern Approaches*,[81] it was said with regard to the effects of severe stress upon children that:

> behavioural disturbances appear to be less intense than might have been anticipated; a majority of children show a moderate amount of fear and anxiety but this subsides; regressive behaviour marked by clinging to parents and heightened dependency on adults appears and then moderately mild sleep disturbance persists for several months; a later less severe stress such as a storm may lead to a temporary increase in emotional distress, although this is variable; enuresis (bed wetting) occurs in some cases, while hyper-sensitivity to loud noises may be evident in others.

(p. 126)

The received view, based on clinical and research evidence, was that major disasters might lead to emotional disorders which would be a handicap to some children but that usually these disturbances were short-lived. This perception was reflected in the authors' assertion that there was no need for a specific diagnostic category for stress-reactions in childhood such as was used in adults.

Until that time the difficulty was that studies had rarely dealt with the effect of major disasters on children who had been at risk of their lives or who had witnessed death and destruction. We now know that post-traumatic stress symptoms, in common with other changes in the child's emotions, often go unrecognised or at least underestimated by the adults in the child's life. In 1987, after the *Herald of Free Enterprise* ferry sank off Zeebrugge, it was suggested that earlier studies failed to identify the extent of children's difficulties after exposure to traumatic events because many had not used screening instruments which picked up post-traumatic stress disorder (PTSD) symptoms, and because they relied on parent and/or teacher reports, and therefore underestimated the level of children's disturbance.[264] Another factor which may be important is that, as in bereavement, the adults themselves may be preoccupied by their own distress and therefore less able to recognise distress in their children.

> In part, it is because adults are understandably very protective towards children who have survived a disaster; and in part it is because adults, unwilling to acknowledge what children may have suffered, deny that children have major psychological sequelae that warrant investigation.[264]
>
> (p. 279)

The third edition of the standard British textbook referred to above has a chapter on post-traumatic stress disorder.[197] There is still some controversy about the diagnosis of post-traumatic stress disorder. It is not the only response to trauma.

We now speak of the 'conspiracy of silence': adults try to protect the children by not speaking of terrible events, hoping that the children will forget or supposing that, if they do not initiate discussion, children are best left alone. Children, on the other hand, more in need than ever of care and nurture, may fit in with and confirm the illusions of the adults by masking or at least remaining silent about their distress, not wanting to upset their carers.

Our current knowledge

In fact, children suffer the effects of traumatic stress in very similar ways to adults. Post-traumatic stress disorder (PTSD) in children has now been studied in relation to witnessed violence, rape and suicide,[179] parental murder,[143] kidnapping,[220, 221] bushfire,[146] child abuse,[89, 92] natural disaster,[93] major transport disasters,[264] community violence,[222] child murder[248] and domestic violence.[156] Studies of the effects upon the siblings of traumatised children, hitherto little studied, are reviewed by Newman and his colleagues with particular reference to illness, disability and death;[162] the effects of crime and disaster require further study.

Like adults, children suffer more intensely and persistently when the catastrophe they witness is caused by a person or people rather than resulting from a natural disaster (see, for example,[188]). In a study at a crisis centre in Los Angeles, nearly 80 per cent of more than 100 children who had witnessed extreme violence inflicted on a member of their family had characteristic symptoms of post-traumatic stress.[179] The same team studied the effects of a sniper attack on schoolchildren in their playground. The sniper was a man who had lost his own family in a mass suicide. Some children were killed. The team found that the children most profoundly affected by post-traumatic stress symptoms were those who had been most at risk for their lives and least protected by an adult. The further away the children had been from the scene of the fatal shootings, the fewer symptoms they showed. Children in other parts of the school, on their way home, at home or out of the neighbourhood, were sequentially less affected and had fewer if any post-traumatic stress symptoms.[181, 182]

This was the first study in which the symptoms of post-traumatic stress in children were systematically and comprehensively catalogued and the direct effect of the stress demonstrated beyond doubt. The authors were able to show, for example, that the children who had been most at risk were almost invariably more profoundly affected than others who were more protected or further away, and that the intensity of the reactions had very little to do with whether the children had been exposed to violence previously, recent major events in their lives or their age or sex. Conversely, the influence of these factors was much greater in those children who had not been in the playground but who developed symptoms later. Interestingly, children who had been exposed to previous violence were not in the main resistant to further stress; if anything, they had been sensitised to violence and their reactions were made stronger by a reawakening of memories related to the violent events they had previously witnessed.

The symptoms of these schoolchildren were by no means transient. Just over a year later, three-quarters of those children who had been in the playground at the time of the attack were still suffering symptoms of PTSD. It was clear that those who had been most in danger of being shot and the most intensely affected at the time went on suffering the most. The less exposed children who still had symptoms had in common a strong sense of guilt, for example about not having done enough to protect younger siblings or friends. Yet severe and persistent *grief* was related hardly at all to whether the children had felt their own life threatened. As one might expect, it had much more to do with how well they knew the victim of the attack. There is the possibility, however, that the grief of some children who had been severely traumatised may have been masked or inhibited by their PTSD symptoms,[158] a theme illustrated, again and again, by children in our study. We are now seeing the longer-term effects of unresolved trauma on children who, never having grieved, have difficulty in trusting those who now try to look after them.

Much of our current knowledge about traumatic stress comes from the assessment of, and interventions with, children and their families in war zones.

As a society, we have been slow to recognise the detrimental effects of war on children. Women and children increasingly are involved in war, especially in the developing world, where they form a large proportion of the population.

Iraqi children who had seen and heard multiple deaths in a bomb shelter have said: 'I feel trapped by these memories.' 'My parents don't know what I am going through. They say, "Try to forget it."' 'This year I don't think I will be able to pass my exams.' 'I feel that anything might happen.' 'God might take my life and I never know when I am going to die.' The effects of stress on these children were comparable with those in other disasters.[65] In an extensive study of affected children in the Lebanon,[135] Macksoud established that, as might be expected, effects were cumulative: the higher the exposure to violence, the higher the incidence of PTSD. Bereaved and displaced children described their feelings of helplessness and their attempts to make plans, to take control of their own lives. When asked to select the most painful of their memories, 60 per cent listed the death of someone close to them. Traumatic stress, with underlying grief sliding into depression, became a part of daily life, although resilience, attempts to plan their lives and strong community ties afforded some support.

In Bosnia, children who had suffered earlier separations were most vulnerable to traumatic stress, depression and associated problems of behaviour.[232] Those with greater symptoms had witnessed the death, injury or torture of a member of their nuclear family, were older, and came from a large city.[88] During 1980–6, Dalianis-Karanbatzakis followed up children whom she had known in Greece during the Civil War of 1946–9 when she was imprisoned along with children and their mothers.[56] This study is particularly helpful in identifying factors related to resilience and survival in the aftermath of extreme events, and we discuss this valuable research further in Chapter 10.

Children who are refugees may have an additional stress. They may become protectors and providers for their parents, receiving bread and other sustenance in preference to adults, so that the latter become dependent on their children. Maturation and adaptation are hindered by premature responsibility and role reversal.[57] We are learning more systematically about longer-term effects. Recent studies[91, 205] have focused on the aftermath of torture, the social effects of exile and the mental health of refugees and asylum-seekers. The numbers alone are frightening. UNICEF estimated that there were 95,000 orphans and other unattached children created by the Rwandan conflict in 1994–5[226] and the Kosovar refugees in 1999 created a new cohort of traumatised children. Models of psychiatric disturbance developed in Western psychiatry may not be appropriate in other parts of the world.[216]

The influence of children's attachments

Securely attached children,[3] who have had consistent, reliable and sensitively attuned care from birth onwards, appear to be more adaptable in the face of stress. They are more sociable and empathic, and have an inherent sense of protectedness, optimism and continuity, and, as adults, are more balanced and autonomous. Insecure attachments may arise as an adaptation to distortions or impediments to the parenting these children receive, but may, in the long term, confer significant vulnerability. Insecurely attached children can be reliably differentiated into:

1   *ambivalent/resistant* infants, who, when separated from their caregivers or when their lives are disrupted, become inconsolably upset, crying, clinging and angry.
2   *avoidant/detached* infants, who, by contrast, show little outward sign of distress (while inwardly highly aroused) and instead may distract themselves, appearing to ignore or avoid their caregivers, and at other times may be aggressive and destructive.
3   *disorganised/disoriented* infants whose attachments are the most difficult to describe, but are potentially of most interest to the understanding of the traumatic response. These children show a prototypical motivational (approach – avoidance) conflict[138] in interaction with a caregiver who is frightening or overwhelmingly (if only briefly) frightened.[139] Thus this is the common pattern of attachment in abused and neglected children,[49] and is also found where the caregiver has not adequately resolved past traumatic experiences or bereavements. These children show distress and disturbance over long periods and are more prone to serious mental health problems in later life.

In the face of bereavement or separation from parents, insecurely attached children are more difficult for surrogate parents to care for and may behave so badly that one set of carers after another gives up on them, increasing their problems.[3] (See also[22, 141, 265] and Appendix 3.)

Post-traumatic stress disorder

We all have ways of dealing with the everyday stresses we encounter. We can, for example, think things through, interpret events, even inaccurately, until they make sense, seek support and advice, or put things out of our mind. When stresses that confront us are so sudden, unexpected and catastrophic that our usual ways of coping are overwhelmed, we are left feeling intensely fearful and powerless to act, unable to put things out of our mind. We call this traumatic stress.

Post-traumatic stress disorder (PTSD) may be diagnosed in children as in adults if certain symptoms, which can be related to a particular stressful event, co-exist in a particular way and persist for longer than a month (see Appendix 3).[5, 6] The symptoms are profoundly distressing. Disturbing images and memories of the event are imprinted and return unbidden. The event may be re-experienced in full as a 'flashback' in response to environmental triggers or memories.

The child with PTSD will try to avoid memories or any reminders of the events, which complicates grieving if a loss has been entailed, since grieving requires the child to bring into their mind an image of the dead person. If their most recent and imprinted image of that person acts as a traumatic reminder, they may try to put this out of their mind and consequently the grieving process is impeded.[176, 180] Recurrent dreams in which the traumatic events are replayed without alteration are particularly common, and only begin to include elements of the child's wishes and fantasies as the child finds ways of coping with the trauma and can begin to grieve.

Initially, a feeling of numbness and detachment with withdrawal is common. Children recount their horrifying experiences from the perspective of a detached observer, which unsuspecting adults may take to mean that they have not been affected emotionally. Numb, compliant children may also be rather a relief to adults struggling with the aftermath of a disaster, so this behaviour is tacitly encouraged. Children exposed to traumatic stress may also become highly aroused, hyper-alert and jumpy, with disturbed sleep and impaired concentration and memory. They may develop new fears directly referable to the traumatic events they have experienced and yet show little of this to adults.

In her extensive review, Terr,[222, 223] a pioneer in this field, identified certain symptoms of PTSD which are particularly profound in children, now clarified by Scheeringa and colleagues[198] (see Appendix 3).

Memory and post-traumatic stress disorder

Traumatic memories are often provoked by sensations (sight, sound, smell, etc.) which are reminders of the traumatic experience. However, children sometimes relive their traumas and troubles at quiet times when their defences are down – for example, when they are bored in class, or at night before they fall asleep (and many are frightened of going to bed because of this) or when they are watching television or otherwise relaxing. Even young children, who cannot express these memories in words, may show by their behaviour in play that they are reliving the traumatic event.

These intrusive perceptual experiences are frighteningly intense:

Dana, aged 15, thought she was going crazy. Two years earlier she had been raped by three youths. This had happened at dusk in a bus shelter. Dana would read until late at night to stop herself from falling asleep and was in trouble for poor and inadequate class work. Often, in the course of lessons, pictures of the rape would flash before her and she would experience sweating and nausea. Her teachers knew that she lived in a children's home because of family troubles but did not know about the rape. An explanation of post-traumatic stress disorder led to considerable relief for Dana and an improvement in her school work even before specific therapy had been negotiated.

Traumatic elements or whole memories are often recalled as sensory fragments, which may seem real and present.[228] Research on the emotional and cognitive processing of memory helps us to understand many of the experiences of trauma survivors.[198, 204, 223] Very young children's sight, hearing, touch, smell and taste work just as well as those of adults but they have difficulty, related to their age and understanding, in processing the information of their senses. Because their experience is limited they have few associations. This makes it harder for them to make sense of their experiences, to *understand*, and to lay down long-term memories. Emotional processing also requires therapeutic skills in working through the experience and children need help in achieving this with the aid of adults whom they are enabled to trust (see[22] and Chapter 8).

Children's ability to *tell* other people about what has happened to them is likewise affected by their age, understanding and the nature and circumstances of a traumatic event. When asked to do so for evidential purposes, they also need specialised help, such as preparing them for the interview, helping them to understand that talking to a police officer does not indicate that the child is guilty of any wrong-doing. Care is needed to avoid making suggestions as to what happened or asking leading questions. The language used should be suited to the child. The interview should not go on too long for the child's attention span, nor should it be repetitious. Video-recording is sometimes valuable. Children may also require preparation for court appearances if they have witnessed a crime. Their help may be invaluable (see Chapter 11).[76, 193, 242]

Repetitive behaviours

Post-traumatic play is joyless, repetitive and leads nowhere. There is no resolution, no relief. Derelict buildings are drawn, masonry tumbles, cars crash, again and again. Stabbing or strangling may repeat themselves in play. One child, whose mother had hanged herself, played many games of hangman and, when embracing her grandmother, tied and untied the neck of her blouse, carrying the ties up behind her grandmother's head as if she were trying to hang her.

Dreaming

Repetitive dreams – often exact recapitulations of the traumatic events but sometimes deeply disguised – are able to be described by children after the age of about 5. These dreams may continue for many years. Younger children, too, commonly have disturbed sleep after a traumatic experience and may show that they are dreaming by making mouthing movements or little sounds when they sleep, or screaming without awakening (so-called 'night terror').

Specific fears

The fears of traumatised children arise anew, their origins are usually explicit and they are more focused and more idiosyncratic than the fears of generally anxious children. A child who had been savaged by a Doberman dog feared that breed of dog above all others. A boy, who had felt the sinking ferry-boat lurch sideways, was overcome by terror on a double-decker bus which lurched as it went round a corner. Dana, raped in a bus shelter, did not tell her friends about her fears of public transport and inexplicably (to others) missed many outings because of this.

Changed attitudes about life

These children, unlike those who have not experienced trauma, distrust and fear their future. They have recognised how vulnerable all human beings are and no longer trust, as do trauma-free children, that life is likely to be good to them. 'The feeling of futurelessness of the traumatised child,' writes Terr, 'is quite different from that of the depressed youngster. For the traumatised, the future is a landscape filled with crags, pits and monsters. For the depressed, the future is a bleak, featureless landscape stretched out into infinity.'[222]

A single violent event produces a clearer pattern but, commonly, children suffer *repeated* blows of fate in the course of war, terrorism or natural disasters which affect whole communities. Terr describes how children may make massive attempts to protect themselves, using denial, repression, cutting themselves off from their own experiences, putting themselves emotionally on the side of the attacker, and attacking themselves. She considers that prolonged traumatisation leads to deep changes in the character of suffering children, who become vulnerable to a whole range of severe disorders in adult life. She sums up the effect of cumulative trauma as absence of feeling, a sense of rage and unremitting sadness, existing side by side with the fears which are common to all childhood trauma.

Some of the children whom we see suffer only a single trauma and then, though grieving and dislocated, are able to put down roots in caring stable circumstances. However, a substantial number fit into the second, more complex, category. Their sufferings may not be as severe or dramatic as those of children caught up in warfare or terrorism but many – though privately and unknown to the outside world – do suffer dislocation and prolonged uncertainty and instability which affect them for the rest of their childhood, as we describe in Chapters 9 and 10.

Biological aspects of trauma

Animals, including humans, are equipped to protect themselves from sudden attack by fight, flight or freezing responses. Freezing is the hallmark of trauma. In general, we show a number of common reactions, varying in intensity with the nature of the threat, which are rapid in onset, occur outside consciousness and are brief in duration (provided that the body's response is both possible and effective). The dilation of pupils to let in more light, rapid beating of the heart to improve muscular blood supply, tensing of the body for action, pallor, sweating and dryness of the mouth, plus interference with digestion, as less essential bodily functions are put in abeyance, are familiar experiences to all alarmed human beings. These responses are meant to be specific to the danger and to abate when the danger has passed. In PTSD they become over-generalised.[229]

This hyper-alertness is not always useful or appropriate in a complex and changing world. It may become prolonged yet ineffective in the face of long, drawn-out or repeated threat, so that instinctive bodily reactions, directed towards self-protection and resolution of danger, instead become a problem and source of suffering. Symptoms of being over-aroused – sleeplessness, irritability, difficulty concentrating, being easily startled, with unstable heart-beat and digestion – may continue indefinitely. If present for more than a few weeks after the threat, they form part of the picture of PTSD.[267]

Sleep disturbance, although so well recognised as an effect of trauma, is under-researched. A detailed sleep history, preferably by standardised question-naire, is of great importance; information should be obtained from carers, directly from children and by observation wherever possible. Specific thera-peutic help is available and is often beneficial.

Developmental stages

The age of the child, and their stage of development, does have an influence on the nature of the symptoms.[121]

Children under 2 years

As noted in our chapter on research, 40 per cent of the children whom we have seen were under 5 years old at the time of the killing, a trend which has continued. Therefore we have now seen, of the first 400 children in the study, more than 160 who were under 5 years old when they lost their parent. We have noted that, particularly when the child victims are 18 months old or younger, emergency services are, understandably, concerned in the main with the children's safety and physical well-being. Caregivers and professionals are not asked to watch out for signs of psychological trauma in just-verbal or pre-verbal children, nor are they routinely offered advice or help, yet problems may be severe.

Ruby, aged 4

Ruby was referred to us, along with her maternal aunt, only at the point when the dead mother's former partner was asking for Ruby to be taken to visit him in prison. Ruby's aunt was horrified at the proposal. She said that Ruby, 1 year old when her mother was killed in front of her, screamed every night for many months, often waking her new family several times from their sleep. Ruby's aunt said that they had been so exhausted they had almost given up on their plan to give Ruby a permanent home. She had not been offered help at that time.

Chad, aged 1

Chad spent several days with his father on the run after Chad's mother was strangled in front of him. After father gave himself up to the police, Chad's weight loss and nappy rash were noted but nothing was written about his emotional state. His foster-parents later told of broken sleep, screaming, greed for food, restlessness and a constant need to be held and carried. These problems continued for many months and Chad's speech was delayed.

Appendix 3 now contains a recent classification scheme for very young children who have been traumatised.

Pre-schoolers

Pre-schoolers, on the whole, do not expect of themselves that they will be able to influence events. For some this means an intense paralysis of intention and immobility or increased passivity. For others it is a protection in that if they do not understand the scene they are witnessing they also do not understand the degree of danger or risk. Many will become regressed and clinging. They may become highly aroused, startle easily and have sleep disturbed by night terrors or sleepwalking.[71]

Primary-school-age children

Primary-school-age children begin to be able to put themselves in the position of other people and so may fantasise their involvement from the point of view of the victim, the assailant, a third person intervening, as well as from their vantage point as observer. Their fantasies of rescuing the victim of the violence depend on the intervention of a third party (powerful super-heroes are particularly popular at this age) rather than fantasies of their own involvement to save the victim, which appear at a later age. Children of this age involve others in their post-traumatic play. Because they are most prone at this age to act out the roles they ascribe themselves within the scenario – whether this means being excessively aggressive and bullying, or passive or provocative, courting aggression – peer relationships suffer greatly. Their dissociation is also particularly marked: a distancing from feelings, and obsessional behaviour and rituals to ward off a sense that there is about to be a repetition of the horrifying experience they have been through. This tendency to try to ward off feelings may also link with psychosomatic symptoms and school phobia is also noticeable.

Secondary-school-age children

At secondary-school age, children's fantasies in relation to the traumatic events are much more orientated to what they might have done or might do if it ever happened again, and they suffer more guilt and shame in relation to these feelings. There is a sense, in many teenagers who come through extreme traumas, that there is no more growing up left to do. They do not expect, as do non-traumatised teenagers, a limitless future full of promise. They may take more risks, putting themselves in danger, getting involved in crime or making attempts on their own lives.

Other relevant research on developmental factors

Some authors[93] have noted that younger children show less extensive symptomatology, and indeed that PTSD is less common and less intense in younger children (although this perception may be a continuing reflection of diagnostic difficulties rather than a validated observation). Young children do develop other behavioural problems, aggressiveness and fears, and may regress emotionally and neuro-developmentally – for example, by wetting the bed at night after they have acquired bladder control. This may be a PTSD equivalent. These authors also comment that younger children may be relatively protected by not fully understanding the traumatic scenes they witness: the degree of life-threat in younger children affects the intensity of PTSD symptoms hardly at all. For children under 5, the reaction of their parents or those caring for them is much more influential than any other factor, and more so at this age than any other. When parents, especially mothers, who were severely traumatised or grief-stricken after a natural disaster, could not adequately attend to the emotional needs of their children, the children suffered more profoundly as a consequence.

Interestingly, teenagers appear to be more affected by their parents' reactions than are their primary-school-aged siblings, possibly because they are expected or expect themselves to take over some of the parenting, or because they share with their parents a more adult perspective on the traumatic events and suffer more adult-like reactions such as 'survivor guilt'. Unlike most other psychiatric conditions in childhood, girls of all ages seem more vulnerable to PTSD than boys, but boys may show more behavioural disturbance after exposure to trauma.[93]

Long-term morbidity, resilience and protective factors

Irrespective of the nature of the trauma, survivors are vulnerable to chronic PTSD and there is a pressing need for prospective longitudinal outcome studies. Single traumatic events appear to have fewer long-term effects on very young children and on psychosocially mature adults than on adolescents, and all suffer more from repeated trauma.[227] There is growing recognition of the need to identify, describe and treat these conditions and to help traumatised people to avoid leading lives which lay them open to repeated trauma.

It is salutary to recognise that in many surveys after catastrophes the majority of people do *not* develop PTSD. Understanding what makes some people resilient and what protects them from the full impact of the stress is critical but embryonic. Perhaps this depends in some on general attributes[80] or specific ones, for example the availability of untraumatised, emotionally available caregivers, the taking of effective action to help oneself or others[148] or genetic/biological factors.

Trauma responses can be built into the fabric of people's lives, no longer circumscribed by being related to one particular event. In these circumstances it is more realistic, rather than attempting 'cure', to think in terms of providing help in survival and coping techniques to be used in the long term[227] and of promoting supportive relationships.

In our view, one of the key research issues for the next decade is an exploration of the interaction between deprivation, traumatisation and the disruption of attachments, throughout childhood, including a proper understanding of resilience and protective factors and cultural variations in response to trauma.

We now know[251, 253] that domestic violence can produce reactions identical to those seen as a result of war or major disaster. Black and colleagues[30] provide an overview of recent clinical and research developments, and we develop this further in the next chapter.

Chapter 2

Children and violence

At last, sounds of a chair falling over,
scuffle of shoes scraping for a foothold
coughs, cries, sobbing.
And then once more
like waves on a shingle beach
the recurring tirade of raised voices,
grating of will against will,
the sound of two rights making wrong.
(Donald Atkinson, 'A sleep of drowned fathers')

SUMMARY

Physical abuse, and subsequently sexual abuse, have been identified as happening to children, with recognition that child protection networks are required. The effects upon children of *witnessing* violence are under-estimated. Women who are abused by their partners are frequently expected to retain responsibility for the protection of their children. Children may adapt to adult violence in ways which distort their development and functioning. Concepts of child protection should be extended to child victims of criminal violence between adults.

Introduction

During the 1960s[124] the physical abuse of children became recognised as an important issue to be researched and debated, and this was followed during the 1970s by similar research on violence to women within the home.[73] Only in the 1980s and 1990s did debate gain currency on the witnessing of violence by children. Accounts have been taken from adults who looked back on their lives, either as abusers or as victims of marital violence, and from teenagers. Other research has looked at referrals of children to mental health services[179] and at the effects upon children of being with their mothers in refuges for battered women.[132]

Lee, aged 8 and 20

Mrs Donald was pregnant with Lee, her first child, when her first husband beat her up. The beatings continued and at 8 Lee was referred to us because he was aggressive, taking risks like staying out late at night, failing to come home from school and not telling his mother where he was, making poor progress in school and at times soiling his pants. He put on a front as though nothing and nobody could hurt him but during only his second meeting with a therapist he began to admit that he was horrified and frightened when he heard his parents argue. He had been beaten himself when he tried to stop his father from hitting his mother but was more afraid for her than for himself since she had been in hospital twice after beatings, the last time with a broken nose and four broken ribs.

When seen on her own, Mrs Donald was able to tell how depressed she was and how afraid to go out of the house. Father kept one appointment with his wife and son and seemed to want help but the rest of the family failed to keep any appointments after the second. Lee was referred to child protection services.

We next heard of Lee aged 12, when he was playing truant from school and sniffing glue. We learned that Mrs Donald had never brought charges against her husband. Lee had 'kept out of his father's way' and had not received further direct physical injuries. His parents now said that they could not control him and Lee went into a local authority children's home. The residential workers found it hard to talk to him and look after him and he was very rude and difficult. But one day he was able to say that he thought he had been sent away from home because he was like his father. By 14, Lee had taken his first overdose of paracetamol and alcohol after an argument with his girlfriend.

Six years later, Lee's first child was taken into care at the age of 18 months with a fractured skull. Lee continues to insist that he had nothing to do with it. The baby's mother, aged 18, backs up Lee in what he says and it has been decided that neither of them is able to offer a safe home to the child.

All child mental health services are familiar with tragedies like this and tend to lose sight of the children concerned, particularly the boys, when they fail to keep appointments and, later, rather than making use of adult mental health services, become involved with criminal behaviour, the court system, unemployment agencies and divorce courts. This story is unusual in that the baby with the fractured skull became a patient of the same child mental health service which had known and failed to help Lee twelve years earlier.

In one quarter of the children seen as a result of one parent killing the other, there is some history of family violence. In some of our cases there had been social work involvement with the children but rarely were they subject to child protection procedures. One exception was a family with four children; they had a baby who was failing to thrive, had unexplained bruises and was under investigation by the local paediatric service which had referred the case to social services. In another case, there was a family feud, with threats of violence, which had resulted in the children being placed on the local authority's child protection register although none of them had received direct injury.

The few families who were known to other agencies had mostly been involved in previous police interventions because of quarrels between the adults concerned. One woman called the police, alleging that her husband had attacked her. When the police car arrived she said that the fight had been resolved and that she no longer needed their help. Twenty-four hours later she died at her husband's hands.

We do not yet know whether there are ways of predicting when violence in families is likely to progress as far as homicide. By the nature of our work, we do not hear about those cases where chance factors or some extraneous intervention have averted homicide. As we study domestic violence systematically, it may be possible to identify warning signs which could be picked up by potential victims, family members, neighbours, social workers or police, a theme which we will turn to at the end of this chapter.

The extent of violence in the home

Until recently, American research provided the most prolific source of information.[111] By the 1970s, work on wife assault was being published which drew attention to the inadequate responses of justice, health and social services, but which did not focus on the needs of children who, unless themselves injured, were considered only as part of the responsibility of the assaulted women. By 1982, a review of the literature on divorce and separation[69] indicated that the amount of conflict to which they were subjected was the most important stressor for the children concerned. This article did not take account of work on domestic violence being undertaken at the same time; thus, the specific effects upon children of witnessing violence were not identified.

Every year in the USA, about one-third of all children in families are either seriously assaulted by one of their parents, witness one parent assaulting the other or are exposed to both kinds of assault.[110] There is known chronic violence in one in fourteen marriages in the USA, and at least two-thirds of women in women's refuges bring children with them.[111] Indeed, in the USA, more women are abused by their husbands or partners than are injured in car accidents or by muggers or in stranger rape.[225] Violence is commonplace in UK society also. The Department of Health[62] records that an average of 32 out of 10,000 children have recorded abuse, of whom the majority are in the category 'physical abuse'. This is the tip of an iceberg, since the accounts of many children who disclose abuse may not be recorded and many children do not tell what is happening to them. In the UK, domestic violence is the second most frequent crime reported to the police, comprising more than 25 per cent of all reported violent crime.[1, 62, 108, 207]

A particularly important work on violence in domestic settings, also in the UK, points out that work linking violence between adults (usually from a man to a woman) and child abuse is recent and not well developed.[156] It is not routine for situations where adults have been injuring each other to be brought to the attention of child protection agencies. Abusive acts between the adults are rarely hidden from the children. In one study, 73 per cent of women interviewed reported that children had seen, and 62 per cent that they had overheard, attacks; half said that children saw the injuries; and almost all of them, 99 per cent, said that children had seen their mother upset and crying. Two-thirds commented that their children knew they were living in an atmosphere of fear and intimidation.[1, 219] As many as one in ten of the women had been sexually abused, and some raped, with children present. The author comments that although women work hard to protect their children or to hide abuse, this is rarely possible. By talking directly to children whose mothers had been assaulted within the home it was discovered by other workers that most of them could talk in detail about assaults which neither parent knew they had seen.[111]

The effects of home-based violence on the mental health of adult victims are discussed in a paper reporting a study which found that many women who attend accident and emergency services are not asked how they came by injuries or are questioned only in the presence of a male partner. The author advises that those who work in health services (particularly general practice, casualty and obstetrics and gynaecology) should be more curious about their patients' injuries. Others make the same point about pregnant women.[149] (When the mother of Jennifer and Anne, whose story is told in this chapter, went to emergency services with a head injury, her story of a fall on the stairs, told in the presence of her partner, was accepted without question.)

In the light of the findings of a number of recent enquiries into the deaths of children through unlawful killing, the Bridge Child Care Development Service (which is funded by the Department of Health, charities and some local authorities) published *Dangerous Care*.[61] This offers an overview of relevant literature concentrating on 'the more extreme end of violence and dangerousness' as it affects children and families, covering mental health, the criminal and civil justice systems, and studies on child protection and dangerousness within families. Information should be garnered about the carer, the children, and the context in which the child lives. Relevant information about the carer includes any history of previous violence or of criminal offending, their past and present mental health, and evidence of any disorders of personality. Concerning the children, the younger they are the greater the risk, and they are more vulnerable if premature, disabled or otherwise disadvantaged. Children who report that they are being harmed or are in danger should be taken very seriously. The context in which the child lives is also important – relevant factors include problems within the family, low levels of social support, high levels of financial and social stress, and disorganisation. All increase vulnerability to violence. Information may not be assessed and evaluated, or communicated appropriately between professionals (see also[163]). The very presence of children in the family may provoke violence. Children understandably may hold themselves to blame when they hear parents arguing about their behaviour, schooling, and how much it costs to raise them.

Finally, there is an organisational context which may contribute to violent events. Thus, child protection services, where workers may be on their own and unsupported, get too close to parents, and inadvertently collude with them in order to avoid difficult issues. Social workers who may be unrealistically optimistic, against the evidence, and become over-involved, yet not recognise that this is happening, or avoid contact because they are afraid for their own safety, may contribute to the escalation of family difficulties into violence.

It is more fruitful when protecting children from violence, directly to themselves or between the adults who care for them, to think in terms of potentially dangerous adults in potentially dangerous situations, the one influencing the other. Women are particularly at risk during or just after pregnancy,[149] and also at times when they have separated from violent partners; this latter theme is illustrated by much of our work.

Thus, the framework for recognising and evaluating the effects of violence on children must take account of the perpetrator, the victim and the situation in which the child exists. Chapter 11, on the legal system, further considers the framework for helping children who live with family violence.

Effects on the child of witnessing inter-parental violence

How the children are affected by their father's violence to their mother has been studied most extensively in groups of children brought by their mothers to women's refuges.[111] Compared to children in non-violent homes they have more behavioural problems – especially over-activity, aggression, rebelliousness and delinquency – more emotional problems such as depression, phobias and obsessionality, more academic under-achievement with poor concentration and poor school attendance, and social problems such as reduced capacity to empathise, to communicate effectively or to assert themselves, resorting to aggression or passive withdrawal when thwarted.

Post-traumatic stress symptoms were recorded in 80 per cent of uninjured child witnesses of violence.[179] Post-traumatic stress disorder is usually more severe and longer lasting if the stress is related to the actions of one person or group of people against another, and is more likely in uninjured witnesses than in injured abused children, whose perception and memories may focus more on their own pain and injury. In violent families the enduring threat of violence and uncertainty aggravates post-traumatic stress or, at least, impedes recovery.[86, 126]

Children react differently to stress and the age and sex of the child contribute to these differences. Pre-schoolers in refuges show a high degree of minor health problems and somatic complaints, sleep problems and negative mood, are fearful and act younger than their age[4] and respond poorly to children and adults.[132] Between 6 and 11 years, children are particularly likely to feel guilty, especially where they feel a conflict of loyalty.

Of the children in refuges the younger fare worst, being more helpless and more dependent on their mothers. The mothers, being insecure, may be emotionally inaccessible, which fuels the children's insecurity. Furthermore, younger children are able to make sense of events around them only from their own perspective which is limited and distorted because of their immaturity. As we indicated earlier, they are prone to blame themselves for what is going wrong around them. Rows about children which lead to violence are more common than rows about sex or money,[214] so children may have reason for their belief that they have caused the violence. Moreover, children see much more of the fighting than their parents realise or wish to admit. Children old enough to talk can describe violence which neither father nor mother knows that they have seen.[111] This theme, that children will tell only when asked (and not always then), occurs throughout all violence and trauma research.

Boys of violent fathers are particularly vulnerable, possibly because their attachment to the mother conflicts with the formation of a male identity. Girls form their identity by becoming like their mothers, boys by becoming different. Boys are more prone to act aggressively because of biological and social factors. This combines with a common reaction to trauma: the attempt to master a response to it through repetitive play, to create a situation in which boys in turn become aggressive, whereupon their mothers blame them for being like their fathers and express fears that the aggression has been inherited. Mothers may then reject their sons. Girls identify with their mothers as victims and are vulnerable to depression and psychosexual problems.[86]

Although girls from violent families show more anxious, withdrawn and clinging behaviour (whereas boys are more aggressive, with more temper tantrums), when asked to describe their own symptoms and behaviour, boys are as likely as girls to acknowledge stress, fears and turmoil. Boys and girls feel the same degree of distress but, as boys act out more, their distress is camouflaged.[111, 113]

As yet there has been little research concerning the interactive effects of psychological trauma, including family homicide, on sibling groups. Birth order, age, gender and stage of development interact with other factors to create a situation where the effect of the same violent event on each child within the family group produces a different picture. For some, the loss may be of a birth parent, for others of a step-parent or cohabitee, known briefly or for many years. Each child is in turn affected by the differing responses of her siblings, making the task of planning their future even more difficult. Several authors provide overviews of what we know about children who live with violence and they emphasise the importance of listening to these children.[29, 162, 164]

Elliot and Lucy, aged 15 and 3

Elliot, aged 15, who lived with his divorced mother, had been visiting his grandparents when his father killed his step-mother by stabbing. He agreed to accompany his father's elderly parents to the prison where his father was serving a sentence for manslaughter. He was able to speak to his father of his horror at the crime but also to feel pride in offering some help to the grief-stricken paternal grandparents. Elliot accepted therapeutic help in coping with these conflicts and invited his mother to meet his therapist.

Elliot continued to live with his mother but visited and wrote to Lucy, aged 3 years, the daughter of his father's second marriage. He understood and agreed with Lucy's need for an adoptive home, since her mother was dead and she had no relatives able to care for her. The adopters in turn were able to accept that Lucy and Elliot should stay in touch with one another and to support this.

Keith, aged 14 years

Repeated experience of violence

Keith Williams, aged 14, kept missing school. He was very anxious when he was there; his concentration was poor and he kept asking to go home because he felt unwell. He often consulted his family doctor because of a range of aches and pains, particularly abdominal pain. The doctor thought that this was anxiety rather than truancy and asked us to explore this. Four years earlier we had seen Gary, Keith's older brother, for the same reason.

Mrs Williams had brought up her two boys single-handed from when Gary was 8 and Keith 4 years old. She had told us that her husband, the boys' father, was a heavy drinker who had beaten her up often, many times in front of the two children. Dad was still in the neighbourhood, and saw the boys from time to time, though he often did not turn up when expected. He had a girlfriend with whom he told them he did not get on very well. Recently, he had asked his ex-wife if they could get together again.

Four years ago Gary had been very clear that he missed school because he did not want to leave his mum on her own; at this time he was very worried that she might get together with his dad and there had been quite a number of violent rows involving dad and other members of his family after dad had been drinking. Mrs Williams was herself very anxious, never travelling on buses if she could help it. Though she managed to hold down a part-time job near her home, she often went off sick and took quite large doses of tranquillisers.

When Gary was referred to us four years earlier, his father refused to come to family meetings, but we met mother and sons several times. She went back to her general practitioner and cut down her medication and began to work closely with the school to make sure that Gary got there. She got legal aid, consulted a solicitor and separated from her husband. Nine months after we first met the family Mrs Williams was rarely off sick. The boys would sometimes see their father at their (paternal) grandmother's house but preferred not to meet him anywhere else. They said he still drank heavily.

Four years later, Keith's story was that he in turn was now his mother's protector. Mrs Williams and he were both very upset because Gary, now 18, went out drinking with his dad, had just lost his job and was, according to Keith, 'laying about all day and going out at night'. Keith, like his brother before him, was worried about being away from home lest anything happened to his mother. After a series of family meetings Gary cut his drinking and Keith was in school regularly. Then mother got a new man friend. At first the boys were rather pleased and the family parted company with the clinic in a glow of optimism about the future. Six months later, they came along for help and advice about how to give evidence in the Crown Court as well as how to deal with their grief, anger and dismay about what had happened.

Mrs Williams's new partner had lost his job soon after they moved in together. He had told her a great deal about how he had grown up in a violent family and how he longed for a peaceful quiet home such as he now had. But Gary and Keith began to worry that this new member of the household drank rather a lot, just like their father, and that he was very irritable. He tended to order their mother about. They kept quiet because their mother still seemed so happy.

This is what they told their doctor after they had taken their mother, as an emergency, to the local hospital. She had been stabbed in the throat and chest and both boys thought that she would have died had they not thrown themselves on the man friend and deflected the arm which was holding a knife. Keith had thought he too was going to die since the stabbing movements continued until Gary had kicked the man friend in the face and chest. Mrs Williams was full of guilt and grief that she had repeated all over again the violent pattern with her husband and that the outcome, an attack and criminal proceedings, was even worse than anything that had happened during her marriage. Gary was horrified that he had been so aggressive and recalled the moments when he wanted to kill the man who had attacked his mother. Keith, as soon as he lay down at night, had vivid flashbacks of the raised knife and the blood spurting from his mother, who he had thought at that moment was about to die. Repeatedly he could hear her screams.

The attacker, in a statement to the police, alleged that the two boys had started the fight and that Gary had hit his mother first. However no charges were being pressed against the boys, who indeed were seen as having protected their mother. The family were focusing their worries on having to appear as witnesses in the Crown Court. This gave them a common bond but enabled them to avoid talking about the immediate horror of the violence in their home. Gradually we encouraged them to talk about what happened. From the sitting-room where the attack had taken place, they had removed the blood-stained carpet and thrown away some cushions, but family finances were such that they could not afford to replace the floor covering.

The family were offered urgent psychological help which drew on literature concerning critical incident stress debriefing,[150] the third of the four responses to trauma outlined in Chapter 6. As indicated in that chapter, we have doubts about the use of this particular term, preferring 'psychological first aid'. Our work did not take place, as is recommended, within one or two days of the disaster but it proved very effective none the less. First, they were asked to set the scene, describing what they were doing, how they were feeling, where they were and what time of day it was, then to describe where they were, what they heard, what they saw, what they smelled, what they did as the violent attack developed. Each took turns in adding to the details so that the whole incident began to come to life.

Next, came questions about feelings. 'How did you feel when that happened?' 'How are you feeling now?' 'Have you felt like that ever before?' As this was a family who knew each other well and where there had been previous memories of violence, we had to do very little at this point since everyone took part and discussed their fears, anxiety, and feelings of guilt and anger. Next, we asked about what stress symptoms they were feeling and the ways in which their life had been changed by the violent incident. This was particularly useful to Mrs Williams who was again finding it hard to travel to work, and to Keith who was very reluctant to go to school in the mornings. It was a relief to them to realise that much of what they felt was normal and understandable.

What this particular family most needed, all three agreed, was some work on coping with how it would be to go to court and give evidence. Mrs Williams sought help from her local Victim Support group (also discussed in Chapter 6) and through this service mother and sons obtained information about the layout of the court, the court timetable and procedure. Our role was to help mother and sons deal with problems as they came up, to support mother in her decision not to go back on tranquillisers or any other form of medication, to help all three to continue to talk with each other, and to monitor their sleeping problems, which gradually diminished over several weeks.

Six months after the attack this family was coping well. Mother had taken no time off sick, Keith was full-time in school and Gary was working. They had used in all about eight hours of clinic time and reckoned this was a good investment. The attacker, however, was still remanded on bail and his case had not yet come to court. Delays such as this, not uncommon in the criminal justice system, can cause great stress to a family and mean that debriefing, support and information about the court system may have to be repeated. This is expensive of professional time and a source of further stress to those who are witnesses.

Why women stay in violent relationships

Until comparatively recently, husbands were given the right and even the duty to punish physically a wife's transgressions.

> Wife-beating was not simply deviant behaviour that was tolerated but rather for centuries was considered to be a desirable part of a patriarchal family system . . . since the nineteenth century . . . for some persons hitting one's wife is now proscribed behaviour . . . . For other persons, it is proscribed except under certain circumstances (for example, 'She won't listen to reason') or is proscribed beyond a point . . . . There are others, however, who continue to believe that hitting one's spouse is tolerable and even desirable under certain circumstances.[94]

Women are disadvantaged in a number of ways by the continuation of attitudes such as this – financially and through their own perception, often reinforced by family and society – that they are of lower status than their partners and that their rights of access to legal protection are insecure. Often they doubt that police and lawyers will have power to protect them.

It has been said of women who stay with, or return to, violent partners, that they are 'hooked on remorse'.[86] The part of the cycle where the man is full of grief and apologies, appearing gentle and promising never to do it again, can be so rewarding that pain and danger are set aside and the risk that the violence will recur is not considered. For women without money, alternative accommodation or family and social support, the urge to hope for better times may be irresistible.

These factors are potent for women from ethnic minority groups, particularly those with strong traditions which sustain them within their parent culture and where patriarchal traditions similar to those that existed until recently in western society are still strong. For example, in our study (Chapter 12) 16 per cent of the men who killed were Asian, compared with 2.5 per cent of the total population of the United Kingdom. These families may have been struggling also with other disadvantages related to their recent immigrant status, but the possibility that cultural factors are relevant to the marked imbalance in these figures needs further investigation.

It may be difficult for those who move from the authority of their father into an arranged marriage, which makes them part of their husband's family, to obtain support from their own kin. This may be disallowed by tradition and, since also by tradition many arranged marriages take place between first or second cousins, the woman does not have independent relatives to whom she may appeal. Her relatives are also related to her husband.

Men, as breadwinners, learn the language of their new country. Women may be expected to continue to speak their native tongue and to teach it to their children. Their choice is between accepting a subordinate position in a familiar society or taking a step into the unknown. Often, if they are badly treated, the women do not know how to contact professionals who may be of help to them, such as health and social services, or a lawyer who specialises in family justice.

Women in all societies may be hindered from asking for help by their social and economic position and by the influences upon them of their own childhood and that of the men who have become their partners. When a woman from an ethnic minority group is abused by her husband, her situation of powerlessness may be linked with cultural and traditional factors.

In violent families children learn that violence is an acceptable way of dealing with conflict. Girls may accept that being a victim cannot be escaped and children of both sexes may take the side of the aggressor, blaming their mother for not doing what father wished. They may practise what they have learned outside and inside the home, being aggressive and demanding themselves. They live with anxiety and uncertainty and are at risk of developing physical symptoms and learning unconstructive ways of resolving arguments and solving problems, seeing themselves as ineffective.[189] They may be further hindered by limited social and coping skills.[111] As they form new relationships adolescents are at risk of becoming victims or aggressors, or of fearing to enter into intimate relationships lest this should prove to be the case. The following story shows what may happen.

Jennifer and Anne, aged 5 and 3 years

Jennifer and Anne Brown were with their mother in a women's refuge. They were referred to us by their family doctor at their mother's request because she found them so naughty and restless. The girls insisted on sleeping with her at night and cried and wet the bed. Their 20-year-old mother said she was exhausted.

The father, still only 22 years old, had lived with their mother on and off for the last five years. He came from a large family of which many members had been in and out of prison for violence and other crimes.

Mother came from an apparently very peaceful and stable family and said she had had a happy childhood until her father died when she was 14. Afterwards she had not got on well with her mother and grandmother. She became pregnant with Jennifer when 14 and after a family quarrel had moved out to live with her boyfriend. He was a violent man who had struck her on many occasions, had sometimes locked her out of the house or in a room, had pulled out her hair and sometimes he left for weeks on end, then returned and asked for forgiveness. More than once mother had gone home to her mother but the boyfriend had sought her out, full of remorse and promises to be different, and she had returned (against the advice of her own family).

The social worker who brought the children to see us calculated that Jennifer had been through fifteen different moves in her five years of life. There had been five brief stays in women's refuges, six or seven spells with grandmother (sometimes being left there without her mother) and short admissions to foster care while the mother, who had neglected her own health, had emergency hospital treatment, once for a miscarriage and once for a head injury. At the time, she said this was an accident and the hospital staff later said they 'had no reason to suppose that this was untrue'. Mother eventually told a worker at the refuge that 'usually' she was bruised and had black eyes but stayed out of sight until she looked better. She had never sought medical treatment at such times.

Mrs Brown said she had twice taken out injunctions against her partner and twice had changed address so as to 'start afresh without him', but each time, just as with their briefer separations, she had contacted him, or he had sought her out, full of remorse, and they had been reconciled. She again said she wanted to be rehoused, from the refuge, to a place away from her own family and from the children's father where she again would 'make a fresh start'. She was rehoused by the local authority and two months after that the children's father moved in and a new pregnancy followed.

In circumstances like this, where the children are attached to their mother, their day-to-day care is good enough and it is very easy for professionals to get hooked into the hopeful part of the cycle. These little girls were clean, well fed, had all their injections, were forward for their age, and somehow their mother's account of how they were also fearful, with disturbed sleep, very disobedient and angry with her, was discounted because of the obvious love between mother and children. When Mrs Brown was rehoused, a meeting of social workers, teachers, health visitor and a member of our team discussed the risks. We advised that the pattern was going to happen all over again, probably many times, and that living with such violent threat to their mother was very damaging to Jennifer and Anne. But the majority view was that the girls got so much from being with their mother that this risk must be taken and that rehousing was going to mean a new life for all three. Three months later, all the anxieties, difficulties and uncertainties were worse than ever and a new baby was on the way to share them.

In our work we have seen two groups of children. First, there are families in which the killing comes 'out of the blue' or where warning signs, if seen at all, were known only to the mother, now dead, and her young children. Second, there are families where the risk is visible and its repetition can and should be foreseen. In the case of Jennifer and Anne, as we have seen, this risk was underestimated. These little girls may never have been struck or otherwise physically hurt, yet at times they showed the frozen watchfulness, continued alertness to their parents' every move, with expressionless faces and inappropriate stillness, classically described in abused children.

Maybe a mother has a legal right to refuse to recognise the risk of letting her partner back into the house even after she has obtained injunctions against him, but she does not have the right to expose her children to the horror and terror of seeing repeated beatings. Child protection services can and should take note of this form of abuse and protect the children. This may mean removing them from danger and helping them to cope with the separation from mother, or it may be that the prospect of losing her children may enable a parent to recognise the danger and to accept help to end a violent relationship. The work on 'Dangerous Care'[61] and the effects on children of domestic violence[1] is aimed at helping professionals who must wrestle with problems like this.

Often when a parent has been violently attacked, and is unable to look after the children, those who plan the emergency care do not know whether or not there has been previous violence. Often no information emerges even with the passage of time, particularly if the children are the only source of information and they are young or reluctant to talk. Others may be unwilling to provide information because a violent attack on someone else may have relieved them from threat of or from actual, violence.

Phil, aged 9

In Phil's family, father, when arrested for the murder of his wife, claimed that his son had thanked him for the killing, which he had seen. Father said that his dead wife, Phil's step-mother, had often beaten the boy with a belt because he told lies and stole from her. Phil was indeed grief-stricken that his father was in prison and blamed himself for the fight in which his step-mother had died.

His own mother had disappeared soon after Phil's birth and he had no contact with any of her relatives. He went to live with his father's parents and regularly visited his father in prison. The grandparents insisted Phil was doing very well indeed and that there was no need for any specialist help for the boy.

We can only guess at the burden that this boy may be carrying. It seems likely that he will blame himself for the disturbed behaviour which his father's new wife found so difficult to cope with, be grateful for what he, like his father, sees as a rescue from danger or injury, be proud of his father yet horrified that he is the son of a convicted murderer. Father is still Phil's legal guardian and Phil will be a young man when his father is discharged from prison. He has said that he wants to live with his dad and make a home for him and he is supported in this by his father's parents, who blame Phil's step-mother for her own death and think that justice has not been done, because their son did not deserve to go to prison.

Predicting violence: What do we know? Can we learn more?

The best predictor of future behaviour is past behaviour. Patterns tend to be consistent within violent families as do other patterns of relationship. In violent families, parents are mostly young and do not think much of themselves. There is a history of impulsive and aggressive behaviour, moods are unstable, with rapid swings. All or most relationships with others present difficulties and there is a tendency to abuse alcohol and drugs.

There may be a history of similar behaviour in the original family, although not all families with broken relationships, young marriages and impulsive, erratic parenting produce children who repeat the pattern when they grow up. A young man or woman from such a difficult background may choose a partner who provides stability, peace, and an opportunity for growth, and a family is created where children thrive. The pattern is most likely to be repeated, tragically, where damaged young people plunge too early into a disorganised life together, incapable of looking after each other. This causes misery to them and their children, although violent death, fortunately, is a rare outcome.

At best, it is difficult to predict the future, but failure to think about it leaves many children exposed to violence and its profound and continuing effects. In our experience, society, in the form of the social services, police and criminal justice system, leaves most responsibility with an injured partner (usually the woman) when there has been domestic violence. Society moves in only if there is direct risk to the children, and is inclined to discount the effects on them of witnessing repeated acts of violence to a parent. Yet child protection services should be involved just as much with the issues of violence to adults caring for dependent children as with direct child injury and neglect.

The issues are starkly illustrated by the story of Sukina[40] told by the Bridge Child Care Development Service, one of the classic child abuse inquiries which led to the later publication of work on dangerous care, which we referred to earlier.

Sukina, aged 5, died in December 1988 following a sustained and ferocious attack upon her by her father. The subsequent inquiry lists, yet again, the lessons to be learned about co-operation between child protection agencies, and the recognition of evidence plainly visible and indeed recorded in a number of hospital and social services records in the months before Sukina's violent and terrifying death. The sixth chapter of the inquiry's report is entitled 'A concept of dangerousness'. It states:

> After we had read the files and listened to the comments of the professionals involved it was clear to us that on the one hand they saw the child as potentially being at risk, whilst on the other the information available about the adults' behaviour was not brought together effectively, so as to place this in context and enable them to evaluate the degree of risk more firmly.
>
> In meeting with professionals at the centre of the case, we were struck by the very wide range of descriptions given of Sukina's father. For example we heard him described as 'gentle, vicious, flamboyant, withdrawn, aggressive, deferential, caring, cold'. It is quite an extraordinary range of descriptions in respect of one individual.
>
> When we talked in further detail with practitioners, it became clear that Sukina's father presented himself differently to different people and in varied circumstances. For example, a member of staff from a particular day nursery said she dreaded being the senior person on duty if Sukina's father was going to collect her. On those occasions he would arrive with a Doberman pinscher dog which he would bring into the nursery, even though he knew he was not supposed to. When this was pointed out to him he would laugh and make it clear he knew that and then remove the dog. The particular individual was fearful of what the dog might or might not do within the nursery. When we talked with other practitioners, some had heard of the incidents but had not experienced them for themselves, yet they too had an account of how they felt fearful of meeting Sukina's father. These observations however did not appear to be recorded in any systematic way in order to allow them to be taken account of in decision making or in professional support or advice.
>
> Crucially, the family was perceived to be one in which 'domestic violence' occurred and yet very little was recorded about the nature of that violence. It has since transpired however that some of Sukina's father's attacks on her mother were of an appallingly vicious nature. For example, what was described at the time as an 'incident' after a trip to London turned out to be an occasion when Sukina's father had tied her mother to a chair, beaten her viciously and cut off some of her hair. 'The attack seems to have been sustained over a lengthy period of time and would appear, with hindsight, not to be untypical for the family.'

According to the records, at no time were Sukina or her younger sister asked about their experience of having seen a violent attack upon their mother. The inquiry records occasions when Sukina is described as seeming frightened of her step-father, yet there is no account of an attempt to find out directly from her what she feared even though she is recorded as not wanting to be taken home early from nursery because 'my daddy will beat upon me'. This may have been a long-standing problem. Two of the mother's previous partners were also violent and Sukina may have been present while her mother was attacked.

The importance of accurately documenting information about domestic violence and picking up on observations made by other people cannot be too highly stressed and it is particularly important to do this when violence between adults affects the lives and emotional development of children. Indeed, children like Sukina may be particularly at risk because they become so compliant, silent and eager to please that they give few clues, or only negative ones, about what they are experiencing and so become even more vulnerable. If they do give clues and are ignored, the risk may be even greater.

Three months after the assault on Sukina's mother described above, a case conference of professional people, brought together to consider the safety of the children, unaware of the full extent of the attack upon mother, recommended that they be removed from the child protection register. So a decision was recorded which could have suggested to Sukina's family that domestic violence was seen as acceptable to those concerned with the welfare and safety of the children.

This historic document about Sukina is the first which, when enquiring into the death of a child at the hand of a parent, shows in such clear and unequivocal terms that injury to a mother is not simply a matter of her own rights within the civil and criminal justice system but involves child protection too.

Although in our own study only one in ten children is *known* to have suffered any physical abuse at the hands of a parent, very many of them witnessed often horrific violence from their father to their mother. From this they could and should be protected.

Chapter 3

Children and grief

There's no construing the hieroglyphs of Death,
It has no grammar for the living.
Faced with it though, one has to try.
I tell what I hope is true,
Making it simple. Yet her cry
Bleeds across the blank of wind
Like the call of some small bird.
(A.L. Hendriks, 'The feathers')

All who live must die
(Shakespeare, *Hamlet*, I, ii)

SUMMARY

Children can be helped to understand the concept of death and, like adults, respond differently to deaths which are expected and those which occur without warning. They can be helped to take part in mourning, sharing their grief with adults. Those who fail to grieve normally can be identified and helped.

The way a child reacts to the death of a parent will be determined by their age and understanding of death, the nature of the death, the prior relationship with their parent, whether and how they have been prepared, how their carers deal with their own grief, and how they explain what has happened and answer questions.

Understanding of death

The child's ability to understand the basic concepts about death has been well studied and it seems that, by 5 years, most children can understand that death is irreversible, universal, has a cause, involves permanent separation, and that dead people differ from live people in a number of respects. They are immobile, unfeeling, cannot hear, see, smell or speak. All their bodily functions cease and they do not need to drink or eat. It is more difficult for young children to understand that dead bodies putrefy and this idea is not fully formed until nearer puberty.[131]

Young children are as intelligent as older children or adults but they lack experience and knowledge. They will struggle to understand what is happening and will fantasise in the absence of an explanation. In *The Daniel Diary*, A. Fabian gives a most helpful description of a 3-year-old's attempt to grapple with his sister's death which[72], along with other accounts, makes it clear that even very young children can be helped to understand what death means.

Because young children believe that they are the centre of the world and think literally, they are likely to believe that they have caused an event if they wished it or did something wrong.

> Lara, aged 4, became very anxious at nursery school after her mother died in a car crash. She wanted to go home as she was sure that something was wrong with her grandmother who looked after her now. Her teacher attempted to reassure her but Lara became more agitated: 'She's not all right – I know she isn't.' Her teacher asked her how she knew. 'You see I told Granny this morning that I hated her because she wouldn't let me wear my new shoes to school . . . .' Lara looked very worried. Her teacher asked if she thought she hurt Granny. Lara nodded, mutely. The teacher explained that feelings could be hurt by words but they would always mend, and no one could hurt Granny's body by words. In a rush, Lara said, 'Yes you can – I was cross with mummy cos she went out that night and . . . .' The teacher finished the sentence '. . . and she died'. Lara had convinced herself that her cross words had caused her mother's death. These ideas can of course be reinforced by parental expressions. 'You'll be the death of me' is a common one.

As children mature, so does their understanding of death. There is no doubt that it is possible to help most children of normal intelligence and many children with learning difficulties to understand the concepts outlined above. What causes many misconceptions is the failure of adults to help the child with an explanation that is appropriate to his or her stage of development. The child often has to struggle to make sense of stories which do not make sense.

Children who lose both parents through the death of one at the hands of the other have particular problems as relatives try to ease their burden by concealing the truth.

Two children, aged 3 and 2 years at the time of their mother's murder by their father, were cared for by their father's sister who took them regularly to visit him in prison. They were told that their mother was in heaven and that their father had gone to live in a big castle. No one addressed their confusion about why their parents had 'chosen' to leave them and the older boy became convinced that he had done something naughty to drive his parents away.

Processes of grief

We understand much about the way in which adults react to the death of a loved one.[168] At first they are stunned and may even refuse to believe the news. They become agitated, wring their hands, call aloud for the missing person, search in places where he used to be. When they search and do not find, when they are faced with the incontrovertible evidence of the dead body, then agitation gives way to sadness, despair, weeping. Movement is stilled except perhaps for a rocking, keening. There may be anger towards the dead person for 'leaving', or towards fate, or a deity or others. The anger may be turned inwards and show itself in self-reproach and punishment. At this time, the comfort of friends and family who care for the bereaved is valued. Expressing grief and sorrow seems to help recovery. Shakespeare knew this when he says in *Macbeth*, IV, iii, 'Give sorrow words; the grief that does not speak whispers the o'er fraught heart and bids it break.'

About a third of bereaved people experience a strong sense of the presence of the dead person in the early stages of grief. In some cases the presence is experienced as a hallucination and may be taken as a sign that they are going crazy, although more often it is a comforting experience and serves to mitigate the pangs of grief.

Eventually, the pain becomes duller and the bereaved person emerges from mourning with a new identity. They are no longer a wife but now a widow, no longer a son but an orphan, no longer a parent but childless, perhaps. Bereaved people fight against the assumption of this new identity and slip back into earlier phases of grief when memories of the dead person are evoked, perhaps by a tune, or a place they visited together in happier days. Anniversaries are particularly poignant times for reminiscence and may provoke renewed mourning in someone who has functioned well until then.

What we have described so far is normal grief. It is universal in men and women in all cultures and even in higher animals as a response to the loss of someone close. It is painful and during the course of mourning we withdraw from the world and let others care for us. Such a withdrawal is probably helpful; it gives us a chance to review our life and try to make the adjustments necessary to continue without our loved one.

For some people, however, mourning does not follow such a straightforward path. Grief can be absent altogether – others marvel at the composure and 'stiff upper lip' of the bereaved. In some cultures, such as our own, it can be admired, but we know that there is a cost. Grief can be delayed and, when it comes, support has evaporated as other people go back to their own lives. It can be prolonged, and become chronic, intractable and burdensome to all around as well as to the bereaved, or it may take deviant forms, such as physical illness.

What causes grief to 'go wrong'? Much research over the past thirty years has helped us answer that question. These bereavement reactions occur more commonly when the loss is sudden, unexpected, untimely, horrific (mutilation etc.), when there have been deaths preceding, or following, in the young, where a parent or child has died, and where social supports are lacking.[167, 20]

How do children react when a parent dies? Do they have similar reactions to those of adults? Can children grieve? For years there was controversy about whether children could relinquish attachment to a parent, because of their continuing need for parenting, or whether they merely transferred their affections to substitute carers.[37–39, 252]

Children younger than 5 have limitations in their understanding, and their need for their mother is so great that it is difficult to help them to grieve, since you cannot grieve for someone if you do not understand that you have lost them forever. Nevertheless a simple explanation should be attempted even with the very young.

Children who have reached school age are as capable as adults of comprehending death, of expressing grief and experiencing mourning. The reactions may appear different because they often take an immature form. The influences on the expression of grief and the ability to mourn in children are related to intellectual, emotional and physical development.

Intellectual development

Children have difficulty anticipating both the death and the prospect of missing the dead parent. There is a developmental progression in the ability to envisage how one might feel on future occasions. For example, it would be difficult for young children to imagine that they might miss their mother when they next go on holiday. Mourning for all the small and large events and situations at which mother will no longer be present is therefore more difficult and, when the event comes, the child is unprepared for the emotional experience of renewed loss.

The illusory or hallucinatory experiences which serve to mitigate the pangs of grief in adults are experienced by young children, who do not appreciate the origin of the phenomena, as evidence of parental return, or as evidence of persecution by the ghost of the dead parent, because of their imagined shortcomings or even death wishes towards the parent. Children devote considerable energy to staying connected with their dead parents through dreams, and by talking to or thinking about them. They try to hang on to something tangible which reminds them of their dead parent.[206]

A child's ability to call up memories is limited especially if there are no tangible reminders of the dead parent.[115] These are often denied them by protective adults who 'do not wish to remind them of their loss'. The places they visited with their parent are not returned to, so mourning is inhibited. Whereas adults can take themselves to the places, in reality and in fantasy, it is more difficult for the child to do both. The dead parent's possessions are tidied away, even photographs may be banished. If a child who has lost his mother at his father's hands is living with father's family, this process of banishing mementoes is likely to be enhanced.

> Marie was 4 when her father stabbed her mother to death. She was asleep at the time. Afterwards she went to live with father's brother and his wife and family. She was taken to visit father every week in prison. She cherished a photo of her parents and herself taken at a family wedding. After one prison visit, the photo disappeared. No one knew what had happened to it.

The loss of a parent is associated with difficulties in learning and failure to maintain progress at school. One study found that one year after bereavement there was a marked falling-off in school work in bereaved children compared with their class mates who had not lost a parent.[230] In another study, the children who were emotionally highly distressed were doing poorly at school, experienced more teasing for having a dead parent, were more preoccupied with thoughts of their dead parent and suffered more health problems.[206]

Emotional development

Young children find it difficult to sustain sad feelings and their capacity to do so increases as they grow older. Not only may they avoid the pain of grief but their apparent lack of sadness may deceive their caregivers into believing that they are unaffected by the loss.

One way in which children come to understand events is through repetitive play which may be distressing to adults because it seems mechanical and without feeling.

> Two young sisters whose father had died enjoyed the game of 'talking' to him in heaven on their toy telephones. Their mother found their glee at this activity unbearable and believed them to be unfeeling about the death. In reality they were coming to terms with his absence through play. When he had been alive, he would have answered their phone calls, so they were experiencing again and again his silence.

Children are often not given help with anticipating the death of a parent, even when it is possible to do so, as adults wish to protect them from pain. Yet there is evidence that it is helpful to them. In one study of parental death, children who were informed about the impending event had lower levels of anxiety than those who were not, even within the same family.[190]

Children need to be able to understand the reality of death in order to mourn and yet they are given less opportunity to see for themselves the physical deterioration, and then the immobility and unresponsiveness of the dead parent. They may be prevented from going to the funeral and protected from the grief of the adults. Where death has been sudden, unexpected and violent, the child is most vulnerable.

> Patricia, aged 5, could not believe that her mother was dead or that father would do such a terrible thing as to kill her. We made arrangements for Patricia to visit her mother's body at the funeral parlour but, as she was still in her father's custody, his permission had to be sought. He refused it and, as a result, it was difficult to convince her that her mother had not abandoned her.

Their concrete thinking and egocentric view of the world makes it more likely that young children will feel guilty and responsible for the parent's disappearance. Longings for death and ideas about suicide are common as part of reunion fantasies but are rarely acted upon.[237]

In the children in our study, guilt about the death and fantasies that they could have prevented it were common.

> Fred, aged 11, and Rosie, aged 4, were with their mother when their estranged father blasted her with a shotgun. Fred ran to get help but Rosie was frozen to the ground with fear and was splattered with blood from mother's wounds. Afterwards Fred was tortured with guilt at his inability to save his mother. Rosie developed frightening dreams in which father appeared brandishing the gun and she yelled at him to stop.

Another aspect of emotional development is the continuing need for care-givers. Children who have lost one parent feel anxious that the other one will also die or disappear. They monitor their surviving parent and may interpret the adult's expressions of grief as illness. Children may hide their own grief in order to protect their parent, and avoid upsetting them for fear that this parent will disappear too. Adolescents in the process of separating from parents may either take a step back and become more involved with the family, par-ticularly if they are the eldest or of the same sex as the deceased parent,[17] or may react by rejecting the family and developing new and possibly premature partnerships.

> June, aged 11, and Angela, aged 8, were living with their father after he had served a term for the manslaughter of their mother by bludgeoning which they had witnessed. June confided to us that they tried to be very good, so daddy would not be cross with them as he had with mummy.

Children may not understand the source of their emotions. The ability to attribute anxiety, depression and other unpleasant emotions accurately develops with maturation.[176] Education about emotional reactions should be a part of the curriculum in schools but rarely is.[235]

Physical development

Very young children who have not yet learned to speak react to loss with bodily responses. Previously continent children may become bedwetters or soilers, lose their appetite, fail to settle to sleep or become restless. If they have recently learned to walk, they may temporarily revert to crawling. Previously secure children may cling to the remaining parent and refuse to separate. Infections and other illnesses are commoner in young children following loss of a parent.[186]

Effects of parental death

Infants and young children

Children younger than 4 probably have little concept of death and their reactions to the disappearance of a parent from whatever cause are similar. Thus a parent away for a few hours, and one absent for longer, evoke the same separation anxiety in children older than a few weeks or months. This is well documented.[37] The longer the absence, the greater the distress until protest gives way to despair and depression, and that in turn to detachment.

Young school-aged children

Children from 5–11 years are more likely to be able to understand the physical changes death brings and are helped by being able to perceive these changes for themselves. They should be allowed to see their dead parent and touch her, in the company of an understanding adult who can help them understand the experience. Adults find this difficult to do and so children are cut off from using their intelligence to make the effort to comprehend death. At this age the characteristic response to the death of a parent is one of excessive activity. About half of all bereaved children develop problems of behaviour or emotions in the year following the death but these are usually short-lived.[31, 78, 184] Serious problems in children bereaved by death from natural causes, whilst more common than in the general population, are fortunately still comparatively rare.[230]

Adolescents

Adolescents are more easily able to express their feelings of loss in a way which resembles that of adults. The capacity to sustain sadness increases with age and so does the ability to express grief directly rather than through bodily symptoms or behavioural disturbances. Adolescents are growing rapidly and hormonal and other influences bring about a desire for greater independence which conflicts with the tendency to become more dependent when bereaved. This may give rise to a seeming indifference or lack of feeling which can alarm and puzzle adults. The oldest child in the family, of the same sex as the dead parent is more at risk for psychological problems.[17]

It is among adolescents too that revenge fantasies become very powerful.

Three children whose mother was murdered by father expressed fierce and persistent hatred towards him, refusing to visit him in prison. They believed he had made other attempts on their mother's life. It was only when they reached adolescence that they began to discuss with their therapist their belief that their mother's soul could not rest easy in heaven until her murder had been avenged. The eldest boy in this Asian family appointed himself her avenger and, although the therapist helped him to understand that his mother would not have wished him to spend his life in prison, it remains to be seen whether she has been successful in deflecting him from his purpose.

Long-term effects of bereavement on children

Children who are bereaved early are more likely to develop psychiatric disorders in later childhood.[31, 129, 194] Goodyer and his colleagues, on the basis of a series of population studies of school-aged children, concluded that recent undesirable life events (such as bereavement) exert a significant (about five times) adverse effect on the probability of being anxious or depressed which was independent of maternal adversities (poor confiding relations in mothers' own lives and the presence of maternal distress). Emotional disorders in the children were best predicted by the presence of all three adversities (bereavement in combination with their mothers' problems).[90]

Adults bereaved of a parent in childhood appear to be more vulnerable than the general population to psychiatric disorder,[15, 44] particularly depression and anxiety, and this seems to be precipitated by further losses. Attempted suicide is more common in adults bereaved in childhood.[16, 106] The longer-term outcome for children under 17 years appears to be associated with the care they receive post-bereavement and this is often dependent on the coping ability of the surviving parent.[99]

Cultural and religious issues

Reactions to loss are biologically based (they occur in higher primates as well as humans) and are therefore likely to transcend cultural differences. Religious beliefs about what happens after death can be confusing to young children at the stage of concrete thinking and so need to be presented with thought given to their developmental stage. A helpful text gives guidance on religious and cultural differences in the conceptualisation of death.[169]

Helping bereaved children and parents

Many of the problems mentioned earlier can be prevented or modified by intervention either before the death (sadly not possible with sudden, unexpected bereavements) or during the period following death. A review of research that has been carried out, testing the effectiveness of bereavement counselling for adults, concluded that it was helpful,[166] and a study of family counselling with children bereaved of a parent showed that it reduced the number of children showing problems by more than half.[31] Others have done sensitive work with individual children, giving pointers to the problems that bereavement poses for children and how they can be helped.[79] Others again have set up programmes offering group meetings for bereaved children and have found them efficacious in reducing symptoms.[152] Camps for bereaved children are available in the USA and Britain,[213] where counselling as a group and individually occurs in the setting of a holiday and where children can learn that their experiences are not unique.

When children are referred immediately after bereavement, mental health practitioners can help ensure that they receive the best care. This may involve periods of relief from the company of a grief-stricken adult, advice about how to cope with other children's questions and adults' expressions of condolence, factual information about the cause of death and the processes of death, burial and cremation, and advice to the carers about viewing the body, attending the funeral, returning to school, and promoting healthy mourning.

> Joseph, aged 4 years, lost his father suddenly when the latter took a lethal overdose of his anti-depressant medication. Joseph was seen by his general practitioner who himself felt guilty at having prescribed the drugs which killed the father. The boy, his mother and the doctor met together for several sessions during which he was able to help clarify for Joseph that daddy had had a sickness which the doctor couldn't get better although he had tried. The sickness caused a pain in daddy's head which was so bad he took lots of tablets to get it better but they had not helped and daddy's body had stopped working. The doctor accompanied the boy to the funeral and helped him to understand why

everyone was crying and what was happening. Helping Joseph in this way relieved mother and also made the doctor feel he was making some restitution. Joseph went on to attend a play-group for bereaved pre-school children run by a volunteer bereavement counselling group, whilst his mother attended some group meetings for widowed mothers run by the same organisation. Joseph gradually came to terms with the loss of his father. He cried appropriately and talked often about his father and he and mother were able to grieve together.

There is no specific pattern of symptoms which results from a prolonged or deviant grief reaction in a child and the treatment is related to the presenting problem. As in all disorders, a careful history will have been taken, and any bereavements evaluated as possible contributory factors. In adults the technique of forced or operational mourning, creating a situation in which the task of grieving is begun, has been shown to be effective, if the patient has depressive symptoms and has been bereaved,[144] but this has not been evaluated in children. In principle, there seems no reason why it should not be equally effective and it has been shown that guiding mourning is not harmful in early bereavement.[32] Bereavement counselling is well-established as an effective preventive intervention.[261]

Preparation for loss

Can we better prepare children and young people for the inevitable little losses of their lives and will this enhance their coping capacities when bigger losses occur, even when these are traumatic and unexpected? The first funeral a child attends should not have to be that of a sibling or parent. Should they not be included in the grief of their community as happens in other cultures, so that, when a neighbour, or a community elder dies, the children attend the funeral or memorial service? If we encouraged parents to prepare their children for the possibility of larger loss by talking about the inevitable small losses, helping them to express their grief and accept comfort, if the opportunity was taken while visiting a church to wander round the tombstones and ponder on the lives of those buried, natural discussion of death and dying and its effects would arise.

A manual for teachers helps to teach about the ubiquity of death and the way in which children can help their mates who may suffer loss. The authors include a useful and full list of children's fiction which deals with issues of death and grief.[235] Most children's libraries will recommend fiction that may help prepare children and some issue lists of books.

When death is near, this educational and preparational work needs to be intensified. Teachers can be very helpful in preparing the class for the impending death of one of their members, and the teachers of the siblings also need to be alerted. They may be the best people to accompany a bereaved child to the funeral, and this should be negotiated by the social worker or hospital teacher so that they can be released from their teaching duties for that day. The bereaved parent(s) can then feel able to give themselves up to their grief, knowing that the children are cared for by someone they know who is less affected by the death.[236] This work is sadly irrelevant to the children in our study, yet a society and schools which educate children about death and dying will be better placed to help all bereaved children.

Contrasting reactions to trauma and grief

Human reactions to loss are different from those to trauma. Initially the bereaved show their distress with a facial expression common to all humankind. The closed mouth, contracted facial muscles and furrowed brow contrast with the staring eyes, dilated pupils and raised eyebrows of the horror-struck.

For the bereaved, the image and memory of the lost person are paramount; the traumatised suffer intrusive memories of the fearful event and often cannot summon up memories of the face of the dead person. The bereaved yearn and are preoccupied with their loss; the traumatised are anxious and preoccupied with their trauma. Bereaved people are anxious about the separation from their lost one. Anxiety settles but sadness is deep and persistent. The traumatised are not sad or nostalgic even when they are also bereaved, but are specifically anxious about threats of danger similar to that which they have experienced. Those who grieve and those who are traumatised are alike in expressing anger, but the former are angry at their loss, the latter are irritable, easily aroused by threat or upheaval and liable to feelings of diffuse rage which cannot be focused. The bereaved feel guilty that they did not do enough for the lost person; the traumatised feel guilty that they have survived when others have not.

The bereaved seek out associations with their loved one; the traumatised avoid reminders of the event. The bereaved see grief as a tribute to be paid to their dead; the traumatised try to clamp down on their feelings and often have great difficulty in talking about what has happened to them. Bereaved people seek out reminders of the dead person, searching for what they have lost. The traumatised are oriented to perceive threat and danger, searching their environment with alert fearfulness. If startled, their responses are exaggerated. The bereaved dream of their dead, dreams which change over time as the loss is accepted. The traumatised suffer nightmares, experiencing terror rather than loss.

The interplay of trauma and grief

Traumatic reactions can interfere with grieving. The nightmares of trauma are always distressing and may prevent the child dreaming more calmly about the dead parent and gaining comfort from the feeling that mother is near. These 'grief dreams' appear to help in coming to terms with the loss. Intrusive daytime recollections also interfere with the child's efforts to remember the dead parent. The mutilated image prevents reminiscence in tranquillity. Traumatic play can be repetitive and uncreative and interfere with the use of play to address and work through grief.

The helplessness associated with the witnessing of the killing of a parent can lead to emotional constriction, sensations of numbing, and avoidance of reminders of the event. Yet to grieve satisfactorily for a dead loved one it is necessary to remember and recollect again and again. The need to avoid the traumatic images interferes with this process. The hyper-vigilance referred to above, which occurs after trauma, leads to a pervasive fearful anxiety which makes it even more difficult for the child to focus on loss.

Children who lose a parent through suicide, or homicide, are preoccupied by issues of accountability and revenge, and these emotions prevent them from developing a grief reaction.

Reminders of the violent death are different in trauma and grief and the reminders of, say, the traumatic circumstances of the loss may be very concrete and have been found to prevent mourning.[70, 185] Pynoos has helpfully delineated the three types of overlapping reminders of a violent death: the reminders of the circumstances of the death, of the loss, and of the subsequent changes in one's life.[177] It helps during therapy to be able to separate the reminders so that each of them is more manageable.

Interventions for traumatic bereavement

The goals in treating children who have suffered a traumatic bereavement are, first, to help them to anticipate, understand and manage everyday reminders so that the intensity of these reminders and their ability to disrupt daily functioning gradually lessen, and then to begin to do the grief work which involves summoning up reminders of the dead parent and grieving for them one by one. The problem is that there are psychological dysynchronies[176] between the resolution of trauma and the grief process, and among the family members. The latter may make it difficult for a bereaved grandparent who did not witness the killing to accept the fact that the child who witnessed it is unable to join in the mourning rituals of the family because the trauma has inhibited grieving.

In our experience, it is possible to address the issues of trauma first, particularly if the children are seen soon after the event, but it may take years for grief to come in. We have known grieving to take place ten years or more after a child witnessed her mother's death and there is good evidence that much adult psychiatric disturbance is related to inhibited mourning reactions.[133]

Chapter 4

Why do people kill their partners?

Art O'Connor

Then dulled thoughts turn
To passion's last despairing cause.
  (Roland John, 'Celebrants')

SUMMARY

Dr O'Connor discusses the psychology and incidence of spouse killing and the impact of the criminal law on adult killers with particular reference to concepts such as unfitness to plead and diminished responsibility. He also discusses death by suicide after a killing, and current sentencing policy. He reminds us that the criminal law and the work of adult forensic psychiatrists remain unconnected with the needs of child victims of crime.

A number of years ago a very dependent man in his late twenties became unhappy and distressed throughout the six months that his marriage was breaking up. He and his partner had a young baby and he wanted the three of them to stay together. He strongly believed that his partner was being influenced by friends in their neighbourhood. She spent more and more time with these people, with the baby, leaving him alone. He was unemployed. He drank very heavily for several months and then, in a fit of despair, drank constantly over several hours. Finally, he downed a full bottle of whisky. He put a kitchen knife into his pocket and went to the house where his wife had started to live with her friends. He pleaded with her to come home. When she refused he lunged at her with the knife and stabbed her once in the throat. She collapsed and died on the way to hospital. He was totally open about his offence and has repeated since, 'I have killed the only person I have ever loved.'

In 25 per cent of homicide cases a husband kills a wife or partner. Why does this happen and why is marriage the one relationship most prone to end in homicide?

One reason is the closeness of the contact with a spouse; the two people live together, have breakfast with each other, spend a significant part of the day and evening together and usually share the same bed. The sexual aspect of the relationship also makes it different from others, as for most partners in a marriage the main sexual contact is with their spouse. It is a long relationship starting usually in the twenties and going on into middle life and even for the whole of life. The two married people often share their own maturation and experiences such as having children, getting a first home, the ups and downs of employment and unemployment, financial successes and pressures, and relationships with in-laws and the general community.

Some of these experiences can be positive and help the individuals involved to grow, but others can be stressful and cause great difficulties for them and their relationship. During this long-term relationship it is easy to expect that people can love each other at some times but will also argue and find each other intensely irritating at others. Who better knows one's weak points and sensitive areas than one's spouse? This would suggest that a spouse is the most likely person to harass, nag and humiliate a person. If this provocation, whether justified or not, is intense enough and prolonged enough it is easy to accept that everyone can reach a breaking point.

Homicide is most likely to occur in the relationship of marriage, or similar situations, and this is not unexpected since it is here that contact between two people is most intense. Both parties have invested so much – in children, families, hopes for the future, affection and love – and walking away from the problem is not as easy as in other situations. The intensity of the relationship issues between the two also frequently means that they are unable to withdraw even if they wanted to. They have also brought to the relationship their own individual pasts with projected notions concerning their own upbringing; they often have expectations of the partner that can be idealised versions of their own parents, lovers, friends, children and others. They also bring a whole range of hatreds and resentments about various people and issues that they play out in various ways in the marriage, with and on the partner. If a man is prone to episodes of frustration and anger with outbursts of violence it is not surprising that the wife is the likely victim. She is available, because of the close contact, is physically weaker, being female, and so is vulnerable and an easy target. She can also be part of the problems and the issues involved.

The intensity of the arguments and the ways of relating within the partnership can sometimes be important in the triggering of violence but this is not always the case. Some people can bring their frustrations and problems home from outside to vent them violently on an unsuspecting spouse. If alcoholism or mental illness is a problem and if these disorders lead that person to violence, then the partner is a likely victim just because of the close contact. Other interpersonal issues are more likely to exist because of what is going on in the relationship itself, and these too can lead to violence and murder.

The following are some of the issues we can meet when asked to become involved in cases where one partner kills another:

1   Violence at home: wife battering.
2   Alcoholism and its relationship to homicide.
3   Jealousy.
4   Extended suicide and suicide pacts.
5   The wife as the murderer.

Wife battering

This problem has always been with us but was brought to the fore in the 1970s with the growth of feminism.[95] Attempts to define the problem have caused difficulties among various commentators. In 1970 the Royal College of Psychiatrists described the problem in terms of women who had suffered serious or repeated physical injury from the men with whom they lived.[192] One writer[82] described battering as repeated attacks and multiple blows, and another as violence, physical or psychological, inflicted on a spouse without her consent.[214] Opinions seem to differ as regards the amount and frequency of violence that constitutes wife battering (see also Chapter 2).

There are also different opinions on the prevalence of the problem. In one Canadian study, it has been estimated to occur as infrequently as in 1 in 500 marriages, and as commonly as in 1 in 10 marriages.[136] It seems to be commoner in lower socio-economic groups and also among the less educated. Why should this be? Can some people in these groups only express their frustrations and anger in terms of violence?

The alarming rise in the rate of violence within the family in the United States has prompted the American Medical Association to complain about it. Dr Antonia Novello, the United States Surgeon General, pointed out that in 1990:

> one third of the women murdered in this country were killed by their husbands, ex-husbands or boyfriend . . . each year approximately 626,000 violent victimisations of women are committed by men they know well. The medical setting may be the first and only place a person who has been abused seeks help.[218]

A third of American women who visit hospital emergency rooms are thought to be victims of family violence but few are identified as such. In Philadelphia 'falls' are the most common alleged cause of injury in women aged 25–34. Noting that falls are common only in elderly people, Dr Novello said, 'Now you tell me what is going on.' A surgeon in the state of Maine has said, 'There are people who have so many "accidents" that the local hospital emergency room staff know them well.'[218]

What are the reasons for this violence? According to Dr Richard Welles, professor of sociology and anthropology at the University of Rhode Island:

> There is tremendous resistance to abandoning models: the psychopathic model, the low social class model, the alcohol and substance abuse model.

There were 2,000,000 cases of wife abuse in this country, but only 800 women were killed. That means that most men, nearly 2,000,000 can control themselves.[218]

This is an alarming response to the gradient between wife abuse and wife killing; the former is regarded as a sign that men can control themselves and only the killing of the wife is a sign of failure.

It is not only wives who are abused, although more attention is paid to this because of the greater degree of physical damage.[210, 211] Various authors have written about husband battering, although professionals are still not in agreement. In one form, it is considered to be the behaviour of a woman acting in self-defence. So it seems to be different from the abuse of wives, where the violence is often unprovoked. Wives who kill their husbands are seven times more likely to be acting in self-defence than husbands who have killed their wives.[212]

Why do husbands batter their wives? Two-thirds of cases are related to jealousy.[82] Sexual difficulties are important causes; husbands say that their wives are frigid and wives claim that their husbands are impotent.[214] Pregnancy has also been highlighted as precipitating domestic violence,[83] with reasons cited such as sexual frustration and stress because of changes in the relationship or the onset of threats, hardships or crises which disrupt family life.

Sexual violence in marriage can be categorised as part of general physical abuse, as part of continuing sexual conflict within the relationship, or as part of a man's bizarre sexual obsession which may involve pornography or rituals.[74]

The majority of women try to talk the man out of the violence and try to pacify him.[165] A quarter fight back or threaten violence themselves. This course of action seems to be effective for some and can cause the perpetrator to desist but, more commonly, it results in more, and more severe, violence.

Nearly 80 per cent of women can only end the violence by leaving the man, but a large proportion of these return. One complaint is that the police do not always take violence within marriage as seriously as they should, although many police forces are improving their services in this respect.

In domestic homicides men constitute fewer than 20 per cent of the victims. This shows that the most dangerous position, in terms of the likelihood of being murdered, is to be a female in a marriage or common-law union; the risk is greater in common-law relationships.[53] In the study that highlighted this, more than half of the 34 cases had a previous history of domestic violence, and in 70 per cent of the cases the violence was related to extra-marital affairs or suspicions about them.

Alcoholism and its relationship to homicide

A farmer in his mid-forties had had a serious alcohol problem since he was in his twenties. He had been married for nearly twenty years and had three teenage children. In the local area he was noted as being an introverted grumpy man with few friends. For most of the marriage he had gone out drinking, especially at weekends. From time to time he got into fights after drinking and had several convictions for being drunk and disorderly. Frequently he would be verbally aggressive at home when intoxicated. He argued with the children about everything and often beat either of the two boys for trivial misbehaviour. Several times a month his wife was the target of his aggression and he would beat her. Her bones were never broken but she was bruised. Sometimes he would threaten to kill her.

One Saturday he returned home after closing time. He was very intoxicated and the shouting and beating started. His wife was crying and he was getting more and more angry. The children were out for the evening and this made him worse. He went into the bedroom and got his shotgun. He was picked up by the police an hour later covered in blood. He had very little memory of what had happened. His wife was found in the house where she lay after the two barrels of the shotgun had been emptied into her. Subsequently he was found guilty of murder and sentenced to life imprisonment.

Alcohol has commonly been associated with homicide, especially domestic homicide, in different studies and populations. In a Scottish study[85] of 367 men and 33 women who had been charged with murder, it was found that 58 per cent of the men and 30 per cent of the women were intoxicated at the time of the offence. An American study[254] found that alcohol was present in both victim and assailant in 44 per cent of homicides. Alcohol intoxication is also common in wife battering. One-third of battered wives report that violence regularly occurs when their husbands are drunk.[82] In violent crime in general it has been accepted for a long time that alcohol frequently plays a part. Researchers in the UK[67] found that 11 per cent of offenders had a serious dependence on alcohol and 23 per cent had a mild dependence. The more serious the crime, the more likely that the offender and victim were intoxicated at the time of the offence. Some social workers would say that alcohol has a special causal role in crimes of violence. Alcohol has long been accepted as having a disinhibiting effect as it diminishes impulse control. When this is coupled with situational factors such as frustration and long-standing interpersonal friction, violence is much more likely to occur. Scandinavian researchers[247] strongly suggest that the only way to diminish violent crime related to alcohol is to limit its availability by rationing, which they claim is much more successful than price control. The story that introduced this section might not have developed if the man's access to alcohol had been limited.

Jealousy

This has always been recognised as a dangerous passion. Blake described jealousy as 'a creeping skeleton around a frozen marriage bed'. It is frequently associated with the violence of men towards women. In a series of 110 homicides where jealousy was the main motive, the violence was directed at the female partner rather than at the supposed rival.[153] Jealousy may involve abnormalities in the sufferer's judgement of his partner's fidelity.[154] In 50 per cent of cases there can be abnormalities of mood which may be diagnosed as depression.[155] The jealous person watches, checks for signs of an affair and endlessly questions the suspected partner for clues or a confession. He wants evidence of the infidelity but also wants the partner's love again.

A certain amount of jealousy is common, but it goes from there, through over-possessiveness, to the excessive jealousy of some people with personality disorders, to jealous states in severe mental illness such as schizophrenia where it may be part of a delusion or a false fixed belief. The sufferer may believe that the partner is having an affair and ignore all evidence to the contrary. There may be other delusions present as well. When the jealousy is associated with a mental illness or is outside the realms of what is commonly understood as normal, then the term morbid jealousy is used. However when we are dealing with a personality disorder or someone who has always been very possessive, we are on less sure ground. There is always the possibility that the jealousy is justified, reflecting the truth about what is going on in the relationship.

Alcohol is involved in some cases of morbid jealousy but the association is not as clear as once was thought. The morbidly jealous alcoholic may return home drunk and demand sex from his wife or partner. She may refuse because of his state of intoxication and her refusal may be taken as proof of her infidelity. He may be impotent because of his intoxication or for some other reason and this he also interprets as proof.

Morbid jealousy is sometimes seen in other medical conditions such as Alzheimer's disease and other dementias, brain damage syndromes and multiple sclerosis.

Clinical management

This can be very difficult; it is usually first directed at the underlying mental illness, if there is one present. This can involve drug treatment, individual therapy or work with the couple, sexual counselling or a violence management group for the man. In the end it may mean separation for the couple, barring orders or a women's refuge for crises. From the psychiatrist's standpoint, jealousy is one of the most important issues in predicting dangerousness. It is a symptom that can remain dormant for long periods but can also re-emerge in a new relationship, leading to more violence with a new partner and even a repeat homicide.

A man in his early fifties had been married since his early twenties, to a woman several years younger. They had three grown-up children. The eldest of the family was a girl, married with a small baby. The two younger still lived at home. Their father was always a suspicious loner and had few friends. He had also been possessive and jealous of his wife from early on in the relationship. At first she thought this was an indication of his affection, but as the years went on she tried to ignore his suspiciousness and questions. For most of their twenties and thirties he drank heavily. He often got drunk at weekends and was sometimes violent at home, especially to his wife. In his forties his drinking became less of a problem but his jealousy continued. From time to time he would beat his wife if she returned late from a night out with her friends from the factory where she worked. He often checked her clothes and would frequently follow her, but never had any conclusive proof of infidelity.

One night he followed her and waited outside the pub. At closing time she left with her friends and there was a man in the company. He was sure this was her lover. He rushed home and waited for her to return. She was later than the short journey usually needed and this further confirmed his beliefs. When she came in he was sitting in the dark. He immediately started arguing with her and accusing her. He started beating her and as they struggled he took out a kitchen knife he had concealed in his pocket and stabbed her several times in the chest. He then went out but was later picked up by the police. At his trial nine months later, evidence was put forward to support a defence that he committed manslaughter in a state of diminished responsibility, but he was convicted of murder.

In this case, I (Art O'Connor) was the psychiatrist for the defence. At one point I decided to do a home visit to assess the family situation. The three children lived in an isolated area with which I was not too familiar. On my way there I became a little uneasy as I realised that I was acting for this man who had made all their lives a misery and had also killed their mother whom they loved. They had every right to feel angry towards him and I wondered whether I was putting myself in danger in going to see them. I was relieved to discover that their anger and hatred had turned to pity for their father and that they just wanted him to get help.

A man in his early thirties was apparently happily married with three young children. He had always been outgoing and well adjusted and very attentive to his children. Over two years he became markedly quieter and withdrawn but this did not give rise to concern. One day he threatened a neighbour, a man who had known him for several years. The neighbour did not respond but later decided to call round to his house to find out what it was all about. When he knocked at the door he was greeted by the man with a knife. He stabbed his neighbour many times and killed him. Subsequently it was discovered that he had been suffering from delusions for many months. He believed that his genitals were being interfered with by some agency and he was hearing voices. He also believed that his wife was having an affair with the neighbour. He was able to conceal all this from his wife and those close to him.

In cases of this sort the usual victim is the wife rather than the supposed lover. This killer was found guilty of manslaughter by reason of diminished responsibility. He was committed to a special hospital on Section 37 of the Mental Treatment Act, Northern Ireland, 1983, with a Restriction Order (S. 41) which meant that the discharge decision would need the approval of the Home Secretary.

Murder and suicide

From time to time, whole families are killed. The typical picture is of several children and the parents being found dead by a neighbour. The murder weapon, often a gun, is found by the body of one of the parents, usually the father. He has killed all the children, and his wife and then himself. Subsequently it is learned that the man had a history of a serious depressive illness. Sometimes the suicide part of his plan is not completed for some reason and he ends up being charged with murder. Typically he has had a serious depression for some months with delusions that he and his family were going to die or suffer a great deal from some illness. Another variant could be that a nuclear war is about to break out and they are all going to have a very painful and distressing end from bombs and radiation. So these killings are attempts by the killer to save loved ones from some dreadful calamity or pain.

In 1965, West (in[84]) studied 148 murder-suicides and compared them to an equal number of murders. Although both groups contained an excess of men he found a greater proportion of females among the murder-suicide group (40 per cent). The murder-suicide group were also more likely to be married and in a family setting. The other murderers were more likely to be young, unmarried males from lower socio-economic groups. West estimated that between 1959 and 1960, 33 per cent of homicides were followed by suicide. In the same time period in Denmark the figure was 42 per cent and in the USA much lower at 4 per cent. In the UK, the rate of murder-suicides in the 1950s was 33 per cent, in the 1970s it was 25 per cent and in the 1980s it was just 7 per cent.[36] It is generally accepted that the incidence of homicides associated with mental disorder is staying steady, but as other homicides are increasing, the percentage rate appears to be dropping.

Suicide pacts are rare. Suicides account for approximately 1 per cent of deaths and suicide pacts make up only 1 per cent of all suicides.[97] Usually only two people are involved but whole families may be. There are two types.[84] In one, both parties commit suicide simultaneously. In the other, one person kills the other by agreement, and then himself. Most of these suicides are couples in their sixties; suicide pacts among young lovers and homosexual couples are very rare. In the UK a survivor of such a pact can be charged, under Section 2 of the Suicide Act 1961, with aiding and abetting another's suicide and this carries a maximum sentence of fourteen years' imprisonment. The person alternatively may be charged under Section 4 of the Homicide Act 1957 for killing or being party to the killing of another in pursuance of a suicide pact, and may be found guilty of manslaughter rather than of murder. Prosecutions under these sections are rare with only one or two each year. Sometimes they can represent criminal deceptions, where one person is trying to take advantage of the other for financial gain. Other cases involve euthanasia, where one partner is dying and the other is trying to save their loved one from suffering.

Female offenders

Women are much less commonly charged with crimes of violence than men; this is especially so in the case of homicide. In a German study in 1973[96] it was found that in the category of abnormal offenders in homicide offences men outnumbered women by 3 to 1, and that in the normal offender category they outnumbered women by 4 to 1. It was also found that women tended to attack children and men to attack women. Planning and intent to kill were more frequent among women offenders. In 1975, a UK study[84] found that 17 per cent of homicide suspects were women and this proportion is probably even lower today. One suggestion is that the increase shown in homicide statistics is related to an increase in homicide by normal males. It is also suggested that the number of homicides committed by women is fairly static, as is the number committed by abnormal or mentally disturbed individuals.

A 40-year-old woman was charged with the murder of her husband. He was eight years older than she was and they had six children. They were married when she was 16 and she always claimed that she had been forced into the marriage by both sets of parents. At the time of the marriage he was a very heavy drinker and over the years the problem increased. Soon after the marriage he started to beat her when he was drunk and this problem also grew worse as time went by. As the children came along, they too were beaten. Despite all this she still felt that she loved him and resisted the urge to leave, which in their close-knit families and community would have been difficult anyway. From time to time he would spend short sentences in prison for being drunk and disorderly, and for damage to property or minor assaults. She often found the periods of imprisonment good, as she got a break from him.

He had spent six months in prison, returned home and immediately went drinking. She knew what was going to follow and put a kitchen knife into her coat pocket to frighten him with if he started any violence. In the late evening she met him in a drunken state near where they lived. He started shouting at her and then hitting her. She was terrified and tried to get away. She took out the knife and threatened him but he continued to hit her. She got away but he caught her and carried on beating her. Eventually she stabbed him and he fell. He got up again and continued to pursue her but she was able to run away. She stayed with friends. She only learned that he had died from the wounds the next day. Nine months later she was found guilty of manslaughter and given a probation order.

The assessment of dangerousness

Sometimes psychiatrists and other professionals are asked to make recommendations about the dangerousness of offenders for the courts, release boards of various kinds and other agencies. This is usually when an offence has already taken place and there is concern about the likelihood of a recurrence. There are different approaches to the definition of dangerousness, as there are to its assessment. The Butler Committee,[46] which looked at all aspects of mentally abnormal offenders, defined dangerousness as a 'propensity to cause serious physical injury or lasting psychological harm'. Scott[199] defined it as 'an unpredictable and untreatable tendency to inflict or risk irreversible injury or destruction or to induce others to do so'. It is claimed that psychiatrists are no better than other professionals in these situations, but others would say that psychiatrists are useful when the offender is mentally ill.[174] There are, of course, differences between the clinical or individual approach to prediction and the statistical or actuarial approach and these can come into conflict (see also[61]).

Scott's paper[199] is still very influential. He reviewed the literature and gave clear guidelines about assessment of dangerousness in criminals. He said that it is important to look carefully at the nature of the offence; the past behaviour of the individual in terms of offending; the personal data for such issues as jealousy, mental illness, mental handicap or brain damage; social circumstances; behaviour in custody and adjustment in society after imprisonment. He concluded that the most important predictor is past dangerous behaviour although other pieces of information are also helpful. He highlights jealousy as particularly ominous because of its likelihood of recurrence in the same or future relationships.

The criminal justice system in England and Wales

A person charged with any offence is brought before a magistrates' court at the earliest possibility, usually the next morning. There it is decided to remand the person either on bail or in custody. The person then appears before that same court for several weeks until the depositions or statements in the case are compiled. At that point the magistrates' court commits the proceedings to the Crown Court. This higher court then hears the case, from anything between six and eighteen months later.

At the beginning of the trial the person is asked to plead guilty or not guilty. If their mental health is in question at that point the issue of fitness to plead may be raised. This happens very rarely and involves a separate trial process with a jury which determines, after hearing expert evidence, whether the person understands the nature of the charges, the workings of the court and its personnel, whether he can challenge a juror, give evidence if he wishes to and give valid instruction to counsel. If the person is found unfit to plead they are committed to a hospital, usually a special hospital, until they are fit again. Problems arise where the patient is unfit to plead because of chronic or deteriorating mental illness, from which he may not recover, or because of mental handicap, so that he may never be available to stand trial. To balance the maintenance of justice against the need for medical care of an alleged criminal who may be innocent creates complicated legal and ethical problems for doctors and lawyers.

The next stage is the trial proper. Here the jury decides, after listening to evidence, about guilt or innocence. Murder is where a person causes the death of another person with intent to kill or seriously harm them. If the perpetrator did not intend to kill or seriously injure the victim, the crime is manslaughter. If the person is convicted of murder the judge must pronounce a sentence of life imprisonment. There is no choice; it is a 'mandatory' sentence. If the person is convicted of manslaughter the judge has total discretion in sentencing. This means that a sentence of life imprisonment or any lesser sentence, even probation or a complete discharge from the court, can be imposed, so it is always better to be found guilty of manslaughter than murder.

To a charge of murder there are several commonly used defences. The first is self-defence. A person is entitled to use reasonable force in self-protection; this includes homicide if a threat to life is perceived. The second defence is provocation, which has the effect of reducing the charge to manslaughter if successful and is very desirable for the defendant. To succeed with a defence of provocation it must be proved, on the balance of probabilities, that provocation was beyond what the 'ordinary man' could have sustained. In recent years the concept of 'cumulative provocation' has sometimes been successfully argued. Here the defendant has tried to prove that the provocation went on over a long period and that, even though the last episode may have been relatively small or trivial in comparison to earlier ones, the killing was as a result of the prolonged provocation.

The next defence is the psychiatric one of diminished responsibility. The 1957 Homicide Act, Section 2 states:

> Where a person kills or is a party to the killing of another, he shall not be convicted of murder if he was suffering from such abnormality of mind (whether arising from a condition of arrested or retarded development of mind or any inherent causes or induced by disease or injury) as substantially impairs mental responsibility for his acts and omissions in doing or being a party to the killing.

'Abnormality of mind' is a broad term. As the definition progresses and case law is established, mental handicap is now being included, as are diseases and an injury. The common diseases involved are depressive disorders and schizophrenia. Personality disorder is covered by the term 'inherent causes'. The critical phrase is 'substantially impairs mental responsibility' and it is on this that most debate in the court is centred. If the defence is successful the charge of murder is reduced to manslaughter and the judge has discretion in sentencing, as indicated above. For the years 1983–4, 5 per cent of homicides were sentenced to life imprisonment, 40–5 per cent were given other custodial sentences and 30–5 per cent were given Hospital Orders under Sections 37 and 41 (a restriction order) of the Mental Treatment Act 1983.[36] Since the mid-1970s there have been between 69 and 99 Section 2 manslaughters per year. To put this into perspective, the outcomes of cases originally recorded as homicide in 1985 are as follows: 132 were convicted of murder, 61 of diminished responsibility, 134 of other manslaughter, and 4 of infanticide.

To summarise in 25 per cent of homicide cases in the UK a husband kills his wife or partner. The closeness of the relationship, both physically and emotionally, can lead to prolonged conflict. Escape from this situation may be impossible for some individuals for many reasons, not least of which may be that they are parents of young children.

Note

Art O'Connor, MB, B.Ch., MRCPsych., is Consultant Forensic Psychiatrist at the Central Mental Hospital, Dundrum, Dublin, Eire, and is the author of *Criminals: Inside the Minds of Criminals and Victims* (1996) Marino Books, Mercier Press, Dublin.

Part II

When father kills mother

Effects on the children

Chapter 5

The children's stories

If I could bring myself to traipse
the path again, that stench of silage . . .
(Peter Dale, 'The Old Path')

SUMMARY

These stories are compiled from the experiences of many families so as to
illustrate in dramatic form the themes of earlier chapters.

Angelo, aged 18 months to 4 years

Angelo was 18 months old when his mother Molly died. She was found
on the ground floor of a café which she had run in partnership with her
common-law husband. It was Sunday and the café was closed. Mario,
Angelo's father, called the police to say he could not get into the flat
above the café and that his wife did not answer the doorbell. As the
police, at his request, broke open a window, father said, 'Can you see
her body?'

When Angelo's father was arrested, he gave his brother and sister-in-
law as next of kin. They were telephoned by the police and came to the
police station to take Angelo to their home. The child had been in his
cot upstairs when the police got into the house. His mother had been
dead for some hours and he was wet, dirty and crying bitterly. No one
knew whether he had been put into the cot by his mother, before the
killing, or by his father after the mother's death. No one knew what
the child had seen or heard.

At the trial, the prosecution case was that Mario had strangled
Angelo's mother and, in an attempt to establish an alibi, had locked up
the house, set off on a visit to relatives and returned to express his

dismay that his wife was not letting him in. He was convicted of murder and sentenced to life imprisonment. Angelo was cared for in the local Italian community by his paternal grandmother, uncle and aunt. He was now a member of a family of five children of which he was the second youngest. At home, the family spoke mainly Italian among themselves. Angelo had heard only the English language until now. His mother had not been a church-goer but Mario was baptised as a Catholic.

Angelo's English maternal grandmother, a widow in poor health living on a disability pension, was bitterly opposed to these arrangements and, obtaining legal aid, objected to him being brought up in the family of the man who had killed her daughter, and still more to this man still being the child's legal guardian, who assumed that he could take over the full care of his son as soon as he was released from prison. She further objected to the change of language and religion. Her view was that Angelo should grow up in a foster family and that he should have no contact with his father, but that she herself, as his grandmother, had a right to see him regularly. She felt that father's family would keep the child from seeing her.

The High Court made a contact order in favour of the maternal grandmother, to be supervised by social services, and appointed the Official Solicitor as guardian *ad litem* to look after Angelo's interests during the court proceedings and to make a full enquiry. Angelo was 3 years old before the High Court hearing took place. By then, he was speaking Italian as his first language and, according to his social worker, seemed happy and settled with his father's brother. He went on regular prison visits, being told that this was a hospital where his father was staying.

The maternal grandmother's health deteriorated and she missed several of the monthly access visits which had been planned for her and Angelo. She told the Official Solicitor that she wished Angelo to know just how his mother had died but did not feel able to come out with this in the course of a Sunday afternoon visit when she had not seen him for several weeks. She dreaded the thought of the child then going back to his family with such knowledge. Besides, since Angelo spoke mainly Italian now, she did not even know whether he would understand if she were to try to talk to him about his mother.

In the High Court, the judge was given conflicting opinions about Angelo's current needs. The social worker who visited the family felt that he was becoming deeply attached to his uncle, aunt and grand-mother and that this was the most important matter to be considered.

The expert advice from our psychiatric service pointed out that the law's delays, before his needs were considered, had allowed him to put down roots but that longer-term difficulties could be foreseen. Angelo was said to know nothing of the killing and still to accept that his father was in hospital, yet all the wider family, including his older cousins with whom he lived, knew just what had happened. Also, the Italian family assumed that father would continue as Angelo's legal guardian and would resume full care of the boy as soon as he was released from prison. The maternal grandmother continued to be bitterly angry that Angelo's needs, and his rights to see her and his mother's family, had been set aside, and felt that he could not do well in a household where he was being told untruths.

As he grows older, how will Angelo feel? He will learn that his father is in prison. The death hit the headlines in the local papers. As he goes to nursery school and later to primary school, he will hear other children speak of it.

At 4 he has become a restless, aggressive child, reluctant to sit still. He sleeps badly, often shouting in the night; sometimes he soils his pants during the day. His uncle and aunt continue to insist that he knows nothing of what really happened to his mother. They have told him she has gone away and they do not know where she is. His mother's mother has died and he has contact only with his father's kin.

Charlotte and James, aged 10 and 8

A story from the 1970s

Charlotte, aged 10, and her brother James, aged 8, had been in a children's home for three years. They were quiet, well-behaved children, friendly with everyone, middle of the road at school and, though they had no special friends, everyone seemed to like them. The residential home records, impeccably kept, told about school, health, dental treatments and outings. The children's nearest relative, their father's sister, had died a year earlier.

A new family placement team had been given the brief of looking at all the records of children in residential care, to see whether they should have homes with families. They recommended that Charlotte and James should be found adoptive parents. The children's home staff were upset at this. They felt that the children were well settled, gave nobody any trouble and should not have their lives disturbed. The family placement team, however, were most concerned to discover how little the children knew about their earlier lives. Their record, prior to their arrival at the children's home, told only that their mother, of Chinese origin, had been killed by their father, a British citizen. He had then killed himself. This had happened in Hong Kong where father was a civil servant and the children had been repatriated to the country of residence of their only English relation. She had visited regularly and the children had gone to her home, until her death from a heart attack.

There was no information about any of mother's relatives. No one knew where Charlotte and James had been when their parents died, nor what they had been told, nor where the parents were buried. There was no information about the parents' estate or about any insurance policies or inheritance to which the children might be entitled and they had no lawyer to represent their interests. They had been maintained throughout by the local authority. Charlotte and James volunteered no information and asked no questions.

Later in this book we discuss children who deal with catastrophe by becoming quiet and compliant, giving no trouble. It can be temptingly easy to look after such children, yet all is not necessarily well with them. They have rights to knowledge about their past, to be consulted about their wishes and to have care and thought given to their future. Sometimes it is easier to notice the problems of children who make demands than of those who keep their heads down.

Safira and Ahmed, aged 16 and 12

A story from the mid-1980s

Safira and Ahmed were born in North Africa, Muslim in religion, black in colour. They spoke Arabic as their first language but had been educated in English. They had been living in England for five years with their father, a businessman and their mother, a nursing sister. When Safira was 16 and Ahmed 12 years old, their father killed their mother with a knife. Safira told us that she came into the room as their mother screamed. The daughter hurled herself against her father as he began to turn the knife on himself.

She described how she dialled 999 and police and ambulance arrived. She followed their mother to the hospital in a police car but mother was dead by the time she got there. Their father, who did not speak after stabbing his wife, was removed by police as the ambulance drove away.

A woman police officer took Safira to the police station and asked where she could stay that night. Safira said that they had no other relatives in England but suggested friends of the family who could be contacted by telephone. Ahmed came back from school to find a police car outside his home to take him to the police station where Safira and the policewoman together told him what had happened. The children were taken in by a friend of their father's who was due to go abroad next day and could offer only emergency help.

Some days after the killing and on three further occasions, both children were interviewed by our team, who were contacted by their social worker. Both children were suffering from frightening dreams, did not cry and spoke little. It was also very difficult for them to talk about their experiences because, each time they came to see us, they were accompanied by different caregivers. Safira and Ahmed had been passed from one to another of their parents' friends; the social worker who had arranged the first placement was becoming very concerned about this and had consulted her managers about the possibility of making the children wards of court (as could happen at that period) to give them some legal security.

The friends of the family were deeply divided. Some saw the killing as an understandable, even just, response to the wish of the children's mother to live an independent life and to have an English education for the children. Ahmed agreed with them. One temporary Muslim foster-home placement broke down when Safira refused to wear a headscarf, a requirement for observant Muslim women. Ahmed, who was visiting his father regularly in prison, now regarded himself as the head of the household and was consulting his father about how to manage their finances.

A relative of both parents, who were related, arrived from North Africa wishing to arrange for mother's funeral to take place back there and for the children to return to their wider family. Safira wanted to go back for the funeral but then to return to England to complete her education as her mother had wished. She told her social worker that she feared that a marriage would be arranged for her were she to return home, which would mean she would not be allowed to study. Ahmed said that he loved his father, who was a good man, and that he would go back to Africa to live because that was what his father wanted him to do.

Meanwhile, Safira described her reluctance to go to bed, how hard it was to sleep and the hours she spent reading in order to put off the moment when she would sleep and face violent dreams. By day, vivid and frightening images of her mother's death flashed before her eyes. Three weeks after the death, Safira had visions of her mother, as though her mother were alive. She described going alone to a nearby park where she could sit on a bench and hear her mother's voice and feel her presence, giving her help and advice. She was both comforted and frightened by these visions. Safira herself understood that these experiences were part of grieving for her mother, but relatives, to whom she spoke of them, became very frightened that perhaps Safira was 'crazy'. This in turn alarmed Safira.

Ahmed slept badly too, complaining of attacks of giddiness and of headaches. He continued to go to school but his work became very poor. Then he was suspended for drawing a knife on another boy. The father decided to plead not guilty to the murder and Safira was notified that she would be required as a witness at the trial. Meanwhile, their mother's body was not released for burial.

Charles and Ellen, aged 6 and 3

Charles and Ellen's parents had been apart over Christmas after a quarrel. On the morning after Boxing Day it was father, not mother, who woke up the children. He told them that their mother had left home and was not coming back and he would be looking after them instead. He shouted at them when they asked questions and ignored Ellen when she cried.

He took them by car to friends and they spent that night there. No one spoke to them about their mother. Back at home, there was no school that week and the children went out only to the shops with their father. Two days later the children's grandmother, their mother's mother, came to the home and asked after her daughter. Charles and Ellen heard their father shout that their mother had left him, 'the bitch'.

Ten days later, the children's general practitioner sought help from our team. We were told that their grandmother had gone to the police, not believing that her daughter had walked out on the children and then failed to contact any of her relatives. On the first day of term father had been arrested and charged with his wife's murder. Her body had been found on a derelict building site and police evidence was that he had taken it from their home and buried it under rubble during the time that Charles and Ellen were with his friends. The children's grandfather had identified his daughter's body and the police who arrested father also alerted social services, arranging for the children to go to the bereaved grandparents.

Mr and Mrs Jones, the grandparents, lived in a retirement flat and had bought bunk beds which were fitted into a corner of their dining room. They were glad of help in talking to Charles and Ellen about what had happened. They said that Charles, aged 6, could remember his mother coming into his room on the evening of Boxing Day to kiss him goodnight. Charles told us he remembered a crashing noise and that he had called out, but his mother told him not to worry. He now knew that his mother was dead, that his father was 'at the police station', but he did not know what his father had done to cause his mother's death. He cried bitterly as he told us that he felt he should have got up when he heard the crash downstairs. Ellen, aged 3, curled up in her granny's lap while Charles and her grandparents were talking and seemed to go to sleep. Later, she played alone with a doll's house. She put the children in the bedrooms, father in the kitchen and mother lying flat in the garage of the house.

We met the family again and the grandparents said they could not go on looking after Charles and Ellen. Grandfather had angina, grandmother was arthritic and both had become more ill after their daughter's death. The children went to live with cousins of their mother, creating an instant family in which there were now five children under 12 years old. The new family was 400 miles from the children's old home and from their grandparents. The new carers decided not to tell Charles and Ellen's teachers about the family trouble, which they felt should stay private.

The arrangement with relatives did not work out and we next heard about Charles and Ellen one year later. By now both children were the subject of care orders and in temporary foster care. Adoptive parents had been found for them, with the agreement of mother's family, but father, now serving a life sentence, objected to the adoption. Ellen was a particularly good and quiet child but Charles's teachers were concerned that he was without friends and liable to unexpected bursts of bad temper. One day he was very rude to his grandmother who commented that he was turning out just like his father.

Anela, aged 15

When Anela was 15 years old, she told us the following story:

At 8, she had come home from school to find her father in tears, saying that her mother had died in an accident after a fall. She and her younger sister went to live with an uncle, father's brother and his family. She can remember few details of this change, but the girls did not see their father for three years, being told he had gone to work abroad.

Anela said that when her father came back he said nothing to them about where he had been. He rented a house and married an 18-year-old and the children went to live with them. A new baby was born and family life was very strict, according to Muslim law, with father the unquestioned head of the household. Anela was beaten when she did not obey. When she was 15 she learned from a cousin of both her parents, who arrived on a visit from Pakistan, that her mother had been killed, and that her father had been in prison for manslaughter. Father ordered this cousin out of the house and said that Anela must not discuss her new knowledge with her step-mother or younger sister. She thinks they must have heard her father shouting these orders but she had not seen her family since she ran away after her father beat her. Anela was taken into care after being found trying to sleep on a railway station bench and we met her soon afterwards.

William and Arthur, aged 8 and 6

We learned the following story from William and Arthur and their mother's parents, Mr and Mrs Thomas.

One morning William and Arthur, aged 8 and 6, were wakened by their grandmother instead of by their mother. She said she had come up to the house to look after them because their mother was not very well and daddy had gone to the hospital with her. Granny made packed lunches and saw them off to school. At the end of the day there was a big crowd round the school gates and some of the men had cameras. They could see granny trying to push her way through the crowd towards them. The boys could see that some of their school mates were pointing them out to the men with cameras: 'That is Arthur.' 'That is William.' The children's grandmother told us she grabbed their arms and rushed them back across the school yard to a side entrance where grandad was waiting with his car, the engine running. 'We are not going home today', said granny.

William and Arthur remembered a long drive, with a picnic in the back of the car. Their granny was crying and their grandfather drove fast and said nothing. It was dark when they got out of the car and found that they were at their auntie Betty's house and would sleep in the spare room which, 'smelled of cold sheets'. William asked, 'Granny, did that man at the school gates say my daddy was at the police station?' Mrs Thomas said she told them not to worry; their mother had had an accident but that there would be more news in the morning. William did not sleep much and was first downstairs the next day when the newspapers were delivered. He was a good reader and his mother's murder had been reported giving the children's names. He told his granny what he had read and she said it was not true. She cried as she told us that she had not been able to bear the knowledge of her daughter's death.

The press are not supposed to name children when their parents or others are involved in criminal acts but many of them ignore this rule. The damage is done when it happens and cannot be undone by disciplinary action on the part of the Press Council or the Ombudsman, although a prompt complaint may act as a deterrent.

These avoidable burdens, added to those of loss and trauma, may tip a child over into profound depression, and if they are living with relatives who are themselves bereaved, as Arthur and William were, they may not receive the support and protection they need.

The team of child psychiatrists, psychologists, psychotherapists and family therapists at the Traumatic Stress Clinic have now met over 400 children during the weeks, months and years after one parent has died at the hands of the other. Where the children live near enough, we can offer therapeutic help when they need it.

Sunil, aged 3, Neesha, aged 1

A child living in the family of the perpetrator

Sunil was 3 years old, and his sister Neesha 1 year old, when his mother was killed by his father. The family had spent the day at a wedding, but, once the children were put to bed, the parents began to argue over money and father strangled mother to death. Father left the home but then telephoned his own father, in a fit of grief, to tell him what he had done.

Although it was traditional for marriages in this community to be arranged, this marriage had been a marriage of love. Both families had serious reservations about the marriage, and mother's parents had refused to attend the wedding. She had lost contact with all relatives on her side of the family. Father came from a large and well-supported family and, although the family knew that the marriage had been deteriorating for some time, the seriousness of father's reliance on drink was being denied.

Father's eldest sister Sameera, who lived at home with her parents, was told that night to go to her brother's home urgently, but she wasn't given the reason. When she arrived, she was deeply shocked to discover what had happened. She had known that the couple were in difficulties, and mother had confided in her, but did not anticipate that such a tragedy could happen. In the middle of the night, she and the children were taken in a police car back to her parents' home.

By the time they attended the clinic a year later, Sameera was living with the two children in a home of her own. She had felt unable to continue living with her parents, as they were denying the enormity of their son's actions. The grandparents did not want the children to know the truth of what had happened, and denied the impact on the children of the loss of their mother.

The children were referred because Sameera had become increasingly aware of their emotional difficulties. In particular, she felt that Sunil was unusually withdrawn and was continuing to have nightmares and sleepless nights. Over the year since father's imprisonment Sameera had been trying to comply with her brother's wishes for contact but this was proving to be more difficult as Sunil was increasingly distressed by his visits to his father. By the time they came for their initial consultation, Sunil was refusing to visit his father at all, and this was causing conflict within father's family.

The team were asked by the Official Solicitor, acting as guardian *ad litem*, to make an assessment of the advisability or otherwise of this contact, ascertaining Sunil and Neesha's wishes. We were also asked to assess the children's psychological needs and advise about treatment.

The team remained involved with Sameera and the two children for a period of four years. Sameera was granted a residence order and has continued to care for the children. Sunil was brought to the clinic once a week for therapeutic treatment, whilst Sameera was seen concurrently to support her in caring for the children. Neesha was not immediately as obviously distressed as Sunil, but her psychological needs were discussed and monitored through the work with Sameera. At a point when Neesha was beginning to ask more questions about her mother's death and what had happened to her father (which coincided with increasing openness on Sunil's part) she was seen, together with her aunt, for a series of sessions to help her make some sense of her mother's death.

There were continued episodes of conflict within the family, as the grandparents wanted the children to talk about and to miss their father, whereas it had become apparent that they were very frightened of him. Sameera, whilst not wanting to obstruct the children's contact with their paternal grandparents, was also concerned about protecting their interests. As time went by, both children were given additional focused work to prepare them for their father's impending release from prison, having served a sentence for the manslaughter of his wife.

Throughout his imprisonment, father continued to apply for contact with his children, but, because of the enormous burden of fear the prison visits carried, the visits were stopped. When father was released, he made a further application, and an initial contact took place at the clinic, following preparation with the children, Sameera and father. The court's decision, following this visit, was that contact would not be in the children's interests.

Pauline and Chris, aged 15 and 12

Chris's father killed his mother in a murderous rage. The parents had been separated for a year when he arrived at the home late at night. Chris and his older half-sister Pauline were in bed. Chris was woken by the sound of Pauline screaming. He ran into her bedroom to find his father attacking Pauline with a hammer. In his attempt to stop his father, Chris was himself hit over the head. When Chris escaped downstairs, he discovered his mother's body, bloody and battered, and ran to a neighbour's house to call for help.

Pauline and Chris had both sustained injuries, and had witnessed and experienced horrific violence. It wasn't the first time that Chris's father had been violent. They had witnessed his cruelty towards their mother on several occasions and over the last few years he had also been threatening towards Pauline, who had coped by spending much of her time at home alone in her bedroom. Whilst Chris had seen the cruel side of his father, he had also enjoyed a lot of attention from him. Chris's father had never been cruel to him, and he was terribly shocked and frightened to see his father assaulting his half-sister.

The children were immediately accommodated by social services and placed in foster care, and staff from the Traumatic Stress Clinic saw them to assess their therapeutic needs. Both Pauline and Chris had returned to school to face the effects of the considerable publicity about their mother's death. Chris was unable to focus on anything but the trauma and he eagerly recounted the details to anyone who would listen at school, also prominently displaying his scars. Chris had previously struggled at school, both academically and in terms of sustaining friendships, and for a while this notoriety gave him the attention he had always lacked. However, he also found himself the target of jibes that he was a 'freak' and a 'pervert'. Chris was troubled by nightmares of the event almost every night, and suffered guilt that he had not been able to prevent his sister from being assaulted, but had been attacked himself. He was acutely traumatised, irritable and over-active.

In contrast to the exuberance of Chris, Pauline became angry, sullen and withdrawn. As an adolescent, she was acutely embarrassed to have her private life revealed to everyone and, whereas Chris was proudly discussing what had happened, Pauline felt profoundly ashamed and tainted. She found it hard to deal with her own trauma or grief because she also felt so responsible for Chris. Whereas Chris was comforted by her, there was no one to comfort Pauline. This made it difficult for her to accept an offer of longer-term therapeutic help and she preferred to talk with her two close friends.

The children's older half-sister came forward to offer care to both of them, but this meant them moving away from the area. Chris was happy to make this move, and had high expectations of what life would be like. However, he was already exhibiting behavioural difficulties and it was recommended that he and his carer would need help. Pauline decided that she would prefer to remain in foster care, so that she could remain near to her friends and would not have to move schools.

Sonny, aged 2

Sonny was a 20-month-old baby when, during a violent struggle between his parents, his mother was stabbed and fell. Sonny was found lying quietly and unmoving by the side of his mother's body when the police arrived. He was unharmed, but his mother had died almost immediately as a result of her wounds. Sonny's father was convicted of manslaughter and was sentenced to seven years' imprisonment.

It is unclear how long Sonny lay next to his mother's dead body before the police arrived and picked him up. The police located a family friend who knew Sonny well, and Sonny was taken to her home, where he remained for several weeks. Sonny's maternal aunt, Dina, was also contacted. She agreed to take care of him but was unable to do so immediately as she was having to make the funeral arrangements for mother, and was arranging for Sonny's grandmother to come to England.

When his grandmother arrived in England, Sonny went to live with her. This arrangement seemed to be working well and grandmother applied for a residence order. It was at this time (when he was about 2 years old) that Sonny was brought to the clinic for an assessment of his psychological welfare and future needs. He came with his grandmother and Dina, who reported that, although he seemed to be happy enough, he would not sleep alone and was not eating well. He was also not speaking and had regressed to the extent that he would not feed himself and was no longer continent by day.

Unfortunately, during the process of the assessment Sonny's grandmother became seriously ill and could no longer care for him. She in fact decided to return to her country of origin, and Dina went with her. Sonny was now faced with the loss of two other carers, in sudden and traumatic circumstances. It appears that Dina's solicitors traced father's cousin, Greg, who agreed to look after Sonny. Greg was married and had two small children of his own. Some months later, following grandmother's death, Dina returned to England with the intention of resuming Sonny's care. However, by this time Greg and his wife had already applied for a residence order. As relatives, they felt duty-bound to care for Sonny and bring him up as part of their family. They claimed that he had settled well and was becoming attached to them. They were equally attached to him and vowed that they would protect Sonny from his father should he want to look after him on his release from prison. But Dina also applied for a residence order and a conflict of interests ensued.

Traumatic Stress Clinic workers were asked by the court to advise as to the best placement for Sonny. Would it be better to leave him with his existing carers, with whom he had settled well, or to transfer him to the care of his aunt? It took eighteen months for the judicial process to be completed, at the end of which it was ordered that Sonny should remain with his father's cousin Greg and his family. Sonny still has regular contact with Dina, but there continues to be difficulty, and tension between the parties, which has increased rather than decreased. The court also ordered that Sonny commence psychotherapy for his traumatic bereavement and emotional difficulties and, two years later, he has just completed his treatment.

Comment

Several of the children we have seen have been left alone with a dead parent for hours or days. Older children are usually resourceful and telephone or call for help. Children under 5 years old are unable to do anything but cry and their voices may go unheard. Sometimes the father kills himself in a public place, and the discovery of his body alerts people and the child is found. Sometimes, after taking flight, father remembers his children and ensures that they are rescued. But much time may have elapsed.

It is difficult to exaggerate the plight of these children, who, as a result of their sudden, violent bereavement, find themselves in a world in which they have no one to whom they can turn as of right. This was poignantly illustrated for us when we became involved in trying to mediate between the paternal and maternal relatives of a 4-year-old girl, Maria, whose father had stabbed her mother. She was living with her paternal aunt and an access visit to her mother's relatives had been arranged with one of our team. She was chatting happily about a holiday spent with her father's parents and mentioned that when she was young she thought she had lived with them. Her maternal aunt, obviously hurt by talk of father's side of the family, said sharply, 'That's not so.' Maria said with a look of distress, 'Oh! I've said something wrong.'

For a 4-year-old to have diplomatic skills of such a high order and an awareness of having offended seems to us to be a tragedy and yet many of our patients find themselves having to tread such a tightrope. The killing produces often unresolvable alienation and conflict between the two sides of the family who fight over and over again the battle between the parents that had such tragic results. The fight not only gets into the families but often into the professionals who are dealing with the aftermath of the killing. We often feel that these children are flotsam on the sea of life and that there is no consistency for them any more. Often no evaluation of the children is made at the time of their tragedy. Referrals relate to subsequent events or eventual recognition of emotional difficulties, as happened with Sunil and his sister. Removal from their home, however valuable in itself, disrupts schooling, social links and therapy (Pauline and Chris). Loss and disruption may continue, compounding the original trauma (Sonny). Maria, now 13, has changed carers six times since her mother died. Few of the children in our study have yet reached adult life; but survivors of these childhood tragedies, now adults, have contacted us and two moving accounts in Chapter 10 illustrate personal views over the perspective of many years.

The problem for individuals who go through the tragedy is that each experience is isolating and feels unique. For professionals in health and social services also this may be a problem encountered only on a single occasion. In later chapters we consider how best to help children, family members and professionals immediately and in the years to come.

Chapter 6

Picking up the pieces

I stand alone in the house
Listening to the unheard echoes
of a life time
    (John Cotton, 'Clearing the house')

SUMMARY

We discuss the immediate effect of the killing, who speaks of it to the children, who takes responsibility, what emergency help and care are available.

IMPACT

These are crimes which are visible from the start. They are committed in the family home, in the street in front of the children, at the home of relatives, often on significant occasions: birthdays, contact visits after divorce, Christmas, New Year festivals, or at the time of other ceremonies which involve family reunions such as Eid, the Muslim celebration which marks the end of Ramadan. In our experience the killing is rarely premeditated: although there may have been previous violence and threats of killing, we have encountered only a few cases where there were previous attempts at homicide.

Since the killings occur in the context of family life, all routines familiar to the children disappear forthwith. It is common for children to be asleep in the house at the time of the killing (or for adults to claim this, even though, in some cases, therapeutic work reveals that the children either saw the killing or heard their mother's dying cries). It is rare, however, for them to sleep in the parental home on the night after the killing and when this does happen it may be because the body has been concealed and the crime is as yet undetected. We have shared with children their horror at realising that their dead mother's body was concealed in a garage or had been taken from the house and hidden.

One family of three children were taken to school unwittingly with their mother's body wrapped in plastic dustbin liners in the boot of the car. On this occasion father gave himself up to the police in the course of the afternoon and the children were taken from school to a children's home. The oldest girl, the daughter of the father's previous marriage, was claimed immediately by her birth mother and step-father. She had been trying to comfort the two younger children, aged 5 and 3, who were now separated from their half-sister and spent that night in the children's home. The police had sealed off their house, having taken a statement from father, and the care staff in the children's home could not obtain their nightclothes or familiar toys for the children's bedtime routine. Indeed, they had no idea what this routine was. The staff did not know how to talk to the children about what had happened to them and were relieved when the children, who seemed dazed, went to bed without protest or question. The next day they were claimed by their nearest relatives, their father's brother and his wife. The new home, never before visited, was in a town one hundred miles from where they had lived with their parents.

We have met children who have been unable to obtain personal possessions months after their mother's death. A boy, due to take GCSE exams, was unable to get his course work and his sports equipment. Father's father had the keys to the family home and would not allow access to it until after the trial of his son who, he was sure, would be proved innocent. Grandfather blamed the 15-year-old for accepting a home with his mother's parents, who were equally sure that father had committed murder.

Often children simply do not ask for their clothes, toys and books, and relatives and other caregivers are reluctant to talk about this for fear of upsetting them. For this reason one girl, aged 8, did not know what had happened to her cat and rabbits two months after she had been placed in a foster-home.

As a matter of routine, a key person, with professional skills and independence, should think for children at this crisis in their lives, not only about grief and trauma, important though this will be, nor just about practical care and nurturance, essential though this is as well, but also about the practical effects of dislocation and the need for personal possessions, toys and photographs. There seems little or no need for such things to remain in a sealed house: the problem is rather that crime detection takes priority. There is no need either for children's personal possessions to become weapons in a battle between angry, grieving relatives.

We have seen examples of very good practice where all these pitfalls have been avoided and police have enabled brothers and sisters to be together in privacy, have cared for them, kept them warm (fear and anxiety make people cold and shivery), talked to them about what was happening and stayed on duty while relatives were found. Family members, despite their own grief, have taken care to obtain toys and meet the need for a bedtime routine. Social workers may have put in hours of unpaid work.

A legal framework, such as the use of an emergency protection order, will allow independent, immediate thought about the needs and rights of the children.

This will create a setting in which the difficult, but necessary, tasks may begin of finding out what the children have seen and heard and collecting basic information about them.

Critical incident stress debriefing

This procedure was developed to help adult witnesses and workers who have been involved in responding to catastrophes, such as airline crashes, earthquakes, major violent crimes and warfare.[150] For decades, reports on adults have shown that firm, thorough and early exploration of traumatic events is important for recovery.[77] Some work on children in a kibbutz[10] confirms this.

Among the lessons learned is that witnesses and those who try to deal with such tragedies have all the normal physical and psychological responses to the horror of human suffering. For at least a hundred years, through study of responses to battles, it has been known that people exposed to war and disasters experience a whole range of symptoms: restlessness, irritability, anxiety, being constantly on the alert, nightmares and other sleep disturbances, changes of mood, depression and poor concentration. There may be a range of physical symptoms such as vomiting and diarrhoea and excessive sweating. It was found in the First World War that people who had witnessed disturbing events could re-experience mental images of the frightening scenes even though they tried to put these out of their mind.

There are four kinds of stress debriefing used with adults:

1   The briefest form takes place at the scene of the disaster or near it and immediately after the crisis. An independent person, who knows about the effects of disaster, assesses the well-being of the people involved and tries to identify those who need a break or a change in duty, working with those who are resting and allowing them to talk about what they feel and what they have seen. The Israeli army takes this kind of debriefing very seriously and finds it most successful in cutting down serious stress reactions in troops who have been in combat.[10]
2   There is an attempt, called 'defusing', to help everyone involved in the disaster to start talking about their feelings and reactions. It is best if this can take place with others who have been through the same terrible experience.
3   A skilled professional is used, within one or two days of the disaster, when those involved have begun to calm down and can deal with emotional reactions which have probably been suppressed during and for a brief time after the crisis.
4   There should be a follow-up some months after the critical incident.

It has been hypothesised that early intervention reduces the likelihood that PTSD symptoms will develop, by helping the trauma victim or aid worker to process terrifying images and to conceptualise and communicate about what has been experienced. However, early claims that 'critical incident stress debriefing' is effective if used as the *only* form of intervention[150] are now being questioned.[187] As our knowledge stands, emergency interventions should be offered, evaluated and followed by more specifically tailored help.

All of this supposes that a basic service should be offered routinely to those caught up in a disaster, whether they are personally involved, available as helpers or accidental witnesses, although there is controversy about the value of a single, especially a group, debriefing. There is an assumption that anyone who goes through such an experience needs opportunities to come to terms with the feelings aroused and to find words to speak about them. This needs further exploration. Techniques used to help workers and victims at the time of a crisis should not be forced on possible recipients, many of whom in any case need more specific interventions in the longer term.

Early psychological interventions with children and adolescents

On the other hand, opportunities for psychological first aid are generally not offered at all to children who have seen violence. Again and again, we find that the understandable, though not helpful, reaction of adults is to avoid upsetting the children further. Thus they seek to protect the children from any reminders of the trauma, and do not provide opportunities for the children to talk. How much worse this is when what the children have experienced or even witnessed is the death of a parent.

When we receive a referral we have to decide whether to see children separately or together, if they have all been involved in the tragedy, and also whether to see them alone or – which can often be very helpful – to have a trusted caregiver or family member take part in the session so that someone in day-to-day contact with the children can understand just what the child has been experiencing.

First, we have the child draw or tell a story about a picture of their choice. It is amazing to us how often they will produce a drawing closely related to what they have been through. Of course, many of the children understand that we are doctors who work with troubles and problems, but we find that the drawings and play related to the trauma are begun almost as soon as we meet the children. Sara, aged 4, for example, found an ambulance and a police car within thirty seconds of entering a crowded, rather messy interview room which also contained her grandparents, a social worker, one of our team and a range of other toys and play materials.

We explore the child's experience, paying particular attention to what the child saw, heard, and smelled, what the child felt and what he did or wished he had done. We pay special attention to any moments of bravery or initiative; children feel less guilty, ashamed and powerless if they did something to help, for example dialling 999, or, in one little boy's case, trying to pour lemonade into his dying mother's mouth 'to make her better'.

The trauma is sometimes 'trapped in' by an avoidance of some detail or moment of particular horror or surprise. Asked about their worst moment, children may be able to describe highly accurate and detailed images. For some, it is the sight of the mother's blood, but for others it is something even more unexpected, such as the smell of the blood. One girl felt her most intense anger at a police station when her father said, 'I'm sorry', about having just killed her mother. Another was intensely distressed when a policeman loosened her mother's bra in order to examine a chest wound.[178] Parental homicide may leave indelible, highly accurate and detailed (mostly visual) images, powerfully recollected as 'flash bulb memories'.[45] If children are not helped to deal with the intense emotion associated with the worst moment, remembering remains threatening. Consequently, discussion that approaches the trauma, whether indirectly, such as talking with the guardian *ad litem* about plans for the future, or directly, for example giving evidence in a criminal trial, may be hindered. (Relaxation training may be helpful for children whose over-arousal prevents them from saying what they want to say.)

We have encountered children who have seen their mother's mutilated body. We try to find out what the child understood of what was witnessed, taking account of fears of loss of control, and find out what he or she did. Often, we have to deal with guilt that the child did not protect the mother or that, if the killing was not witnessed, the child may have relived, again and again, the possibility that the killing could have been prevented if only he or she had woken, gone to another room or been with the mother when father arrived. Sometimes children remember sounds overheard such as a door banging or a raised voice and relive those moments, wondering if they marked the time of their mother's death.

We try to find out in detail the child's perception of what happened after the killing so that we can help put right misperceptions common in young children. What did the father do, what did the child do, were there any adults available, what happened with the other children? We ask the child to draw or play or act what happened and try to tap their fantasies of avenging mother's death so that we can deal with them. We take time to discover any events or feelings important to the child which may otherwise be missed.

Sometimes we ask a social worker or other family member to tell the child just what did happen. It may be useful at this point for us to use dolls, other play materials and drawings and to help the adults now caring for the children to communicate with them about the tragedy.

We try to relieve children's fears that they may either have caused their mother's death or could have prevented it. They need to know also that they were not and are not to blame for the violence of which they are the victims. Although the adults around them may weep and be angry on behalf of the children as well as on their own account, and may have great difficulty in talking about and otherwise expressing how they feel, they, the children, are not to blame for these miseries.

The interview must be rounded off in a fairly formal way, finding time and words to express the child's loss and to begin to discover just how he or she is mourning, if mourning has begun at all. Because this style of interviewing may increase preoccupation with the horrifying past events, it is useful at the end of the interview to orient the child to the present (to reinforce the message that memories reflect *past* experience and are not in themselves real) and to the future (including the immediate future, for example asking what the child will be doing after the session). It is also helpful to establish with them who they can turn to, if distressed in the future.

Follow-through

Then we talk to those looking after the child and those legally responsible, about protection, legal rights and about immediate plans as to where the child will live. Usually there is need to consider matters such as whether mother's body has been released for burial, whether it should be seen by the child and whether the child should take part in the funeral ceremonies and, if so, in what way. It is important to think about how the child goes back to school, whether a change of school is involved and what will be said to teachers and school mates.

We try to be available to the child and the family or to local school and health services during any civil proceedings about the future and during any forth-coming criminal trial.

Bearing in mind the very real risks of continued suffering, we also give advice about the need for a more detailed assessment of the mental health and well-being of all children who have lived through this tragedy, although therapy starts with the psychological first aid.

> Howard, aged 6, drew a picture. His uncle and aunt, with whom he had lived since his mother was killed by his father, thought that Howard did not know how his mother had died or where his father was. Howard's picture shows he does know and may have witnessed more than his relatives realised. The picture shows two children asleep in bed when father hit mother with an axe. Mother falls dead with blood around her shoulders. A drawing of a child taken from his own house has no legs and no face (indicating his reluctance to leave his home, and his longing not to have seen what he did). A building with barred windows indicates that he is aware that his father is in prison although told he was in a hospital.

Those who care for the children must be alert to what they do and say. Certain developmental immaturities in children make it difficult for those caring for them to understand events from the child's point of view. These include increased difficulty in knowing how long events lasted or in what order they took place, elaboration of detail, deciding that previous events were omens of the tragedy, re-enacting, in sometimes dangerous ways, the traumatic events, and repetitive play which never reaches a resolution. Thus, those who listen to the child must be aware of fragmentary, disconnected communications which may be of great significance, and must be alert to this and to what the child may wish to tell them. There may be differences between what a child says and how he or she behaves.

As children grow older and their vocabulary increases they begin to understand previous events in a more complex and subtle way, and these new memories, with words to describe them, may lead to added distress.

Anela (whose story is told in Chapter 5), who was taken into care at 15, could understand in retrospect the time she was told that her mother had died of an accident and her father's subsequent disappearance. Looking back, she recalled how unhappy and angry her mother had been, how often her mother had wept. Now Anela wept to think of her mother's isolation, loneliness and danger.

We bore these problems and principles in mind when drawing on the work of Pynoos and his colleagues (see Appendix 1) to create the framework described above for an interview with children seen immediately after the killing. It may also be useful for those children who are referred sometimes weeks or months after the event, and with whom it has not been discussed, and for work with children who have witnessed other crimes or catastrophes.

It is not possible of course for a child mental health team to meet all the needs uncovered at such a time of tragedy. Police, relatives, other witnesses, social workers, family members and foster-parents all have differing needs and skills, just as all who take part in a severe and sudden tragedy are affected by it and, if the children are to be helped, consideration must be given to everyone.

Individual social workers, for whom this may be a unique event, have told us how they too can experience sleeplessness, digestive upset, periods of poor concentration and the like, just as helpers in other major disasters may. Relatives, also shattered by grief exacerbated by anger, go through similar but worse experiences.

There are problems of 'parenting by default' where, because of the death of a parent, usually by violence, as in manslaughter, murder, suicide, or murder followed by suicide, a sudden task is imposed upon relatives. They manage both to over-protect and yet subtly to reject the child whom they have taken on.[42] We have found this a common pattern among the families we have seen. The principles for working with these relatives are similar to those for any emergency which disrupts the lives of children. There may be a particular need for couple therapy for the bereaved adults who have taken on an unexpected and unplanned parental task, and for work which considers the original children of the family group as well as the needs of the newcomers.

Initial exploratory interviews with children or adults should lead to continuing evaluation and in the meantime we have to be pragmatic. Of the children we have seen within a few days of witnessing the killing of a parent, the majority have described nightmares and these have ceased in most cases after interviews where we have helped them to understand and deal with some of their experiences.

To summarise, the task in the early days is to provide nurturing and, as much as possible, familiar people, objects and routines for the children. It is necessary to allow the children, carers, professionals and family to speak of their experiences and to be on the alert for the need for more intensive later help. There is a need to recognise the transitional period of numbness and the intense feelings that may succeed it.

Above all, it is right to help the adults understand that children are going through similar experiences to themselves and indeed are suffering to an even greater extent. It is always difficult for us to bear the suffering of young children and, in order to protect and help them, we must avoid masking from ourselves its depth and intensity.

Other early problems

An early trauma is the *identification of the body*. One grandfather told us how he had bent to kiss his daughter's forehead and his lips had stuck to the frozen surface. No one had prepared him for this and he wept copiously as he described it. It is difficult under such circumstances to offer advice on whether other family members should also see the body, yet what evidence there is does indicate that doing so does help the process of grieving.[51, 119] Workers with disaster argue that not being able to see the body may contribute to later difficulties. It may be horrifying to see a loved one who has been mutilated and people should always be prepared for what they are to see and feel (like the icy touch of the frozen corpse) but what is imagined may be more horrible than the reality. Many mourners also need to see their dead in order to know that they are dead, to have a visual image and memory of the death, and to say goodbye. All of these factors apply just as much to children as to adults. In our culture it is not customary for children to see bodies, but a careful weighing-up of the pros and cons, by adults and professionals, with consultation involving the child who often has his or her own views, may be of great help. Even if the decision is that the body should not be viewed, a careful discussion helps the process of grieving whereas avoidance does not.

Tara, aged 4

Tara was brought to see us by her social worker a few days after her father killed her mother. She had heard the sounds of fighting but had fallen asleep. Her father told her that her mother had gone to hospital because of an accident. She went to live with foster-carers and cried endlessly to see her mother. Her social worker asked for our help in breaking the news of mother's death and father's imprisonment. We explained that mummy and daddy had had a fight. Daddy was very strong – maybe he didn't meant to do so but he hurt mummy so much her body had stopped working. We went through all the ways in which it didn't work any more. When people's bodies don't work any more they die. Tara could not believe this and demanded to see her mother. We advised the social worker to take Tara to the mortuary and show her that her mother was dead, after preparing her for what she would see. The social worker had never seen a dead body before and needed some convincing that this was the right thing to do. To her credit, she overcame her own fears and carried out the task admirably. Tara was encouraged to try to talk to her dead mother, and shown that there was no response. The visit was helpful both for Tara and her social worker and Tara began to grieve appropriately for her mother. We worked with Tara, her foster-carers and her devoted social worker for the next few months. Tara was eventually placed for adoption and we recently had the pleasure of seeing her again, at the age of 8, well settled with loving new parents and doing well at school and at home. She is able to speak to her new family about her early memories.

Many families have spoken to us about the stress of the long delay between the death and the funeral. This is a common problem where there are repeated post-mortems and disputes about the cause of death, and where an alleged killer is pleading not guilty. We have encountered one family unable to bury their dead for eight months and a delay of three to five months is not uncommon. One 5-year-old was carefully prepared and helped to know that his mother was dead, that her body did not work any more, that she could not breathe, move, eat, or cuddle him, and that her body would be put into the local churchyard. By the time the body was released the little boy had become convinced that the funeral had already taken place and could tell a story about it. His grandparents, with whom he lived, were unsure whether the advice given to them, that the little boy should go with them to the funeral, was the right response after so long a delay. Their personal decision was to have a quiet private cremation and later to take the child to his mother's memorial garden to plant flowers. It is likely that their careful thought and concern for their grandchild and their ability to consult and then to take decisions on his behalf will lead to healing.

Contact with father

Early decisions have to be made about whether and how the children should visit their father in prison or in prison hospital. The principle to be guided by is that contact is the right of the child not of the adult and that the child's welfare is paramount. Fathers may wish to keep plans for their children's place of residence 'on hold' until they are released and they will need help to recognise that this is not appropriate and that the children's needs must come first.

Advantages

The advantages of contact with the perpetrator and perpetrator's family are that:

1 Contact may maintain worthwhile relationships and attachments. Even though the father may have killed the mother, he may be the only family the children have left. In some cases, although the man's relationship with his wife had been problematic, his relationship with his children had been good. With the sudden loss of their mother, young children especially may need to see their father to be assured that he at least is still alive.

2 If the child's last and enduring memory of their father is a terrifying one of him in an out-of-control and violent state, seeing him in a different light, when he is calm and the child protected, is likely to bring some relief and comfort. Many children want to know that, in spite of what he has done, their father is being taken care of.

3 If the father can take responsibility for his actions, contact may help to prevent children from blaming themselves for the breakdown of the family and for the mother's death. Most important of all, contact may enable a father who has caused the untimely death of the child's mother to apologise to that child.

4 Contact is one way of informing children about a parent who is mentally or physically ill. Children whose father is in a psychiatric hospital or a prison hospital may be helped to understand that illness is thought to be related to the behaviour which led to their mother's death.

5 Contact can help to ensure that children who must move from one home to another achieve this as smoothly as possible. For example, if father approves of the children going to live with relatives or a foster family, and can tell them so himself, the children will be relieved and helped by this assurance. For the same reason, contact with father may be very helpful when children who have been in emergency care move to a permanent home.

6 In the longer term, contact is one way of keeping children informed about the family from which they originate. This may be of particular importance if children are to live with the victim's kin. If father is of a different culture or religion from mother, contact is one way of keeping children in touch with these roots.

Disadvantages and difficulties

There are, however, many practical and theoretical difficulties which may make regular contact impossible or undesirable.

1   When those who care for the child feel threatened or angry about proposed contact visits, these feelings will be sensed by the child. If the child then develops problems of behaviour it will be necessary to weigh up the benefits of contact against the peace of mind of the caregivers. If the caregivers become depressed or otherwise disturbed by the visits this may interfere with the care and peace of mind of the child.

2   The father in prison may use contact as a way of trying to blame the mother for her own death, to deny responsibility, to disturb or interfere with the relationship between the child and those caring for him. Unless the father, in this case, can be helped to a less destructive attitude, the disadvantages of contact for the child may outweigh the advantages. Also, children in any case may decide for themselves that they do not want to see the parent who deprived them of their mother.

3   Many prisons make pay-phones available to prisoners, which is in general a highly desirable contact between them and the outside world. It may, however, be an inappropriate intrusion upon children to receive telephone calls unexpectedly and in the absence of trusted adults who can help them deal with the situation. In our view it is better that telephone contact should be carefully considered and in general used sparingly, if at all. If it is seen to be in the children's best interests, it should be by appointment and, again, it should take place only with the agreement and consent of the child concerned and his carers and professional advisors.[24]

Victim support services

Adult relatives of the dead parents tell us that these can be of great value. So far, as described to us, such services have been made available to these adults – grandparents, aunts and uncles of bereaved children – rather than directly to the children themselves. For example, Support After Murder and Manslaughter (see Appendix 4) may be of great help to grandparents whose daughter has been killed by her husband. The benefit to the grandchildren is indirect. CRUSE, the national organisation for bereavement care, with branches in many parts of the country, now trains its volunteer counsellors to offer bereavement counselling to children as well as adults and has extended its service to those bereaved by disaster as well as by illness.

In 1990, Victim Support, which offers support to all victims of crime and is routinely contacted by the police, published a report on its Families of Murder Victims Research Project.[55] This was designed to identify and describe the heavy toll on families and friends of the victims, to identify needs, and to examine how victim support services, in conjunction with other relevant agencies, might work to provide advice and support. It found much unmet need among adult victims and their adult relatives but made brief mention of child relatives and their particular pain. Thus, most families in the project learned of the murder from the police rather than, as with our children, being there when it happened. All the families confirmed the need for accurate information right from the start and it was clear that families in shock needed to be given the information on more than one occasion. Sometimes relatives first heard of the killing from the media and this was a particular problem where the closest family members longed to break the news as gently as possible to their wider family, this wish conflicting with the need to broadcast details of the killing to aid the criminal investigation.

Many relatives reported that they could cope a little better with the terrible news if they were in familiar surroundings, a comfort usually not available to the children in our study. Where the family home was the site of the murder and the location had been sealed off by the police, with the family not permitted access, there were huge practical and emotional difficulties. Access to clothing, money, cheque-books and problems about the settlement of bills and even paying for food were instanced. There was no framework in which families could express how it felt to have their privacy thus invaded.

Moreover, when the home was re-opened, no one was responsible for restoring it to the state it had been in before the killing. There was often no help with cleaning, repairing damage, replacing articles taken for forensic purposes, or dealing with blood-stained walls and carpets or the marks of finger-printing. Simply visiting the site of the killing was immensely painful for relatives of the murder victim.

When it came to identifying the body, the tendency was to find a male relative. On occasion, advice was given that the sight would be too distressing and identification by non-family members was encouraged. Afterwards this might be regretted and relatives stated that imagining the condition of the body was far more distressing than actually viewing it. When Victim Support volunteers went with family members to view the body, in general this was seen as far better than not undertaking this task. Repeated post-mortems, and delay in releasing the body for burial, were sources of great pain and anxiety.

The project found that families appreciated the need for media coverage and felt that such reports could be helpful in crime detection, but it gave many examples of the use of photographs without reference to families, incorrect details appearing in the press, pressure on relatives to provide stories and, on occasion, the publication of details of the victim or of the murder which the family had not known.

The project's major recommendation was that victim support should be extended to families of murder victims. Family members should be offered the opportunity, not just formally to identify the murdered person, but to view the body as part of the process of grieving. The numbers of post-mortems should be limited. There should be detailed, sensitive involvement of the family in the criminal proceedings, with seating available in court, and a visit to the court before the hearing. Relatives should not learn details hitherto unknown in the course of the hearing. It should be possible for families to 'defend' the victim against defamatory statements which might be included by the defence in mitigation of the alleged crime. We strongly endorse these recommendations. All the findings are relevant to the families of the dead parent when they take on the care of children.

One 14-year-old girl read a newspaper account of her father's trial. He admitted killing his wife but defended himself by saying that she had had numerous affairs and had taunted him with his impotence, provoking him to assault her. The daughter had visited her father in prison while he was on remand, but had not been told that this would be her father's defence. She then felt that, by visiting him, she had endorsed his blame of her dead mother. The word 'taunting' crops up quite regularly in reports to us of pleas in mitigation. There is a stereotyped quality about the information that is presented in evidence and afterwards reported. Relatives often quote these phrases. Very painful, acutely traumatic events are reduced to the vocabulary of tabloid newspapers.

At the time of the killing, another family had been awaiting repossession of their home. At his trial father blamed all their financial difficulties on his dead wife, saying that she was a greedy incompetent person who had spent money on herself and lied to him about the state of their finances. He adduced no evidence in support of this claim and indeed, since he was found guilty of murder, it seemed likely that the jury did not accept that he acted on impulse as a result of provocation, which would have justified acceptance that he was guilty of man-slaughter. It would have been possible to interview the children of the family, who had clear memories of their mother's attempts to get father to look at the household bills, thus enabling additional evidence to be available. Such evidence, which as indicated earlier may be helpful in criminal investigations, is also valuable in planning the children's future.

Victim Support recommends an extended role for the Criminal Injuries Compensation Authority (a government-supported agency which offers recompense to victims of violent crime for their psychological or physical suffering, via a tariff system) so that, in cases of unlawful killing, consideration could be given to an automatic payment for funeral expenses. They also recommend an increase in the standard bereavement award. Financial help does not heal grief but families encounter such severe and immediate financial problems that practical help is not to be underestimated.

With regard to reporting the effects of crime on victims, the Press Council has published a helpful code of conduct.[173] This says that newspapers and journalists serving them should in general avoid intruding into personal grief. Enquiries should be carried out with sympathy and discretion. Newspapers should also refrain from publishing pictures which needlessly exacerbate grief or cause distress. Children's names should not be published.

Victim Support recommends that copies of this code should be made available to families. They also suggest that a press conference, where a statement can be made and a photograph provided, is a preferable option for families who wish to speak to the press without inappropriate intrusion at times not of their choosing.

The work of volunteers

Volunteers can act as intermediaries with police, mortuary officials, funeral directors, doctors, coroner's courts, social security services and other agencies. They can help with practicalities like cleaning up the scene of the crime. They make links between the families and the world outside and can be on standby after the crisis, to provide further help as needed. Some can listen to the expressions of pain, grief and anger and offer comfort. Like any other workers with disaster, volunteers need training and supervision of their work. Many find it helpful to work in pairs. Besides being of direct use to families volunteers can help other agencies and individuals to become alert to the needs of families in disaster and to think how their services may be extended and made more helpful.

There are particular difficulties when the alleged perpetrator of the crime is a member of the family. Victim Support's present view is that it is better for volunteers to work with victims rather than to attempt to also work with an offender. Volunteers who do this work need back-up to deal with their grief, breaks in which they can refresh themselves and ready access to advice from specialists in law and counselling. Many families have told us of the valuable help obtained from this service.

What can the police do to help?

The primary job for the police is criminal investigation but they too have to learn the stressful tasks of breaking news of the killing to family members, answering questions, and collecting data from people who are stunned and grief-stricken. A police liaison officer can be of great value to families who need regular, consistent information about such matters as the return of property, procedure at an inquest and dates of trials and other court hearings. These officers can ensure that the family of the victim knows about the evidence that will be presented in the criminal trial, so that their first knowledge of the details of the killing, or of their daughter's alleged infidelity, is not at the trial itself. Liaison between police and victim support services is valuable to families during the impact of their disaster and requires co-ordination, which, though on a smaller scale, is similar to that needed when a major disaster has affected a community. Where families with children are concerned, this sort of assistance to the adults helps them to think more clearly and act more effectively towards the children. Families of the victims appreciate being told of the impending release of the killer, but rarely are, so the first news might be a sighting of him in the vicinity of the children's home by a neighbour, or worse still a startlingly unexpected face-to-face encounter.

AFTERMATH

What happens in the two months or so after the killing of a child's parent may determine a pattern of further disruption of that child's life for the rest of his childhood. Decisions about where children will live, with whom they will be in contact, how they will be made legally secure and their financial affairs safeguarded, require active forward planning.

Patsy and Ken, aged 7 and 5

Patsy and Ken were referred to us when 7 and 5 years old. Both children were under 3 years old when their father killed their mother by strangling her. No plans were made on their behalf at that time so an emergency placement drifted into a long-term one without the consequences being considered. As a result the children's lives were disrupted again when their father was released from prison.

At the time of the killing the two children were living with their mother's mother and father but, just as before the killing, they regularly went to see some of father's relatives. From prison after his conviction for manslaughter, father said that he approved of the two children being with their maternal grandparents provided they could also visit his family, particularly his mother. The social worker had been involved in setting up contact arrangements while the children remained in the legal guardianship of their father, no legal advice having been sought on their behalf.

There was a long history of family conflict. The parents had married when only 18 years old, mother being pregnant with Patsy at the time. Both sets of grandparents, and numbers of uncles and aunts, lived in the same village and there had been much effort to support the young couple in becoming parents, combined with a lot of anxiety and some recrimination. Some of the family thought it right that the marriage had taken place, others thought it a great mistake. The latter group were not surprised when the young parents had a series of quarrels and separations and mother's parents often took over the children's care when quarrelling between the parents reached a crescendo. However, nobody in either family foresaw the violent climax.

The children's father pleaded guilty to manslaughter but, at his trial, claimed that his dead wife had been unfaithful to him and had provoked him, describing how she had slept with other men, and 'flaunted' this in his face.

We first saw the children four years after the killing when father was due for release from prison. He had received a six-year sentence of which one-third was remitted.

The social worker had helped the family to make an application to the Criminal Injuries Compensation Authority but compensation for the children had been refused on the grounds that the children were being well looked after by their grandparents and did not need compensation for loss of parental care.

At the time we saw the children and grandparents their apparent calm disintegrated. We were told that the two families had decided together that the manner of mother's death was so painful that the children must never know it. They knew that she had died and were taken to see her grave and put flowers on it. They were told that daddy had gone away from home to work, and father, on the occasions they visited him in prison, went along with this story. All the family said that the children were particularly well-behaved and good, were doing well in school and that it would be absurd to upset them by giving them any new information. But all of them were uneasy about how the situation would develop once father came back to live in the neighbourhood.

The social worker, still informally involved from time to time, expressed her doubts about these decisions. Everyone in the village had known about and been horrified by the killing, and father's return was likely to start new discussion. Many children in the wider family, older than Patsy and Ken, knew and could remember just what had happened and many of these children would also have heard the more recent discussions about how to handle matters when father came home again.

Patsy helped an impossible situation when she told her Sunday School teacher, apparently out of the blue, that she knew that her daddy had killed her mummy. This relieved the impasse and enabled some work with the grieving families, but since father came back to live in the village the two sides of the family are no longer on speaking terms, the children are behaving badly in school and their mother's parents are saying that they can no longer look after the children.

We have encountered other families where the killing has allegedly remained a secret until the children are into their adolescence (see Anela's story in Chapter 5).

Marital conflict by proxy

After what is in fact the loss of *both* parents, the extended family often steps in or is invited to step in to offer the children a home. Both sets of relatives may lay claim to the children in the service of their own emotional needs, rather than with the best interests of the children as their paramount consideration. These children, like Patsy and Ken, who have suffered multiple losses and traumatic disruption of their lives, who need security and stability of attachment more than most, may find themselves caught up in a protracted and often ferocious tug of love between competing relatives, which replicates the conflict there had been between their parents. The children are embroiled in conflicts of loyalty, and have to placate relatives on both sides to prevent what they fear will be another catastrophic resolution to a dispute over them. We found that one in three children who had interested relatives from both sides of their family were subject to what we referred to as *marital conflict by proxy*[122] (see also Chapter 12). Perhaps surprisingly, two out of three were not. To some extent this may be accounted for by the relatively high number of first-cousin marriages (mainly Asian) in our sample and the timing of our assessment: many of the relatives were seen *before* the father's criminal trial, which, as we shall see later, is a time of heightened tension between the families. Thus the one in three affected is likely to be an underestimate. Our impression, subsequently, is that one in two would be more accurate over a longer period.

Motivational factors for the father's family will necessarily be different from those for the mother's family. It is important that the opposing families recognise this. For the father's family, the primary organising principle is the resolution of shame and guilt; for the mother's family it is the resolution of grief and mourning. These two processes interact systemically and either aid resolution or impede it. For some, the resolution will have occurred at an earlier stage in the family life cycle. The father's family members may have distanced themselves from his violence and may have supported their daughter-in-law (and the children) during previous episodes of marital conflict. The mother's parents, in two cases at least in our study, had experienced a kind of loss of their daughter through hostile and premature separation during her stormy adolescence, with long periods when there was no contact. They were able to identify with their son-in-law's exasperation and to acknowledge their daughter's part in the escalation of marital conflict.

Where the maternal kin were able to forgive their son-in-law (and his family) after the homicide, the families could be reconciled and resolve issues of residence and contact in a child-centred way. Mother's family were more likely to forgive:

1   if the father accepted responsibility for the killing and showed remorse;
2   if the father's parents acknowledged their shame, and especially where they shared a genuine grief for their daughter-in-law;
3   where at the criminal trial, if there were pleas of provocation, descriptions of their daughter's behaviour did not go beyond their own experience of her as provocative, nor arouse their shame and blameworthiness for their upbringing of her;
4   if the sentence of the father was regarded as fitting.

However, there are a number of processes that militate against a favourable resolution. Long-standing marital conflict had, in many cases, enlisted the extended families' partisan support while the mother was still alive, polarising the families even then. This pre-existing feud was exacerbated by the killing.

With the mother's family, when the depression linked with grief cannot be resolved for whatever reasons, family members may attempt restitution by having the child or children as a replacement for the mother. This seems to bereaved parents to be natural justice and what their dead daughter would have wanted. They are outraged if the father's family lay claim to the children.

Yet father's family may be motivated by a genuine sense that they are in the best position to offer the children a home: for example, they may be the relatives who know the children best. However, their motivation may be based on the wish to keep the children in contact with their father, awaiting his return from prison, when he can again resume their care. They may assume this to be his right as the surviving parent and in the children's best interests. Furthermore, driven by a need to overcome or avoid their shame and guilt at having, within their family, a man who has killed his wife, they may see their bringing up the children as the best way to make reparation and to be forgiven or exonerated from blame. They may minimise father's culpability and copy him in blaming the victim. This is often most intense and dramatic at the time of the criminal trial, if the father's legal representatives try to have the charge of murder reduced to one of manslaughter on the grounds of provocation: that is, the wife provoked the husband beyond what he might reasonably have been expected to tolerate. In these cases the lawyers paint the worst picture of the dead woman, sometimes wildly exaggerating transgressions or character flaws, knowing that neither she nor her family can defend her. (The victim is not represented in criminal trials.) If the mother's family is not already hostile, this is bound to make them so, especially if the criminal court accepts the father's version, and gives him a lenient sentence on that basis – the verdict appearing to the father's family to support or justify their application to have the children reside with them rather than with the family of the 'shamed' victim. (This echoes the views of Victim Support.)

Of course, this is even more powerful when the mother's relatives are angry in their grief, feel cheated, deprived unfairly, reproach themselves for having done too little to protect the mother, and see blame and retribution as the best solutions to their grief. They idealise the mother and see no good at all in the father, disallow any more balanced memories of their parents that the children may have, withhold the children from father and father's family as retribution, and vigorously fight over the 'possession' of the children, in the civil courts.

Blaming and feeling blamed (and shamed) are reciprocally connected in the two sets of relatives, and an escalation on the part of one generates a symmetrical escalation in the other, a particular problem within kinship marriages. Blaming and retribution, while understandable, are the antithesis of forgiveness and compassion. Collaboration between the two sets of relatives, difficult though this will be, may help them to think first about the children's needs, but is very hard to achieve in practice.

Help from social work and health professionals

The role of the social worker is a thread running throughout this book. In the aftermath of the child's disaster a crucial role is that of liaison, with police, health professionals and teachers. This should be done with the active involvement and agreement of adults and children and, wherever possible, the social worker should enable survivors to make their own connections, seek help as they need it and work towards solving their own problems rather than having others take over. The delicate task, always, is to identify and to speak for young traumatised children; there is a difficult balance between addressing the rights and needs of the grieving adults and those of the children. As ever, this is a difficult role for social workers many of whom, despite often very sensitive and thoughtful work, have found themselves blamed and treated as inadequate. For example, the worker for Patsy and Ken, who had got on well with paternal and maternal families while father was in prison, found that all the adults rounded on her after his discharge. She could have said, like Mercutio in *Romeo and Juliet*, 'a plague on both your houses' (something which growing children also may say when their families go on fighting over many years). As with volunteer workers, it is essential that social workers have ready access to competent supervision, support and legal advice.

The complex patterns of trauma and grief delineated in Chapter 3 create fruitful ground for referral to a range of health-care services. Family practitioners and health visitors can add to the often scanty knowledge about the children who are suddenly bereaved, and are likely to have knowledge of their early development, health and behaviour which may be of value to later carers and to therapists involved in helping the children. They are likely to be familiar with the local health resources and can obtain specialist help as appropriate. Child psychiatrists, psychologists, psychotherapists and other professionals based in child psychiatric clinics should be able (and have the resources) to offer skilled emergency assessment, individual and sibling group psychotherapy, bereavement counselling, assessment and help for educational problems, and treatment of any psychiatric disorders (post-traumatic stress disorder, anxiety, depression, conduct disorders, etc.). Paediatricians may be needed to treat sleep and habit disorders, difficulties in development or medical problems.

As social workers, concerned adults and the children themselves begin to plan for the future, it may be valuable to have a consultation with a member of the child mental health services. Many of our referrals are related to problems about where the children will live, with whom they shall have contact, whether they should see the body, how they should take part in funeral ceremonies and how they and their family should communicate with friends, school mates and teachers.

Help in school

It is important that teachers know about trauma in the lives of children and this may seem to be accepted good practice. Guidance to schools on preparation for possible traumatic events has been circulated to all schools in the UK.[262] But the desire to protect children may mean that efforts are made to conceal all evidence of the past from education services. Schoolteachers, however, should not be told about tragedies without this first being discussed with the children concerned, according to their age and ability to understand the issues, and some children may decide for themselves that they do not want teachers to know about their troubles. But in our experience the commonest pattern is that decisions to tell or not to tell their teachers are made on behalf of the children instead of with them and that it is helpful to children to know that school staff are aware of their problems.

When teachers do know about the tragedy they may be falsely assured that the children are doing remarkably well. Children are likely to come to school after disturbed sleep. They may be afraid of the dark, of being alone and, as they were falling asleep, may have suffered flashbacks and intrusive memories. They may be having difficulty in separating from those who are looking after them and be clinging and demanding in ways which seem much younger than their years. This can be particularly difficult when the new carers themselves are full of grief. It can be hard for family and teachers alike to deal with a tired, unhappy, irritable child who does not want to go school. Once in school the children will show changes in their ability to concentrate and to understand and may well fall off in their school work compared with what they were achieving before the tragedy.[231]

Moreover, these children are alone in their difficulties. When a whole school is hit by tragedy, as happened with the children of the *Jupiter* boat disaster and the children of Lockerbie,[171, 263] or when other major disaster affects a community, at least there is a general understanding that everybody is in trouble and is suffering from the effects. Our children may be in a new school, perhaps at a great distance from where they were living; they may lack school-books, project work and have been in the middle of courses different from those now available. They are likely to slip behind not just in learning but in social skills such as going to the toilet when necessary, taking turns, sharing, keeping calm and not interrupting in class.

If children go to school after a domestic tragedy of which the teachers are ignorant, they are at risk of being labelled as trouble-makers or as having inexplicable learning difficulties. If teachers know of the bereavement, but not the extent of the child's knowledge of it, they will be inhibited and uncertain about picking up cues from what the child does or says.

The starting point should be a recognition that children bereaved by domestic violence are not well and happy; indeed, if they are behaving as though nothing has happened to them, this should be regarded as a problem. Bright children, who adapt and carry on within the middle range of school achievement, may nevertheless be under-achieving considerably, with serious impairment in their ability to trust others and to make reliable friendships with other children. Teachers should also know that children are likely to experience intrusive thoughts and images and recognise that these may occur not just at night but at quiet times in the classroom. Like other professionals, they need sources of advice and consultation about such problems.

Summary

It is important that all professionals should be on the alert when children have been violently bereaved. They should be aware that knowledge in brief of a child's experiences, coloured by optimistic views of a child's adaptability and resilience, may allow the child's suffering to be underestimated. It would not of course be appropriate or possible for family doctors, social workers and teachers to work in the very intensive way described in Chapter 8, and many children need specialist help. But there is now a substantial body of clinical work about the effects of disasters on children. Professionals in community services who know about this will be sensitive to the effects of trauma on children and their families and this will enhance the home and the school environment and the health care available to the children and those who look after them.

Chapter 7

When mother kills father

Diseases, desperate grown,
By desperate appliance are relieved
Or not at all
    (Shakespeare, *Hamlet*, IV, iii)

SUMMARY

We outline what is known of women as perpetrators of violence, considering biological and social factors. There are differing effects upon children of loss of father at the hands of mother and the response of the law may differ also. We consider whether children may ever return safely to the care of one parent who has killed the other.

Women appear to be much less violent than men and this is reflected in our group of 425 children. In only 22 families, with 44 children altogether (10 per cent), did the mother kill the father.

The events which led up to the killings were different from when father was the killer. In some cases, the mother had been repeatedly physically, sexually and emotionally abused by the father and, when they were both the worse for drink, and mother in fear of her life, she slew him. It seems to have been touch and go which one killed the other first. In over 50 per cent of the women perpetrators there was a history of childhood physical and/or sexual abuse. This may also have contributed to their initial passivity in relation to their violent partner's abuse of them or the children.

Women are probably biologically less violent than men and this difference is emphasised by social factors such as the differential reinforcement of aggression in boys compared with girls. It may be a reflection of this that in English there are numerous Latin-derived words for the act of murdering another – such as a monarch, sibling, parent, wife (uxoricide) – but no word specifically denoting a wife killing her husband.

Our sample, while too small to enable us to draw any firm conclusions, reflects in its proportions the total group of husband killers in England and Wales. Home

Office statistics[108] tell us that, between 1982 and 1988, 164 women were charged with murder of a spouse, cohabitee or lover, and 13 with their manslaughter. During the same period, 753 men were charged with murder and 32 with manslaughter, giving a male:female ratio overall of 9:2. However women were acquitted of all charges in 22 per cent of cases compared with 5 per cent of men. Ten times the number of men were convicted of murder (278 men to 27 women).

Probably at least half of these couples would have had children so it is again surprising how little concern and thought is given to them. For example, a study of women who kill their partners, ranging from the eighteenth century to the present day, by an American journalist,[116] mentions the children only in the accounts of the trials, where they appear sometimes as witnesses, often speaking in their mother's defence. Other than an occasional remark about their going to live with relatives, we gain no idea of the children's plight or fate. We have found no other literature which looks specifically at the children of mothers who kill their partners, although the literature on the effects on children of severe domestic violence is growing (see for example,[29] and[156] for reviews).

Previous domestic violence is known to have occurred in all but one of our mother-kills-father cases but in only two-thirds of the father-kills-mother ones. In one case the police had been called on over fifty occasions by neighbours because of father's repeated attacks on mother before she finally killed him. Many of the women had left home again and again because of their husband's violence only to be dragged back from a refuge or persuaded back by his remorse and promises of reform. In the end they believed that they could only be free of him by his death.

Courts in the UK generally deal more leniently with husband killers than wife killers.[98] In only one of our cases was mother convicted of murder, and in three cases she was convicted of manslaughter but released immediately on probation. In five cases she was convicted of manslaughter and received a custodial sentence, although in one case this was reversed on appeal. Three mothers had their cases dismissed (usually on grounds of self-defence). In two cases mother was mentally ill and needed treatment in a psychiatric hospital. The others still await trial at the time of writing and most of them are on bail and either live with their children or see them regularly. One mother, convicted of murder, died of natural causes after five years in prison.

A significantly higher percentage of the children whose father killed their mother had witnessed the killing (79 per cent) than those whose mother killed their father (54 per cent). It is possible that when a mother kills she may take more care to protect her children. The following case vignettes illustrate children's responses to their mother's homicidal act.

Madasir, aged 10 years

The mother of Madasir had endured her husband's violence for many years but had stayed with him for the sake of the children, and because in her Asian culture, women did not leave their husbands. The two families were intimately tied by generations of first-cousin marriages and indeed those who did not marry a relative were considered to be outcasts. Such in-breeding not only increases the risk that any genetically based disorders will be enhanced (and many psychiatric disorders and alcoholism, as well as physical illnesses and disabilities, have a genetic component) but it also may make it difficult for a woman, faced with an unhappy marriage, to find understanding or sympathy from her immediate family, since they are also the husband's relatives. Mother had tried to leave her husband once but her parents had persuaded her to stick it out. She was too proud to tell them again of the violence and degradation she experienced, but one day with the help of her sister who had taken her side in the family arguments, she murdered him. Madasir, unknown to the sisters, had witnessed the killing although he had not at the time appreciated what was happening.

The next day the children were told that father had left home but Madasir found that his possessions and even his suitcase were still there. A few days later he told his father's mother of his worries and she went to the police. When father's body was found, mother and her sister were arrested and Madasir had to give evidence against them. Mother had previously had profound depressive illnesses and was found unfit to plead. She remains in a secure psychiatric hospital and Madasir as he moves into adolescence is struggling with his ambivalent feelings towards his culture, his religion, his race and his family. He feels responsible for his mother's incarceration, the losses his two sisters have experienced 'because of me', the deteriorated relationships within the wider family, and the shame that a once proud family are suffering.

Ina, aged 14 years

Ina was referred to us by her social worker for an opinion about how best to help deteriorating relationships between herself and her foster-mother. She was doing badly in school and had recently stolen several small sums of money within the home. Ten years earlier, Ina's mother had killed her father. Neither the foster-mother nor the current social worker knew Ina's story other than by hearsay and through reading very unsatisfactory case records. They knew that Ina had been in the house at the time of the killing but not what she had seen or heard. Although the foster-mother, a neighbour to the family, had taken on the emergency care of Ina and then, when it turned out there were no relatives who could offer Ina a home, had become a long-term carer, she had never been given any information about the killing and had not liked to ask.

What was known was that Ina's mother had been arrested but never came to trial, instead being referred to a psychiatric hospital. At some point, according to the record, there was a case discussion about the possibility of returning Ina to her mother's care, but mother failed to keep appointments with social workers and by the time Ina was 8 years old mother's whereabouts were unknown. Then the foster-mother had lost her husband and had brought up Ina, with her own children, single-handed.

It was startling to realise that there were so many gaps in the knowledge of Ina and her foster-mother about what had happened comparatively recently. Her foster-mother remembered coping for months with Ina's nightmares and described how Ina had been so slow and unresponsive in school that a teacher had wondered if she needed special education. Ina and her foster-mother, separately, expressed worries about whether the girl could have inherited some form of 'madness' from her own mother.

We attempted to help Ina by work on fears of inherited illness, buried traumatic memories and the lack of a trusting relationship between Ina and her foster-mother, which may well have been linked with the child's early trauma and failure to grieve. The traumatic events were distant and yet they were still reverberating and affecting Ina's life. She is still in a limbo with no parents she can claim as her own, living in long-term foster-care. This has been found to be the worst option of those usually open when children are taken into care because of deficiencies in their parenting. (Others are a return to their family, adoption or a residence order.)

When a group of children taken into care because of their parents' difficulties was followed into adult life, it was found that those who did best were the ones who had been adopted and those who did worst were those placed with foster-parents. This had perhaps originally been as a short-term measure, but the situation had been allowed to drift on without decisions about a permanent placement. The foster-parents usually did their best to give the children a good home, but they, like the children, were uncertain about how long they would be living together or indeed whether they would ever see each other again if the children were returned to their parents or adopted by others.[33, 34] Unless, as can be achieved, skilled social work has established the long-term nature of the foster-home placement, with no legal conflicts about its continuance, in such circumstances it would not be surprising if both children and foster-parents held back from that process of 'falling in love' necessary to the formation of those mutual bonds of attachment which we now know to be an essential contribution to the mental health of children.[37]

These findings illuminate Ina's story. She has lacked a secure home since her father's death. Neither Ina nor her foster-mother wanted to be hurt by yet another disruption of attachments, which both had experienced in the past. The consequences for Ina were disastrous. She began stealing from her foster-mother. Some might say that she was taking from her illicitly what she needed and could not get in any other way. Money is often a symbol for love and children who are not loved and wanted are more likely to take what they feel they need and have been deprived of. If Ina had been given immediate help in establishing whether she had undergone the trauma of seeing her mother kill her father, if she had been nurtured in a family where mutual attachment could grow, and if she had received counselling to help her mourn her father's death and the loss of her mother, and been given some explanation of the role mental illness played in her mother's actions, plus help when her foster-father died, it is probable that her life would be more settled and she would be functioning more healthily today.

Greg, aged 3 years

Greg was only 3 years old when he saw his mother kill his father. In contrast to Ina, he was brought to see us a few weeks later by his foster-parents, with whom he was now living. Their family doctor knew of our interest and had suggested the consultation. Greg's parents were both heavy drinkers and in financial difficulties but had been too proud to confide in anyone. After the killings it came as a shock to both sides of the family to learn of the straitened circumstances of the young couple. During a drunken quarrel after mother had been very upset because her husband had made her steal a bottle of whisky and she had been apprehended, she had picked up a hammer and smashed his face. She passed out and did not regain consciousness for over twelve hours. No one knew what Greg had seen or how he had fared for that time. But when mother regained consciousness she phoned her cousin who took him to her house whilst mother gave herself up to the police and went to prison.

Greg had been mute after his father's death but the following day he had told his carer that his father was dead and demonstrated how his mother had hit him, showing the parts of his father's face that had been hit. He followed his foster-father around anxiously and did not want to be separated. His sleep was disturbed but he reported no nightmares. Although he was now, a few weeks later, just becoming a little more outgoing and happy, he played at home with little building blocks which he built up and knocked down compulsively and repetitively. He had cried for his mother and father.

In his play during the assessment session with us Greg was preoccupied with the killing. He spontaneously re-enacted it using doll figures to represent his parents. He picked up a toy scalpel belonging to a set of toys we use for children being helped to prepare for a surgical operation and, putting it in the hand of the mother doll, he used it as a hammer, repeatedly hitting the face of the father doll.

Greg's anxiety, clinging and repetitive compulsive play were signs of post-traumatic stress disorder. His sensitive foster-family had almost certainly prevented more serious symptoms by their ability to receive his early traumatic communications and not attempt to suppress them. Their willingness to seek and accept advice and help made it possible for us to offer him psychotherapeutic help. Over the course of the next year Greg visited his mother regularly in prison, and in sessions with a psychotherapist began the journey to understanding and healing. Mother, who said that before her marriage she had been sober and hard-working with no particular difficulties, described how she had been reduced to despair by her husband's extravagance, alcoholism and refusal to work. Drink became an anodyne to dull the pain of her unhappy marriage and the worry about their debts which, however hard she worked, never lessened. The therapist learned from Greg that, with both parents drinking, violence between them escalated. Mother had endured many beatings. Greg demonstrated in play and drawings that he had witnessed her humiliation and her hurts many times.

Mother was charged with murder, but the Crown Prosecution Service accepted her plea of manslaughter due to diminished responsibility, and on the day of her trial she was given a non-custodial probation order. She began slowly to rebuild her life, obtaining accommodation and a job before resuming Greg's care.

Greg was helped by sensitive carers and a therapist, whom he saw regularly for two years, to come to terms with his experiences (as described in the next chapter). His family managed to avoid a continuation of the battle which had killed his father. Father's mother kept in contact with Greg's mother throughout her imprisonment and showed she forgave her for killing her son. Greg's symptoms of post-traumatic stress subsided and his development and adjustment have to date been good.

Frank and Julie, aged 7 and 4

Frank and Julie's mother killed their father in a state of mind altered by alcohol and chronic fear resulting from years of brutal physical and sexual misuse by her husband. This really was a case of the 'worm turning', and of a woman who killed rather than be killed, the damage to her body which her husband had inflicted just before she killed him necessitating her subsequent hospitalisation. Mother had recognised that father's denigratory and contemptuous attitude towards her extended also to Julie. At her trial it was successfully argued that father had so terrorised her that she had felt unable to leave him, believing he would surely seek her out and retaliate.

She was released from prison and resumed the care of her children, determined to make up to them for her absence and for the killing of their father (which fortunately they had not witnessed). She brought them for family therapy sessions which were aimed at helping them to reintegrate as a family and enabling the children to express their grief for their father's death. Another aim was to help mother address the issues around discipline and control which were distorted by the children's anxiety about her.

In our sessions we found that mother repeatedly discouraged the children and the therapist from addressing mourning issues. She was unable to face taking them to visit their father's grave. Her exhilaration at having freed herself from her sadistic husband made it difficult for her to recognise that the children's experience of him – or at least Frank's – might have been more rewarding. Her fear that Frank might have inherited his father's cruel traits led her to avoid the children's need to mourn their father and to discover his positive attributes.

Julie's self-esteem had undoubtedly been affected by her father's inexplicably changing attitudes towards her, with praise one minute and denigration and taunts the next. For Frank, father had set an example. Frank's sudden small cruelties to the cat caused us considerable concern. Both children could benefit from their own separate therapists to help them with these problems but it may be difficult for their mother to acknowledge their needs.

Like Greg's mother, Frank and Julie's mother has retained the friendship and practical support of her mother-in-law. She struggles courageously to rebuild a shattered life, with few material resources and much opprobrium from her community, but the future for her children, growing up in a home where painful subjects are taboo and the children are aware that the ultimate sanction for bad behaviour is death, is uncertain.

Children, even more than adults, need adult help to remember and to make sense of their memories. They have to develop a rounded picture of the parents who made them and whose inheritance they share. For children to be fed on a diet of hatred, for them to believe that their dead parent had no redeeming features, does violence to their own self-image. 'If daddy is bad, half of me must be bad too as half of me comes from daddy', one 8-year-old told us. Therapeutic help for children should address feelings like this.

Gaining a rounded picture of the killer parent or dead parent becomes impossibly difficult if the child lives with relatives who themselves are bitter, or filled with hate because of the loss of their son or daughter through the death or imprisonment.

Emily, aged 6

Emily's mother, Frances, is a pretty, young Cypriot woman whose family repudiated her when, at 16, she became pregnant by Tony. He was a handsome young man whose parents came to the UK from southern

Italy in the 1950s and were well-established, proud and prosperous. Father's family befriended her and took her in and, although the couple drifted apart after Emily's birth, they remained friendly. Mother basked in the warmth extended to her by father's family and found their support and practical help useful.

When Emily was 9 months old, father's parents baby-sat while Frances and Tony went to a mutual friend's party. Frances was jealous of the attention Tony gave another girl there. A quarrel ensued, and Frances, fearing that he would hurt her, as he had in previous fights, pulled out a little knife she kept in her sock to defend herself with, warning him to keep his distance. He either did not see it, or did not heed it. The knife entered his heart and he died immediately.

Frances was arrested, convicted of manslaughter and served a prison sentence, where she matured and learned a trade. Tony's parents looked after Emily, and although they took her to see Frances in prison they opposed Emily's return to her on her release, arguing that the child was settled with them, and did not really know her mother who had no home and no job and was unreliable in her contact with Emily. Frances yearned for her daughter but felt guilty that she had deprived Tony's parents, who had befriended her when she was homeless, of their son. Her inconsistent behaviour reflected her extreme conflict of mind. Her solicitor, recognising her agony, arranged for her to see a psychotherapist who helped her to have the courage to begin to function again. She developed new relationships and kept a loose contact with her daughter, always wanting to be with her, but not wanting to challenge her grandparents who had safeguarded Emily's placement by making her a ward of court. When Emily was 6, we were asked by her guardian *ad litem* to advise the court about where she should live and what contact she should have with her mother and others.

We found that Emily was confused about who Frances was, and who her grandmother was in relation to her. She called grandmother 'mummy' as she heard others do (Tony was the eldest of four children, now all living away from home but returning often), and was not discouraged from doing so. She also knew that 'mummy's' name was Agnes. Grandmother had told Emily on her visits to Frances in prison that they were going to visit 'first mummy' to help differentiate her from 'second mummy' (herself), but mother was also referred to as Frances within the extended family. Emily showed us her confusion by telling us that mummy was married to grandpa (pointing to her grandparents) and that her father was 'under the ground' and had been killed by Frances. Asked who Frances was, she replied, 'She's a lady I visit but she's gone to Cyprus.' Later, seen alone, she told us about her dreams of her mother who had gone to Cyprus who was called Agnes. 'There are two Agneses, you see', she explained. 'The other mummy moved to another house and swapped her name.'

Offered a free choice of toys, Emily enacted a scene with much violence where an elephant repeatedly impaled a man on his trunk and a lion bit off a little girl's head. Emily said she was showing us the scenes in her dreams.

Emily's fantasy world was a violent one. Although she was cared for devotedly by her grandparents, their grief over the death of their son, their sense of betrayal by a girl whom they had succoured, and their attachment to and concern for their granddaughter led them to wish to prevent Emily from knowing her mother or learning about her. They were not malevolent, and they believed they had Emily's best interests at heart. But their hearts are sore at the loss of their son when his heart was punctured. Frances is heartbroken about what she has done to Tony, his parents, her daughter and herself, but little Emily may never open her heart to her mother or forgive her for depriving her of her father and turning her world upside down.

Should women killers be treated differently from men in the penal system?

Many penologists and writers on women's issues have argued that women should not be imprisoned.[48] In 1970 the Home Office suggested that by the end of the century there would be 'fewer or no women at all being given prison sentences', yet the likelihood of a woman being sent to prison has in reality doubled in recent years.[63, 107] If a non-custodial alternative is appropriate should we not use it? Other countries have found it possible to use day prisons, bail hostels, and community service instead for women and their recidivism rate is no higher than ours.[18] Most women who kill a mate are themselves battered and under-privileged. By imprisoning them, we punish not only the killer, but the innocent children who lose both parents suddenly, traumatically and simultaneously. The children's fate is dire. They have on average four or five different carers before their mother is released, with homelessness, poverty, unemployment and stigma to contend with, and if she has been away for a substantial time she may be unsuccessful in gaining a resistence order, or like Frances, ambivalent about having the children back, loath to uproot them yet again.[249] In our study, all of the children of the women who were killers were living with their mothers at the time, but nearly half of the fathers who killed were living separately from their wives and families at the time of the killing. In these cases, and especially where young children are concerned, the loss of a mother is much more significant and may be more immediately traumatic than the loss of a father.

Although our numbers of mothers who kill their partners are too small for us to make comparisons with the fathers who commit the same act, other studies of women killers have shown that, unlike men, very few of them are in general violent or dangerous and most of them have children who suffer by the separation.[19] Furthermore, when women are imprisoned, the children often have difficult journeys to see their mother and keep contact with her, because there are relatively few prisons for women, compared with the number for men, and undergo in addition all the difficulties (loss or imprisonment of a parent, violation, disruption of schooling, financial disadvantage), described in Chapter 9.

Two eminent judges have stated that 'it is important to avoid subjecting anyone to the damaging effects of imprisonment unless this cannot be avoided'.[258] Society, however, in dealing with domestic crime, fails to distinguish between the paying of a debt to society, assessment of the risk of further violence and that of future parenting capacity, and these issues should be considered in relation to men and women. Can a mother or father who has killed retain the moral capacity to parent children and should mothers who kill be assessed differently from fathers in this respect? The majority of the children in our first series who have returned to their killer father had not yet grown up when we followed them up a few years later. One did disastrously – running away at 16 from a father who physically abused her throughout her childhood. She is very depressed and has attempted suicide. Another, who returned to her mother's care, is living independently, having run away repeatedly from her mother. Yet a third is in prison, having been convicted of the murder of a peer. Many of the children of mothers who kill return to their mother's care (in contrast to the children whose father kills mother, where a return to the father's care after his release is uncommon). Few of our children have reached adulthood yet. Those we know of have not done well and this seems related to the fact that normal disciplinary measures are problematic – the children fearing that if they step out of line the same fate may befall them as befell their father. One boy of 6 started dressing in his sister's clothes. He told us that he thought he would be safer if he was a girl as mother 'only killed men'.

So far, we have been asked for advice on this issue more often where the mother has committed the crime, which is why we discuss the issue in this chapter, but our principles for practice remain identical irrespective of the sex of the surviving parent. Our observations are that younger children who return to the killer parent are wary, anxious, over-compliant and placatory.

June, aged 11, and Angela, aged 8, were living with their father after he had served a term for the manslaughter of their mother by bludgeoning which they had witnessed. June confided to us that they tried to be very good, so daddy would not be cross with them as he had with mummy.

In adolescence they disconcert their parent by defiantly repudiating the killer parent's right to have authority over them: 'You killed my mother/father – why should I do what you tell me?' This opens the way to homelessness, delinquency, and danger of sexual exploitation, in addition to the burdens that were the legacy of the original trauma.

Often the children side with the mother in the domestic violence which preceded the killing and, seeing her as a victim and sometimes as their protector, are less likely to be condemning of her than are the father-kills-mother children of their father. Nevertheless, living with a perpetrator parent of either sex carries the same risks as they both fear the parent and find it difficult as adolescents to accept his or her control. Mother-kills-father children may also fare less well in therapy, as keeping loyal to their killer mother makes it difficult to acknowledge angry or sad feelings necessary to benefit from therapeutic help. We found that those children living with the perpetrator parent of either sex were less likely to be brought for treatment, as it was difficult for the parent to recognise and acknowledge that the children might have been harmed by the crime.

We know only of those cases referred to us and advocates for parents due for release from prison point out that there may be successful reunions with children of which we do not hear. We doubt, however, whether a man or woman who has killed can be an effective parent to the children, dealing with unspoken fears, compliance or rebellion and providing a reliable model for dealing with aggression. We think that as mental health professionals it is our duty to advise civil courts which are asked to return children to a parent who has killed, that they must consider not just the debt to society, which may have been paid, nor the risk of further homicide, which may be small, but the need of the children for competent trustworthy parenting for the rest of their childhood.

Chapter 8

Healing the trauma
Help for children and those who care for them

My childhood's ceiling was no protection
against the snakes and fat herbivores
that struck or licked at my dreaming self . . .
    (Alan Harris, 'Trapdoor')

SUMMARY

The concept of psychotherapeutic help is discussed. Clinical illustrations
compiled by therapists from work with many children illustrate longer-term
therapy with individuals, groups of brothers and sisters and families.

Children who have had one parent killed by the other have many needs. In this
chapter we look at how early intervention might prevent later problems and at the
use of different forms of therapy to heal the wounds which have already been
acquired. We also consider how social workers, general practitioners and foster-
carers can help children to grow straight when fate has dealt them such a massive
sideways swipe.

We will follow through a few children from the time we first saw them. We have
disguised these stories by mixing them up as well as by altering distinguishing
features. They will, we hope, be useful as guidance for others wanting to help
children in similar plights.

This chapter deals in the main with psychotherapy. All words with the prefix
'psycho' pertain to the mind. Thus psychology is the study of the mind, and
psychiatry, the study of disorders of the mind. Psychotherapy, therefore, is the
treatment of the mind and is usually used of treatments which do not involve
drugs, surgery, electric convulsions and the like. The agents or tools of treatment
are the therapists themselves and they use their sensitivity, honed through training and personal psychotherapy, to understand the communications of their
patients and help them to make sense of their experiences, dreams, fantasies,
anxieties and fears. They must create a safe and predictable treatment setting for
children and they do this by, as much as possible, meeting them in the same

room, at the same time regularly week after week, warning them in good time when holiday breaks are coming up. The therapist will provide some drawing and play materials for the child and make sure they are kept safe and undisturbed from session to session.

During the hour of therapy, therapists learn in their training to clear their minds of all their own preoccupations – they force themselves to concentrate only on the child's communications, however they are expressed. By giving themselves up to the children and their world, psychotherapists can catch subtle expressions and tentative communications which might go unnoticed otherwise. There is some evidence that this structured, reliable experience for the child is therapeutic in itself. For example, some of our younger patients might believe that they made mummy disappear because they were naughty. But if the therapist standing for the mummy pops up reliably each session, even after the child has made it clear she hates him, or tests him to the limits, then it might be possible to believe that he or she is not at fault after all. The therapy setting lends itself to the child transferring patterns of behaviour, learned in other relationships, into the one with the therapist. Therapists pay attention to the children's behaviour, and the feelings it evokes in the therapists can be used to help the children.

For therapists to concentrate on material which is often distressing, dealing as it does with primitive feelings, violent emotions and actions and frightening fantasies and realities, they must themselves be supported and enabled to take a step back and think about what they are doing, and ensure that they are not misinterpreting the material that they are experiencing, or becoming over-whelmed and depressed by it. All therapists, no matter how senior, usually arrange to meet from time to time with an experienced colleague to ponder together on the substance of the therapy hour. With this supervision they are more likely to avoid one of the most dangerous pitfalls of psychotherapy, over-identifying with their patients. This can happen particularly when their own experiences have been similar. For example, perhaps one therapist had a violent father, or another lost their mother when young. They will have come to terms with whatever effect this had on their personalities and functioning during their own personal therapy as part of their training, but in this field as in others the price of success is eternal vigilance.

Family therapists and their supervisors often use videotaped sessions, or even have the supervisor view the session live behind a one-way mirror. Sometimes two therapists will lead a group session – one more experienced than the other – so that they can receive another kind of 'live' supervision.

Continued supervision throughout their career is one sign of true professionals in this field; another is the willingness to submit their work to being tested by comparative trials using research techniques (see for example Kolvin *et al.* (1981)[128], still a model for others to follow). Finally, they must spend time at conferences and reading the literature so that they are aware of advances in their field to be put at the service of their patients. Good descriptions of a child psychotherapist's work are to be found in two books: Boston and Szur's

Psychotherapy with Severely Deprived Children[35] and Szur and Miller's *Extending Horizons: Psychoanalytic psychotherapy with children, adolescents and families*.[217]

Psychotherapy has to take place in a context. Children do best in therapy when they live in a home which is permanent and where their carers, counselled by the therapists or their colleagues in the clinic where they work, can deal sensitively but firmly with any disturbed behaviour which may result from the painful working through of the traumatic experiences during therapy. To have such a setting is not always possible; many of our children have several temporary homes before they settle. We do not believe that therapy should be delayed pending a permanent home and so therapists may have to work under less than ideal conditions, like the children they serve. Often society hopes that the therapist can make the children right so that they can be settled in a good home, whilst the therapists are hoping that the home can be provided first, to make their therapy more effective. The reality is that there are no guarantees of either and we must all work with what is available.

Other forms of help

Chapter 3 discusses **bereavement counselling**

Some children benefit from **cognitive/behavioural therapies**, offered usually by a clinical psychologist and aimed at helping children to receive, conceptualise and process accurate information about their circumstances and thus to modify how they think and behave in the light of increased understanding.[125]

Social skills training may help children to cope better with predictable problems: for example, how to deal with intrusive questions at school, what to say to friends, how to respond to expressions of sympathy. This is often useful to children at sea among new experiences.

Pharmacotherapy, the use of medication, so far has but a small part to play, but may be useful in the short term for the relief of specific symptoms so as to enable psychological therapies to be more effective. It is likely, with continuing research, that more specific and appropriate medications will be developed to relieve the immediate and often severe bodily suffering (which we discuss in Chapter 1) which follows a disaster (see also Chapter 10).

Eye Movement Desensitisation and Reprocessing (EMDR) is a relatively new treatment for post-traumatic stress disorder. Subjects are taught lateral eye movements which, it is theorised, synchronise with brain wave (electro-encephalogram) patterns similar to those seen in rapid-eye-movement sleep, which in humans coincides with periods of dreaming. In a waking state, subjects are taught to reproduce these eye movements, while being helped, under carefully planned and controlled conditions, to re-experience traumatic events. Studies, so far in the main with adults, indicate effective, reliable relief from psychologically disturbing symptoms of PTSD. These methods increasingly are being evaluated for adolescents and children old enough to collaborate in exploring their experiences in this way. The method was pioneered and developed by Shapiro between 1989 and 1995[200, 201]; it has since been evaluated[250] and its use for children and adolescents reviewed.[9]

An overview of the current classification, diagnosis and treatment of post-traumatic stress disorder is provided by Black and colleagues.[30]

Our first vignette describes development over a period of ten years and illustrates the problems that arise when a child witnesses the killing of her parent and is not relieved of the traumatic images by immediate debriefing.

Philippa, 4 years to 14 years

Philippa came to see a therapist with her two older sisters when she was 4 years old, brought by her social worker a few weeks after her father killed her mother by bludgeoning her to death with an axe. Philippa had been asleep when her mother had burst into her room, hoping no doubt that father would hesitate to hurt her in the child's presence.

The social worker was seeking to know what Philippa had witnessed and what help could be given. The children were being cared for by their father's parents and father was in prison. Philippa was one of the team's first cases and from treating her we learned much of what we now know. Pynoos and Eth had not yet written their seminal paper[180] describing an interview for children who had witnessed violence to one of their parents, and a description of critical incident stress debriefing was still a few years off.[150] What we decided to do was to offer family therapy sessions for the three children, their carers and their family to try to help the children to express their grief and begin their mourning for their mother. Already the families on each side were lining up for a battle and so it seemed important to try to mediate between them. We were like fools who rush in where angels fear to tread and have since discovered how very intractable such enmity is and how rarely mediation is successful. Philippa's maternal grandmother could only repeat again and again what a wicked poisonous man her son-in-law was: 'That murderer!' she would spit whenever she saw his mother, the children's carer. We have also learned over the years that children who witness violence to those they love cannot do their grief work until the trauma is addressed and dealt with (see[70] and Chapter 3).

In the first session, it was clear that Philippa knew less than her sisters, to whom father had confessed what he had done although they were not witnesses. Philippa had been told that her parents had had an accident and that mother was dead and father in hospital. She parroted this story to us and then disarmingly added 'but I don't think it's very true'. Asked what was true she replied that she thought that her parents might sneak back to their house and no one would tell her. The following week we arranged that the grandparents with whom she lived would meet with us, and the other children and Philippa would be told that mummy and daddy had had a big fight and that daddy had hurt mummy so much that she had died, her body didn't work any more. Because daddy had hurt mummy he had to be punished and he was locked up in a prison where he had to stay for a long time.

It was disconcerting to discover, the next time she came, that Philippa was announcing proudly to all who would listen that she had the strongest daddy in the world. He was so strong that he could kill people! Philippa was very proud of her father. They had a good relationship. At the time of mother's death, child and mother had been locked in a battle about Philippa's intransigence over going to bed. Father would come home from work and, because of the marital difficulties, would tend to undermine mother's authority, giving Philippa permission to stay up longer. Years later, when Philippa was talking to her therapist, she would remember her initial triumph that mother was dead and that she could have father all to herself – that she had won father from mother. Her guilt in later years led her to be savagely self-punitive and nearly led to her death.

The father's parents tended, as most do, to excuse their son's behaviour. 'She drove him to it – she was nothing but a whore.' They took the children to visit father in prison regularly and made a home for him in their house when he was released three years later. The older children felt less affection for their father; they found it difficult to condone his actions and elected not to live with him, moving to maternal relatives and effectively losing touch with Philippa, who after a time moved with her father into a little flat. No one knew what happened until, when she was in her teens, she ran away and asked to be taken into care. The story she told her social worker was as follows:

Father had been a stern disciplinarian and had alternately beaten her for slight misdemeanours and lavished affection on her. He had bound her to him with tales of his suffering at mother's hands, provoking her sympathy. He told her that he had not killed her mother and that he would prove it to her. Philippa had found herself in adolescence provoking him again and again to hit her. One day, she had been beating him on the chest with her fists, when she had a sudden feeling that she had experienced this before. All the feelings of bewilderment and terror suppressed for years flooded through her. She knew in a flash that, if she did not leave, she would drive her father to kill again. To protect him, rather than herself, she left home.

Philippa was profoundly depressed when she came back to see us ten years after her mother's death. She cried interminably, she could not sleep, she was painfully thin. She felt pangs of guilt at having left her father. His anger at her putting herself in care echoed the fatal rage when he was told by her mother that she was leaving him, all those years ago. Philippa punished herself by cutting her arms, her abdomen and her hair and by turning to drugs and sex. The feelings of bewilderment and terror she had experienced, which had led her to run away, we now recognise as a flashback phenomenon – a cardinal sign of post-traumatic stress disorder, and one that can occur years after the trauma.

In long sessions with her therapist, Philippa came to realise that she had been compulsively re-enacting the final moments of her mother's life – seen and heard from the bed in which everyone thought she was fast asleep. Again and again she had tried, without being conscious of what she was doing, to prove that her father had not been a killer by pushing him to the limits, in the hope that he would show that he was not capable of losing control. She would have preferred to deny the evidence of her own eyes and ears, her own memories, if this could have exonerated her father.

Philippa's state of mind was very disturbed. Years of abuse, years of having the evidence of her eyes negated and rubbished, years of being compliant for fear she would be meted out the same fate as her mother, and, more recently, months of defying fate and challenging it to do its worst, had left her with a severe psychiatric disorder. We thought then that this was a disorder which a skilled and patient therapist might influence if Philippa were to accept help and stick with it. She found it hard to let people help her. She had little trust in an adult world, preferring to rely on herself and her friends, but lacking signposts and markers to help her to choose friends wisely. She found herself used and then abandoned by friends and masochistically laid herself open to exploitation. And yet she could evoke love and compassion too in those whose lives she touched. She was beautiful and intelligent, and there was an inner core of sanity and stability which must have come from the security which was her mother's gift to her. She did not remember it but it shone through even when she was at her most destructive.

It might have turned out differently for Philippa, if we had known then what we know now. Then we would have been more active in ascertaining what Philippa had witnessed and we would have debriefed her more skilfully. We would have tried to provide her with a legal framework of protection so that she did not have to return to an abusive father. We would have been able to keep a watchful eye on her progress and to intervene swiftly to offer help before things went so badly wrong. As an adult, Philippa did meet the right therapist and her story is continued in Chapter 10.

Harry, aged 6

Harry had a different experience at our hands. He came to see us with his uncle and aunt only a few days after his father shot his mother and then killed himself. By that time people knew of our interest and we had learned to offer immediate interviews to traumatically orphaned children.

Harry was a bright, attractive, serious and tall boy, very self-possessed. We asked him to draw us a picture after explaining that we were doctors who tried to help children where there were worries and problems – 'worry and problem doctors'. Harry immediately chose the yellow felt-tipped pen and first drew a small man holding an enormous gun. He talked as he drew, telling us that his father had come back to his home where he lived with his mother, after they had been out together. The parents had had a quarrel and dad had killed mother. We asked him to draw his mother. He peered at us quizzically: 'Are you sure you want to see it? I can only draw sad faces.' And he did indeed draw mother, small and with a very sad down-turned mouth.

We asked him where he was when dad hurt mummy. He said he had gone upstairs but had come running when the loud noise had happened. Daddy ran away and Harry tried to revive mother by pouring water over her as he had seen on television. Then he had tried to ring for an ambulance but the phone had not worked for him and he had fallen asleep. Next morning he had tried again and this time someone came. He told us proudly how he had taken the police to his auntie's house all by himself. Then he fell silent and we wondered out loud if he was feeling that he should have been able to be a big boy the night before and stop daddy from hurting mummy. He looked at us in surprise. How did we guess?

We asked him where his daddy was and he proceeded to finish off the drawing by adding a car which had crashed into a tree, 'daddy's car'. We told him what a brave and clever boy he had been to try to help mummy and to remember how to use the phone to get help, and we explained again and again that he could not have stopped daddy as he was not there, and anyway daddy was too strong because he was grown-up and Harry was only a child. We explored his understanding of death and helped him to express and grasp the basic components,[131] which we know (as described in Chapter 3) are understood by the majority of 6-year-olds: that dead people are different from the living, that they cannot move, or breathe, or see or hear or eat or talk, or cuddle their children; that death has a cause, that it is universal, and that it leads to permanent separation.

Over the next two years, Harry saw the same therapist, a member of our team, every week. There were many themes in his play.

Families

Harry frequently played with families of dolls and families of animals. A common theme was fighting between the parents, something that we presume he must have experienced even before the final fight. Often the play involved three generations, indicating how important a part his grandparents continued to play in his life. Early in the therapy there were usually several children in his play families. He used to talk openly about his hopes that in his 'forever family' which his social worker was seeking he would have brothers and sisters, indicating his loneliness as an only child. However, when he went to live in a family with other children, his play families had just one child and this theme was often repeated, hinting at the difficulty he had found in sharing and the problem of coping with his jealousy. At times when there were other child dolls around, he would throw them away from him in a very dismissive manner. At other times he openly expressed his jealousy of his foster-siblings.

Another family-oriented game that Harry often played was a racing game with toy cars. He described them as 'the daddy, mummy and Harry cars'. He would push the cars across the room and the one that got closest to the wall would be the winner. He would frequently crash the daddy car so that it would lose. When his therapist said he thought that Harry was telling him about his anger with his father, Harry would say he was angry with his father for killing mummy.

Burglars

In his second session, Harry found a wire doll of a balding old man. Someone earlier had coloured the bald patch red and Harry said it looked like a bishop's hat. He returned to this doll many times during his therapy. The doll always represented something bad, usually in the form of a burglar who would break into the doll's house and smash things up, kill people or kidnap babies. By making a senior respectable person do bad things, Harry was showing us his cynicism about adults in authority and, perhaps in particular, his father. We learned that his father had told him after the killing that he would be back, but of course he never returned. He would also have felt that his mother had abandoned him, or that perhaps she should have been able to prevent father killing her. Harry's cynicism towards adults manifested itself in other ways. He would ask his therapist questions but would not believe the answers if they did not fit with his thinking, even on mundane things like whether, when you mixed blue and yellow paint together, they made green.

Violence

Harry's play during his sessions was full of fighting. For months he was obsessed with a television cartoon programme about some turtles, frequently drawing pictures of them. They were 'goodies', fighting against crime. At times Harry would identify himself as one of the turtles and act out some of their fights. However there was another side to this obsession: he would draw the turtles in the most accurate detail. If he made any mistakes he would become very frustrated, either completely blacking out his mistake or tearing the picture and throwing it away.

His play with the toy animals was frequently violent. He would enjoy throwing the animal, who in his play was killed in a fight, across the room. Often all the animals but one would be killed. The games he played with cars which represented people often contained violent themes such as car crashes.

Wish to be given things

Harry would frequently ask to be given something by his therapist. He would find biscuits in the therapist's drawer and ask if he could have one, or he would ask for his pen or for a present. This behaviour subsided when he went to his adoptive home and was probably a measure of the insecurity he felt in temporary foster-care. The giving of something concrete also allayed his anxiety that the therapist was a 'bad' adult.

Boundaries

For many sessions, particularly early on, Harry would test out how far he could push his therapist before he set limits. He tried to rummage through drawers, or look in the therapist's pockets. At times he took sweets and biscuits and ate them even when told he could not have them. For many months the only way of stopping him from going into drawers and pockets was physically to restrain him. Sometimes he then threatened not to like the therapist or not to come to see him any more.

Harry would try to start his session early by going into the therapist's room before he arrived and then end the session early by leaving or going to the toilet.

Other examples of the way he transgressed boundaries included sitting at the therapist's desk pretending he was the teacher, and the therapist the pupil. He would then instruct the therapist to fetch things for him.

Harry's crossing of boundaries probably represented another example of his feeling of deprivation as well as his cynical view of adults and need to feel in control of his world, a world that had shattered with his mother's death at which he had felt totally helpless. One way of dealing with this is to identify with the aggressor-daddy and see if the therapist could be like an effective policeman and stop him like a policeman-daddy would. It was important that the therapist could accept his wish to reverse roles and his need to split the good and bad parts of people, but nevertheless establish his own limits firmly. Harry was helped to understand the source of this and other behaviour through the therapist 'thinking out loud' about what he thought Harry was feeling as he acted. Often the therapist could understand Harry's feelings because of the way he experienced Harry's behaviour to him within the therapy session. The theme of identification with the aggressor is one we find repeatedly in work with children where one parent kills the other.

Feeling left out/not knowing

Harry often drew secret patterns and then asked his therapist to guess what they were. Sometimes, particularly when he was living in his foster-home, he would sing songs which he knew his therapist would not understand. At other times he would be openly rejecting and dismissive of the therapist. One of the themes underlying these behaviours was the wish to convey to the therapist Harry's own feelings of being rejected and abandoned by his parents, by making the therapist the object of his own rejecting behaviour.

At other times Harry would draw something and then cover it over with typist's correction fluid. Then he would hide behind a chair or under a desk and check whether he could be seen. We felt that Harry was letting his therapist know what it felt like not to know things, to have things kept from him. He must have felt this way frequently after the death of his parents when decisions were being made about him by people whom he felt he could not influence, decisions which sometimes he would not know about until much later.

This theme persisted until the last sessions. He would draw puzzles which were like mazes, expecting his therapist to find the right path to get to the end. If he managed to do it correctly Harry would make the puzzle more complicated and place all sorts of obstacles to prevent his therapist from emerging from the maze. Harry must have had similar feelings about the maze of his life which he had difficulty in finding a way through.

Dismissing the past

Harry would often speak contemptuously of his past. He would frequently look at his old drawings done in previous sessions, and say they were no good, or even tear them up. A favourite activity was making paper aeroplanes. He would always say that he could do it better now and that the ones he had made before were rubbish.

After living with his adoptive parents for just one week, he was keen to change his name to theirs. On some of his possessions he immediately changed his initials. Coincidental with the move to his permanent home, a new doll's house had replaced the old one in the therapy room. He took to the new doll's house with great enthusiasm and was very dismissive and rejecting of the old one, referring to it as 'rubbish'.

Harry's wish to diminish his past experience is a common one with traumatised children. It is difficult for them to hold on to memories of good events and people prior to the trauma, and this rubbishing of the past can be seen as a defensive protective device, to avoid recognising the great loss or losses they have incurred. Unless worked with persistently, such selective amnesia prevents mourning and makes it impossible for the child to progress to making new bonds with a substitute parent. Harry's therapist was able to help him to recognise what he was doing and, by his consistent, non-judgemental behaviour, approaching each session in a reliable and thoughtful way, he was able to help Harry to work through his disturbed feelings and attitudes and to some degree restore his mental health, which had been put in peril by his multiple losses and lengthy wait in the limbo of short-term temporary care. Harry was able to acknowledge that his parents were dead and could be grieved for.

In the last few therapy sessions, a few months after he had moved to his adoptive home, he became more settled and contented. He was able to accept his losses, and he became less challenging and rejecting of his therapist and less cut-off from his feelings. He was able to accept the therapist's interpretations and respect boundaries. He was able to express his sense of loss at the prospect of ending therapy and to acknowledge what he had gained.

Whether Harry has been completely healed will not be known until he has grown up. What we do know is that we were able to prevent symptoms of PTSD developing, by our initial debriefing session, and we were able to influence to some extent his placement. Finally, his therapist gave him the opportunity to experience the fact, session after session, that he could not destroy him, however hard he tried. So perhaps he could be convinced that it was not he who had destroyed his parents, nor his actions that had driven them away. Harry was eventually adopted by a loving family, who arranged for him to have further therapy when he was a teenager and needed to rework some of his confusion and loss.

Greg, aged 3

We told something of Greg's story in Chapter 7. Here we relate some of the work that his therapist did with him during the two years after he had witnessed his father's death at his mother's hands and been left alone with father's dead body and mother's unconscious one for twelve hours.

After his debriefing session with us a few weeks after the killing, Greg started weekly psychotherapy sessions with one of our therapists. She provided him with a set of toys which were kept for him in a box labelled with his name. They included a family set of 'pipe cleaner' dolls, some wild and domestic animals, the hospital set he had had in his debriefing session, plasticine and some drawing paper and crayons. The room where they worked had a doll's house with furniture in it and a Wendy house with a tea set.

Greg's early sessions were conducted with his foster-father in the room as Greg clung to him and would not be parted. Later he began to trust his therapist and would come by himself to the therapy room. For many of the early sessions, he would choose his 'family', which was the foster-family, and would be incredibly aggressive to each doll, throwing them on the floor, and using the surgical knife to kill each one of them. In a subsequent session he found the crocodile and made it have a battle with the male dolls which they always won. Later he re-enacted the same fight with the Greg doll and made himself win too. The same fights with the elephant had the same results. In another session he found a second crocodile and was intrigued that it had a hinged mouth which opened, naming it a 'bad' crocodile, and the first one a 'good' one. After a while the bad one became the good one and he repeated this several times before putting all the animals in an 'animal farm house' and carefully closing it.

The tendency, seen also with Harry, for Greg to split the good and bad, and the breakdown of a reliable understanding of what was good and what was bad, are a result of his witnessing of the killing, leading to a confusion in his mind of what constitutes good and bad.

In the next session, he took a female 'mother' doll and shut her in the house, paying no more attention to it. In the following session she had a fight with the male doll he had called by his foster-father's name, although at other times he called it by his grown-up foster-brother's name, and the mother doll was called variously 'mummy' and 'auntie' (the name he called his foster-mother). His play was extremely aggressive – the dolls fought, and he threw them repeatedly to the ground.

Greg's play was not directed by the therapist at all but she tried to understand what he was portraying. By conveying her understanding in words which he could take in, she could make the unbearable a little more bearable and help him to use his intelligence to make sense of confusing, frightening images.

In one session, about three months after the killing, Greg picked up the mother doll, saying in reply to a question from the therapist, 'my mother'. He placed it on a sofa which he had earlier said was like one in his foster-home. The therapist wondered if Greg would like mother to come to join him in 'uncle's' house and he did not answer. Then he took the toy knife and began cutting the doll's arm. The therapist commented that he seemed to be very angry with his mother and was maybe cutting her arm because it was the arm that killed father. He remained silent, took the mother doll and put her in the same house as the crocodiles.

This house has bars on the window. The therapist wondered whether he thought that his mother was as dangerous as the crocodiles and had to be put in prison. He nodded. There was more aggressive play and then a car came to take the mother doll and the crocodiles away. After that his anger towards various animals showed itself in his throwing them one after another on the floor. The therapist struggled to understand these communications and was able at last to say she thought that Greg was longing for mother and very angry with her at the same time because she had killed daddy and gone away.

At this time Greg was visiting his mother in prison twice a week. When we had first met him, three weeks after the killing, he had not seen her at all and we advised that regular visiting should start at once. Young children like Greg are very dependent on their mothers, and cannot understand sudden disappearances. They tend to think that they have done something wrong and that they are being punished by her leaving. It was important to let him see that she had not gone by choice but because she was having a punishment herself.

For a long time Greg's play, using wild animals, was preoccupied with issues of good and bad. An elephant was both, in the same session. He talked about the mad elephant and made its eyes red. Then he put the Greg doll into a cupboard. When his therapist understood that he was showing her the little boy who had hidden, frightened, in a cupboard, after he had witnessed his good mother change into a red-eyed bad or mad one, and was able to put this into words, Greg seemed immensely relieved and looked at her as if he had been woken up from a dream. This sequence had to be repeated again and again by Greg in subsequent sessions before he could understand and come to terms with what he had witnessed. Although in his sessions he appeared disturbed, his foster-parents were reporting that his nightmares had diminished and that he was clinging to them less. He started at a nursery school and was able to separate for a few hours without pining.

Greg now began showing that the fights between his parents had been initiated by father most of the time and played this out compulsively – both in his sessions and at home. In the sessions at this time he showed his fear of being a small boy and wanting to be strong and in control of everything. But he also worked hard in the play sessions to try to sort things out in his mind.

One way of dealing with feelings of powerlessness which he showed was to identify with the aggressor. Being big is powerful and enables him not to be at the mercy of the killer.

Nine months after the killing, mother stood trial and to everyone's surprise was released on probation. She went to stay with her cousins and Greg and was rehoused eventually. We offered mother weekly meetings with our social worker who tried to help her with her depression and guilt about the killing. When Greg went to live with his mother alone his play became much more disturbed. He indicated his fear and anxiety by re-enacting some of the aggressive games which had been a feature of his early sessions and which had since subsided.

In his play at this time he was showing how worried he was by the use of a mouse which he made with plasticine. This mouse clearly represented him. He put the mouse in a toy teapot, saying aggressively that he had smacked his mummy's face. The therapist tried to make some guesses about what this meant without success. Finally she said, 'I wonder if the mouse had to be locked in so he wouldn't hurt mummy because after that mummy might get angry and hurt him.' Greg stared steadily at her and released the mouse, saying, 'He wants to see his mummy.' He became very anxious and ran to the waiting room to see if his mother were there.

We wondered if he was experiencing unpredictable behaviour from his mother and it did not surprise us to find that mother was not coping and had turned to secret drinking again. Things looked bad and Greg went back to his cousins. But mother's probation officer found her a place with Greg at a hostel run by a voluntary organisation, which offers rehabilitation to offenders and is staffed by social workers and child care workers. Greg's therapy continued. He showed us how he liked the hostel. There were other children and he felt that mother was happier and therefore safer to be with.

During this period, helped by our social worker, mother showed Greg photos of father. She told him what had happened, how it was an accident as a result of their drinking, and she promised him that things would be different now. She had to come to terms with her own anger at her husband's violent and anti-social behaviour and found it difficult when Greg talked positively about him. But with guidance she managed to present him with a good image of his father; they visited his grave together and went to see his family.

When the time came for therapy to end, Greg showed that he could express appropriately his sad feelings about his therapist's departure and could mourn her going in anticipation, showing a new ability to express feelings rather than acting them out aggressively.

When reviewed a year after he and mother moved into accommodation independent of the hostel, Greg indicated that he still had fears that his mother might start drinking again and he feared that she might then be violent. We arranged for him to resume therapy with a different therapist, nearer his home. The most healing thing for Greg, though, was that his mother became more predictable as she gradually, with help, got her life together. We do, however, have reservations about a child returning to the care of a perpetrator parent, however much one empathises with the provocation which drove them to kill. This is discussed in Chapters 7 and 9.

April and Jules, aged 6 and 2

April was 6 and Jules only 2 when their father strangled their mother after she had told him she was leaving to live with her boyfriend. Jules was asleep on the sofa in the same room and April was upstairs. The children went to live with mother's sister and her husband who kept them in touch with father's family but were reluctant to take them to visit father in prison. The children were seen locally at the child psychiatric clinic and the doctor there felt the children would benefit from contact. By this time the children had been made wards of court and, acting on this advice, the judge made an order that the children should visit the prison to see father every month. They went with their father's parents, at first happily and then with increasing reluctance to be separated from their carers, and there were unhappy scenes at the prison gates, which is where the judge had suggested the separation occur so that the carers could receive the children back after the visit to deal with any anxieties or upsets they might have.

Hearing of our interest, the local doctor suggested that we evaluate the situation, and the guardian *ad litem* commissioned us to see the children and recommend what should happen. We saw them a year after mother's death. Jules was suffering from post-traumatic stress disorder, with troubling nightmares, bedwetting, and difficulty in eating. April had begun to attack Jules viciously, and in our interview it became clear that she held him responsible for mother's death. She believed that Jules, who had witnessed the killing, should have called out so that daddy stopped what he was doing.

We felt that the visits were traumatising the children, who had not been helped immediately after the killing and who needed therapy before considering further contact with father. This was so ordered and for a year they did not see him whilst they had regular sessions with their psychiatrist. The therapy sessions and the relief from the contact visits appeared to help and their symptoms improved. They made good progress at school and were much happier.

The time came near for father's release from prison and the court needed to consider their future. Father wanted them to return to his care; the aunt and uncle, who were caring for them, wanted them to stay with them. After seeing father, who had made impressive strides in his personal development in prison, and considering all the pros and cons, we recommended that they should stay where they were until they were grown-up but that there should be a family meeting with the children, father and one of us to assess the advisability of restoring contact. We felt that a meeting in the presence of a therapist, who could help father to apologise to the children for killing their mother, explain the arrangements for their care decided in court and begin to make some reparation to the children for their loss, was an essential preliminary to this.

We met in a pleasant venue provided by social services, the children having been prepared carefully for the session by visiting the setting the previous week with their social worker and by having been informed of the court decision by their guardian *ad litem* who had looked after their interests during the court hearing. We thought that this was important in order to allay any fears they may have had that meeting father was a preliminary step to returning to him. Even so, the tension was high and there had been a return of their symptoms before the meeting. We met first with father to help him to think about the children and their needs. As we often find, he was preoccupied with his own feelings and the exercise of concentrating on the children was helpful. The children came to the centre with their aunt who then returned home. With our help, father talked frankly about how he and mummy had had a fight because she was unhappy living with him and he had lost his temper and hurt her very badly, and although he had not meant to, because he was stronger than her, he had killed her.

He used the analogy of a broken toy: if it isn't too badly broken it can be mended but mummy's body was too badly broken and the doctors could not mend it. It was his fault and he was very sorry that he had caused them to lose their mother. The children listened to this with great concentration and said that they understood. Jules sucked his finger and was looking very tense and uneasy. Father then went on to tell them that because he had done this very bad thing he had been punished by having to stay in prison, but his punishment was nearly over and he had learned many things in prison. He had learned to keep his temper, a lesson he wished he had learned when he was younger; he had learned to help people and was hoping to get a job looking after elderly people, and he had learned that he had no right to think that, just because he was married to mummy, he could control what she did. He realised that one could not own people.

He then went on to ask the children about their activities and it was striking how April was able to respond warmly to him and talk about the race she had just won at her school sports day. Jules remained wary. It was unlikely that he could really understand all that had been said, as he was still only 4. When father asked April to demonstrate her skill at reading she looked at the books we gave her but was reluctant to read and finally refused.

Father talked about the decision that they stay with their aunt and uncle, endorsing it and approving of their care of the children, and saying that he hoped that he could be available to them if ever they needed him. He gave them some small presents he had made and said goodbye.

We saw the children afterwards; April said that she would like to see dad again 'in a little while' but Jules remained silent and wary. With our help, father had done a good job, in very difficult circumstances, but it was clear that for Jules there were memories that made him reluctant to accept this man into his life. He was only 2 when his mother was killed and he had not had the immediate therapy that might have prevented the traumatic memories being stored in his long-term memory.[227] Not seeing his father for a year had been helpful in diminishing his traumatic symptoms but it meant that father was a virtual stranger to him and it was appropriate that he approached him with wariness. Jules will be needing more intensive individual therapy and it would probably be wise to postpone more meetings with father until he has had some further help. This family session was helpful not only in assessing the children's reactions to father, but it had an essential therapeutic component in helping to heal the trauma by enabling the children to hear father's apology, his acknowledgement of his responsibility for the killing and, for April in particular, his firm proscription of violence as a way of solving problems.

Work with a group of siblings, aged 10, 8 and 4

Two sisters, aged 10 and 8 years, and their twin brothers, aged 4, were referred for group therapy after they had seen their father stab their mother to death. At that time there was no knowledge of earlier family violence but on each visit to their therapists (a man and a woman working as a team) the children showed what it had been like to live in their household. Acts of murder and assault were described, acted and drawn in every session and the therapists were threatened, bullied and intimidated by the children who attempted to destroy the room and its equipment. The girls also bullied their brothers and all four children challenged the therapists to protect them and prevent them from causing harm whilst seemingly trying to demonstrate that these were impossible achievements. This piece of work, a series of ten meetings between therapists and children, could not resolve such severe difficulties, but provided the basis for a more realistic appraisal of the damage and disruption which they had suffered and of their specialised future needs. A specialist foster placement with continuing psychotherapeutic help was planned with advice from the therapists.

As described at the start of the chapter, the continued availability and resilience of the therapist are an essential component of treatment.

Long-term therapy: Astra, aged 10 to 14 years

Astra was in therapy for four years after her father killed her mother when she was 10 years old. She was 11 when, unprotected by a screen, she was asked to give evidence at her father's trial and did not succeed. She shook for several days after this ordeal and afterwards for the first time used colour and story design to depict herself as a sad clown, who concealed and revealed her grief. A series of paintings now illustrated her dreams, nightmares and daytime visions. She drew her mother as perfect in heaven, her father in hell. Sexuality was a snake-haired, Medusa-like woman, covered in blood, attacked by a snake-like male figure. Therapy became an intermediate space between inner worlds of nightmare, hallucination and grief and the outer world of the trial and public knowledge.

Two years later, continued therapeutic sessions revealed fear, abandonment and physical abuse which had preceded the killing. Astra continued to idealise her mother and to blame her father, although the pictures of mother were sometimes witch-like. Astra was convinced that she would have the same destiny as her mother.

During the next year, therapy had to continue within the precarious framework of Astra's remaining family, mother's relatives, who, guilty at having failed to save the mother, shamed by public knowledge and angered that father had been found guilty only of manslaughter (whereas, had Astra been capable of giving evidence, he might have been convicted of murder), found it difficult to accept help. Astra's mother was idealised by her family and Astra's fear that she was also her 'villainous' father's child was hidden from relatives.

In the fourth year, Astra was able to use twice-weekly therapy as a resource, having feared it as an attempt to remake her as a perfect and trouble-free person. Her therapist considers that she has moved into adolescence as an individual in her own right, an adolescent with her own future rather than one fated to repeat her mother's destiny. Astra now understands more of her own state of mourning and can compare herself with others who suffer. She has become able to relive good experiences with her therapist and to round off their relationship. She has understood that separation does not necessarily lead to death and that she can and does survive.

Therapy for children is a rare commodity often regarded as an expensive and unproven luxury, yet not to provide this service to traumatised children is misplaced parsimony. These stories illustrate the grief, rage and terror of children who have suffered family violence. Society does not have the resources to offer the help they need. To allow this situation to continue will be a false economy.

Often therapeutic help is offered intermittently ('pulsed intervention', see Pynoos (1992))[176] and relates to increasing maturation of the children, with increased capacity for communication about their difficulties, further traumatic events (a criminal trial, publicity), new ways of showing grief (pathological mourning, problems of behaviour, an inability to trust adults) and changes in the lives of those who offer care (unresolved grief, the birth of new children, financial problems, continuing disputes between family members). There may be additional court hearings which add to the children's anxieties. The following stories illustrate themes such as these.

Chloe and Tom, aged 10 and 7

For many years Chloe and Tom had been exposed to domestic violence. Their father was a chronic alcoholic who had been in and out of work, losing jobs because of his alcoholism. He sometimes disappeared for days or weeks on binges and, when he returned, he would be violent towards their mother. The children often witnessed these scenes, which would escalate to a point where mother would have to escape from the house and seek refuge. Eventually she left father and moved to another part of the country to live with her older brother and his wife.

Father quite quickly traced his wife and would arrive at their new home unexpectedly, often drunk, trying to see his children. One evening he was particularly aggressive and smashed a window, and as a result mother sought an injunction prohibiting him from coming to the home. Eventually father's visits stopped and mother was rehoused by the council. The family had not been in their new home for very long when father broke down the front door and began a violent argument with mother.

Chloe and Tom were getting undressed ready for bed at the time and on hearing the commotion downstairs Chloe, dressed only in her vest, ran out to find out what was happening. What she saw was a prolonged attack on her mother, before she escaped through the battered door to get help from the neighbours. Tom was found at the bottom of the stairs when neighbours arrived and it was thought that he had not witnessed anything. Father had run away and was missing for two weeks, during which time the children returned to their uncle and aunt. He was eventually traced and arrested two weeks later.

Chloe and Tom were seen with their uncle and aunt at the clinic a few months later, having been referred by their general practitioner. Uncle described the children as being demanding and attention-seeking, but in different ways. The couple were also surprised that the children hardly mentioned either of their parents and did not talk about what they had witnessed that night. They had decided to leave well alone and not raise the topic with the children, but their general practitioner had suggested they should seek advice from us. The difficulties that Tom had shown ever since he started at school had become so acute that the school also was seeking advice. He was described as a 'Jekyll and Hyde' character, oscillating between being in a world of his own and disconnected from what was going on around him, and being hyperactive, unfocused and unmanageable in his behaviour. Chloe would easily become upset over the smallest of things, collapsing into floods of tears, but would burst into giggles whenever her mother or father were mentioned, showing inappropriate emotion. She was troubled by nightmares that she could not remember.

Chloe was to be called as a witness in her father's trial, and we worked to prepare her, but fortunately her father pleaded guilty and she was not required to appear. However, the trial was given a lot of publicity locally and the children's names and address were published. This led to Tom being teased and bullied at school. New information also emerged at the trial, which indicated that Tom had seen his father attacking mother, and that he had called out for help.

The children's uncle and aunt were newly married when they took on Chloe and Tom. After a year, they wanted to start their own family but, in view of the increasing demands of caring for Chloe and Tom, they felt that they could no longer offer a home to them. The children were placed in a bridging foster-home while the local authority assessed what kind of placement would best meet their needs, and explored the possibility that other family members might be able to offer Chloe and Tom a permanent home. This was another significant loss for the children, and a lot of work was needed to prepare them for this move.

Yasmin, aged 16

Yasmin was the second eldest of five children, living with their mother. Her father had left the family following violence towards mother and the children. Yasmin had always been close to her mother and, when injured by father, mother would often spend the night in her bed. This made Yasmin a particular focus for father's anger, although at times all the children were terrified of him. The happiest time of Yasmin's life was when father left the family. The oldest child in the family, a boy, had left home because of father's violence, and this left Yasmin as mother's main support. She helped mother to take care of the younger siblings, and also often interpreted for her mother. She had avoided making friends herself, feeling overly protective towards her mother.

One evening father returned to the family home and was let in by one of the younger children, who had woken up and come downstairs. Mother was watching television in the lounge when father burst in and began to physically assault her. It was a long attack and mother died of internal injuries and blows to the head. Yasmin and one of the younger children were the first to come downstairs when they heard the shouts and screams. They saw their mother bleeding but were afraid to approach her because of their father. He told them that mother had fallen downstairs and that Yasmin must help him to clean the body and change her mother's blood-soaked clothes. She was then told to call 999 for help. It was quickly clear to the police that mother had not died of natural causes, but initially Yasmin and her younger sister, Nazia, confirmed that mother had fallen and that no one else was involved. Father stuck to his story, denying that he had been to the home. However, he was arrested and remanded in custody.

Placements had to be found for the children but it was not possible to find a foster home for the four of them. Yasmin went to join her brother at the home of one of her aunts, whilst the three younger children were placed with foster-carers. Regular contact was arranged between the children. Social services referred the children to us for advice as to the children's psychological needs and recommendations for future placement.

The three younger children made good use of the short-term bereavement work which was offered to them as a group. They have continued to remain with these carers, and have begun to thrive. However, by the time we met her, Yasmin was a very troubled and distressed young girl. Her aunt was finding it very difficult to know how to manage her at home. Yasmin was unable to leave her aunt's side, following her all over the house. She insisted on sleeping with her aunt at night, and suffered from terrifying nightmares about her mother's death, and the previous abuse she had suffered and witnessed. On occasions, she had outbursts of rage and had threatened to kill herself when her aunt tried to establish a more normal routine. Yasmin continued to insist that her aunt spend all the time with her, and prevented the aunt from spending time with her own children, causing tension and conflict within the family.

Yasmin was troubled by visions of her mother crying and calling for Yasmin to join her. Yasmin was badly traumatised by her mother's death and the part she played in what she felt was a collusion with father. She felt guilty that she had not been able to stop her father from killing mother and had not been able to protect her mother. Even though she had contact with her younger siblings, she remained very worried about their safety, whilst at the same time trying to hold them back from fully enjoying their new home.

Yasmin suffered from pathological grief, not allowing herself to enjoy anything in life and poring endlessly over photos of her mother and items of her clothing. Yasmin's aunt tried to help by spending time with her at school, but Yasmin often refused to attend school or would fall asleep in class.

As time went on, Yasmin became increasingly distant from her younger siblings, who did not want to see her because she bullied them. The younger children, however, with their growing confidence, were beginning to open up to their foster-parents and social worker about the true events surrounding their mother's death. They were initially worried about what Yasmin's reaction to this might be, and Yasmin needed to be prepared for the disclosures her siblings were making. The process was a slow and painful one, but eventually Yasmin and her siblings were able to talk truthfully and together about what had happened.

The three younger children have continued to do very well in their foster placement and their carers noticed an enormous change in them as they were released from the terrible secret they had kept. Yasmin's older brother has gone on to university, but Yasmin is still struggling with her pathological grief and symptoms of PTSD.

Karl and Robert, aged 5 and 8

Karl and Robert were at school when mother was attacked and killed very suddenly and unexpectedly by their father. This family had been a stable and contented one until father was made redundant. The family were in considerable financial difficulties and father became depressed, with a sudden onset of mood swings. He consulted his GP on one occasion, but did not return for treatment and the extent of his depression was not recognised.

After he had killed mother, he hid her body in an outhouse and then went to collect the children from school. He told them that they were going on a trip and should get ready and, when they asked where their mother was, he told them that she had gone to care for a sick relative in another part of the country. Father took them to a railway station and tried to leave them there but, having second thoughts, he returned to the children, who were becoming increasingly anxious and bewildered about his behaviour.

They returned home late at night and were sent to bed. Both children slept fitfully. They could hear their father talking and shouting to himself downstairs, and they could not make sense of their father's behaviour. Suddenly their father broke into the bedroom and tried to suffocate Karl. Robert's screaming and Karl's waking made father withdraw, and he fled the home. Father tried to kill himself by jumping off a bridge, but only injured himself. When admitted to hospital he told the police that he had killed his wife and that the children were alone. The police immediately went to the home, and arrived to find the children still in their beds, but wide awake in fear.

When we saw the children, they were living with their maternal grandparents, who themselves were very traumatised by their daughter's tragic death. The police had already interviewed the children, who had begun to reveal what they knew. They had been told that their mother was dead, but no one had talked with them about the nature of her death They had also been told that their father was ill in hospital (he had been admitted to a secure psychiatric hospital). We met the children with their social worker to try and piece together for them what had actually happened, and to give advice to the social worker about how to support them.

The children were both extremely shocked as a result of their own experiences with father and, when they saw us for the first time, it took some time to calm them so that we could begin our task. Their state of shock seemed to prevent them from being able to think and concentrate in order to begin to make sense of what had happened. It took several sessions with the children to piece together, bit by bit, what they could remember. Much of the unspeakable and unthinkable horror was conveyed through the children's play, as it was so hard for them to express this in words. The children were extremely worried about their father, who had previously been a loving and caring man. They had been as attached to him as they had to their mother.

The children formed a good relationship with their social worker, who brought them a considerable distance to their sessions and participated in the sessions. Following our initial work, we referred the children on to their local service for further therapeutic help. Father had suffered a mental breakdown and the children needed help in understanding that the mind could become sick, as the body could, and that, when it did, a person might think in distorted ways, just as a broken leg could be distorted. This was why daddy had behaved the way he had and, although doctors could heal him, nothing could repair the damage he had done when he was ill.

Jack, aged 4

A six-year contract for psychotherapy (Scandinavia)

When Jack was 4 years old his mother was strangled to death in their home by his father. When the police arrived Jack sat on his father's lap with eyes red from crying. Father gave very little information about what had happened except that his intention had not been to kill. Following father's suggestion, Jack was placed in the care of his mother's sister. He himself was taken to a hospital for psychiatric care which was to last for several years.

Referral to the child and adolescent mental health services

The clinic was contacted by the social services after a period of several months; they suggested that the boy and his foster-parents might need help. To the clinic came a restless and intensely-talking little boy. Prior to the trauma the staff at Jack's day-care centre had noted a close relationship between mother and son. Jack had some conduct problems which staff felt were a result of mother's difficulties in limit setting. Father had not lived on a regular basis with mother and child. It appeared that father had suffered from increasing paranoia; when they lived together as a family they had on his wish become more and more isolated. Thus Jack had not seen his maternal relatives for a year before his placement. At his day-care centre Jack was defending his father when he was called a murderer by the other children. Jack had fantasies that his mother was not dead but would return; sometimes he had fits of inconsolable crying and intense longing for his mother, especially after having attended her funeral.

When the foster-parents came for counselling their main concern was that there was no legal protection ensuring Jack's right to stay with them if father claimed the little boy when he was discharged from psychiatric hospital. At home he scarcely ever talked about his earlier life, which led them to think that he had put it behind him. Clinical evaluation showed that this was not the case.

On our recommendation a psychotherapeutic contact was initiated offering Jack weekly psychodynamic play therapy. At the same time the foster-parents would come for counselling by another psychotherapist. This treatment was to continue for six years.

Themes in therapy

Aggression

A lot of aggression, chaotic in form, was expressed in Jack's play. Gradually he formed more coherent scenes when he was playing in the sand-pit. Sometimes mad or mean persons would be imprisoned, sometimes groups of soldiers would be fighting each other. Jack put himself on the winning side. He directed the play so that the therapist would always be defeated.

Jack's play was seen as an effort to regain power and be the one in control in contrast to what he had experienced while his father killed his mother. Identification with the aggressor could also be seen in Jack's play with water and sand, where soldiers would all the time be drowned in the water or in the quicksand. This might also be seen as Jack's way of identifying with the victim, dealing with the fact that mother died because she did not get air. For a long period Jack wanted to make 'poisonous water', mixing sand, water and colour. This might be under-stood both as a potent weapon and as something that could protect him from dangers in a more magical way. It was also a way of dealing with his past experiences. Father had become increasingly suspicious and had accused Jack's mother of poisoning his food. As time went by there was more reparation in Jack's play: an interest in building bridges between separate worlds was emerging.

He told his therapist how frightened he had been, when his father had his mother in a stranglehold. He had tried to prevent it by hitting father in the back, but father had shouted to him to stop whining. Jack had experienced this as if his own life was threatened.

Attachment – transference and countertransference reactions

Jack expressed very positive feelings towards his therapist and evoked in her a feeling that he was something of a special gift in her daily work by being so affectionate. This could be understood as a way of dealing with his loss of mother with whom he had had an affectionate and loving relationship.

Jack demonstrated a wish to bring together past and future. He would claim when visiting places with his foster-mother that he had already been there with his mother. In therapy he would ask if the therapist would protect him, as mother had done, if he were caught in the elevator. He loved hiding and being found by both therapist and foster-mother in the waiting-room.

He wanted his therapist to come home and often asked to have things from the therapy room, like broken pencils or toys. It seemed as though he wanted to bring together his foster-mother and his biological mother by means of the transference reactions to his therapist as therapy went on. This need was met by having joint sessions together with foster-mother (occasionally also with foster-father) and her therapist.

Jack also wanted to have material from the therapy room to use for protection. After his first visit to father he had been more frightened at home. He wanted to be in a little hut that he had constructed in the garden, but he did not have the courage to go there by himself. He asked for and got some of the 'poisonous water', which he thought could protect him in the hut.

Another way of identifying with the therapist was when Jack wanted to play and walk about in her much too big shoes, slipping up and down in them. In therapy Jack would act in a way which provoked the therapist to hold him, something he seemed to enjoy. Gradually he demonstrated an increasing wish to defy limits set by the therapist.

After three years of therapy, termination was planned, since Jack's overall behaviour was much improved and he seemed to be at ease. However Jack very clearly stated that he did not at all want to stop coming. He wished to continue the therapy until he had 'got his driver's licence, a car and a home of his own'. It became clear that listening to the strong voice of the child was the right thing to do and continuation of therapy was agreed upon. As a result deeper material emerged in Jack's therapy. Jack expressed even stronger aggression than before and gave more examples of how he could master it in a socially acceptable way. He would also tell his therapist about sadistic behaviour he had shown against a younger boy, unbeknown to adults. This could be talked about in the therapy session as a parallel to the situation when Jack had been completely at the mercy of his father on the night of the killing.

Grieving for mother

Jack in his play often brought in ambulances and rescuing devices. He seemed to ponder about and feel guilt about the fact that he had not been able to rescue his mother, which the therapist firmly declared had not been possible.

In therapy Jack related how he would talk to his photograph of mother at home and how he would beat his head on the wall beside it when there had been a dispute between him and his foster-parents. He would re-enact the trauma of the last night in his home, pretending he was stuck (like mother had been) under a bed nearly suffocating. By managing to get away he was forming another outcome of the trauma in his fantasy. This seemed to be soothing for him, helping him to move on.

After that came a period when the main theme in Jack's play was that of rebirth. Jack posed questions indicating that he should not think so much about what had happened earlier in his life but rather engage more in his daily activities. He asked his therapist: 'I am trying to forget. Do you think I should remember?'

Contact with father

This was a recurrent dilemma during the six years. Father, who felt lonesome and was afraid of losing contact with his son, wanted him to visit him at the hospital. Foster-mother declared that she could never again meet the man who had killed her sister. She thought it could be nothing but harmful for Jack to visit him. She was prepared, however, to let Jack go if his therapist said it was in his best interests. Jack's therapist therefore accompanied him. After a few years foster-father would come too.

Before therapy started, Jack had been taken by the child protection team (two women he had hardly met before) to visit father at the hospital. Since they had noted nothing but a talkative, happy-looking 4-year-old child, in their opinion there was no obstacle to arranging further visits except perhaps the foster-parents' objections. Jack's reactions after his meetings with father were so violent, though, that his therapist recommended a break for more than a year before Jack was exposed to this again.

After this Jack met his father once a year. This activated the trauma and produced more material to work with in therapy sessions. Jack's therapist also met with father twice a year as a way for him to feel involved in his son's life and to help Jack heal his trauma. During all these years there was insecurity for Jack and his foster-parents since father had hopes that Jack could come to live with him after he was released from hospital. These meetings helped him to accept that Jack had become deeply rooted in his foster-family and that he would not be able to care for his son.

Jack's reactions

Compared to what could be seen on the surface, it was shocking for Jack's therapist to learn how upsetting and frightening his meetings with father had been for Jack. Usually there was an immediate follow-up in the therapy room. When the second meeting took place, Jack's teacher, who knew nothing about this meeting, contacted the therapist to ask if something special was happening in therapy. Jack had been very difficult in school, abusive to both pupils and adults, threatening one boy with a wooden paling and getting a little girl in a stranglehold. He had also said that he did not want to live. No sign of these profound fears could be seen during the contact meeting. Jack talked a great deal and tried his best to keep father in a good mood, which he succeeded in doing. Leaving the hospital he immediately fell asleep totally exhausted. In therapy vivid expressions of aggressiveness and fear followed for a very long period. Other visits were followed by regression at home and acting out in school. One example was when he scared a substitute teacher, threatening to kill her.

In preparing for the next visit, Jack said he really had only one question to ask father: namely why he had killed Jack's mother. In his opinion it was impossible for anyone to pose that question since father might get so angry and aggressive that a hundred policemen would not be able to hold him back.

Later on, the therapist could talk to father about Jack's questions and fears, but it was not until the sixth year of therapy that it was possible for father and son to talk about the subject. Father was able to say he was sorry and describe what had happened.

The goal had been to help father and son to keep in contact so that they would not be strangers to each other when Jack was mature enough to decide for himself about contact. Looking back at the age of 11 years, Jack said that he had been pleased with meeting father once a year. At the end of his therapy Jack said he regretted the fact that at his wedding it would be impossible to have both foster-mother and father attending, a sign of how it had been possible in Jack's mind to build bridges between his family of origin and his future life. More and more he identified with his foster-father. This seemed to help the introject (the image within his mind) of his terrifying father to fade away.

Final part of therapy

During the last years of therapy Jack expressed even stronger aggression than before. He loved to wrestle with a huge doll, which he would hit so hard that he would be sweating and exhausted afterwards. He wanted the therapist to watch his struggle, but also act as a referee, giving warnings for fouls. He would proudly declare that he had won silver and gold medals in these fights.

At the end of therapy Jack gave examples of many situations when he had been a loyal friend wanting to help others out.

Comment

Maybe the transference reactions that develop when a young boy comes to therapy after experiencing such a traumatic loss as Jack had take on a special significance. In his case, therefore, it seemed right to extend his therapy to as long as six years. Jack's placement with maternal relatives gave him a natural feeling of affinity. Though he at times was a very trying boy there was never a risk that he would be sent away to another foster-home. There was mutual love.

A disadvantage of placing Jack in his mother's sister's home was that he was not free to communicate about the trauma and it was difficult for him to make connections with his former life. Had he not had the opportunity to express himself in the therapy, the trauma might have suddenly made itself known through Jack repeatedly acting out his fear by scaring those weaker than he. As a safety-valve Jack was also given the opportunity to come back once in a while as a teenager.

It is unusual for under-resourced children's services to offer treatment for so long a period as this and individual psychodynamic play therapy is a rare and valuable resource. Without this help, Jack's life may have been very different.

Chapter 9

For the rest of their childhood

Home no more home to me, whither must I wander?
Hunger my driver, I go where I must.
    (Robert Louis Stevenson, 'Home no more home to me')

SUMMARY

Here we correlate what is known of family violence and its effects on children with knowledge on PTSD, bereavement and the problems of finding secure long-term homes for dislocated children.

What was happening before the crime?

In planning for children we need to take into account the growing body of research on the effects on children of family violence. We have worked with children from violent homes, those for whom their bereavement and loss have come out of the blue, and those where the extent of the violence is not known and may emerge only over time. Information about the family, emerging during the early days, may help with long-term planning and some of the research developing from the issues discussed in Chapter 2, on children and violence, is particularly relevant. Thus, children from violent homes show a wide and diverse range of symptoms and troubled behaviours which will affect their ability to adapt to new circumstances. One study[251] showed that boys from violent families could be distinguished from boys of the same age but from non-violent homes: the former were at a disadvantage with regard to competence at school and home, aggression, delinquency, depression, obsessive behaviour, over-activity and poor communication. Children who have seen violence between their parents are less likely to assert themselves (perhaps in self-protection) but do become either very aggressive or unduly passive when thwarted.[189] These children seem less able to understand the feelings of others.

Post-traumatic stress disorder is likely to be more severe and longer-lasting if the trauma is caused by fellow humans, and especially if it is seen as intentional rather than accidental. It is more likely to occur in witnesses, such as our children, who were not themselves attacked and whose ability to feel and remember remains unhindered by physical pain and injury. Moreover, the threat of violence remains in the mind of the child and is expected long after the threat has been removed.

Boys of violent fathers are in particular difficulties; they love their mother yet want to be like their father. Indeed, boys are expected to develop their gender identity by becoming different from their mothers, whereas girls are meant to be like their mothers.[86] When a boy becomes a son of a killer, this exacerbates social and biological factors which lead to expectations that boys will play more roughly and are more prone to act aggressively.

When finding long-term homes for children it must be remembered that those who are trying to come to terms with post-traumatic stress disorder may act in ways reminiscent of the terrible event, as did Ahmed (Chapter 5) who was suspended from school for attacking another boy with a knife soon after his father had been arrested for stabbing his mother. Boys who act out may indeed be labelled as like their father and this is an additional burden for them to bear. Girls, by contrast, are more likely to become depressed, show problems in sexual relationships and place themselves in situations where they are victimised. However, this is only true of about one-third of children who survive violence in childhood and we need studies of factors which help the other two-thirds to survive without repeating the pattern of their parents.[137]

Many children may have been showing a range of troubled behaviours before becoming involved in the crisis of death. The more serious the situation the children have suffered, the higher the rate of problems, which interact with one another to exacerbate difficulties.[111, 195] According to one study, the most important influence on the child was the amount of overt battling seen and, as parental conflict increased, so did the aggression of the parents towards the child and the lack of care offered.[114]

So, in planning children's futures, as much as possible should be discovered about them: their relationships, health, educational records, social circumstances and family relationships (see Appendix 1). There are circumstances which may help reduce their distress and protect them from future problems of behaviour. A good, trusting, affectionate relationship with the lost mother means that the bereavement will be all the greater but the possibility of healing will be better than for a child who had no such relationship. A trusting relationship with an adult outside the immediate family (teacher, aunt, grandparent, godparent), success at school and other achievements and good relationships between siblings are all factors which may help a child adjust to the future.

A new home and family

Placing children together or separately: 'The children are all the family left to each other'

This was a statement made by their social worker about three children who were living in a children's home. An assessment was being made as to whether they could safely return to the care of their parents, when their father strangled their mother. The view of the two older children, aged 15 and 14, was that their mother had started many fights with him, that the battling was as much her fault as his and that he had never meant to kill her. They hoped that he would get a short sentence and in the meanwhile wanted to stay where they were, continue at local schools, study for their exams and visit him regularly. They also wanted frequent contact with their mother's mother, being old enough to realise that she too was grieving.

The youngest member of the family, a boy of 4, had quite different needs – for reliable, secure and immediate parenting. Work with father in prison, the elderly grandmother, who wanted to keep contact with her grandchildren but was not well enough to care for them, and the two older children helped everyone to make a plan that the 4-year-old should be placed in a foster-home. It was agreed that he should stay there long term and that it might be in his best interests to be adopted, but that it would be important that he keep in touch with his older brother and sister, grandmother and father.

This was an unusually flexible solution. Children who have passed through a violent crisis may be closely attached and drawn yet closer together by their loss; it may be unthinkable to them and to others that they should be separated. However, it should not be assumed without careful thought for each individual that they should stay together under any circumstances. Whatever the age of the bereaved young person, the need for parental care and thought about individual needs should take precedence over the links between siblings. This may seem a hard principle. But we have been alerted to the problems of keeping children together in groups, without consideration of other factors, by a number of tragedies, losses and uncertainties which have arisen. There are practical difficulties too about placing a large sibship together with foster-carers or even with relatives, and if a permanent placement is sought for a large family of children they may have to wait an unacceptably long time.

Three children were placed together with family friends after their father had been remanded in custody for killing their mother. They were Muslim in religion, their extended family did not live in England and time was needed to plan their future. The little boy and girl, aged 6 and 4 years old, were cared for by their 17-year-old elder sister to whom they were attached; the little one soon began to call her 'Mummy'. The family with whom they boarded were very relieved by this turn of events and praised and supported Sulima in her role as 'little mother'. She meanwhile passed her eighteenth birthday, enrolled at a college of further education, as had been the wish of her dead mother, and fell in love with a non-Muslim fellow student. She was trebly burdened – by her wish for further education, by her longing for a romance which would allow her to feel loved and valued, and by the pressures upon her to care for her little brother and sister as a mother – and lacked advice or help. Eventually, when mother's relatives in Pakistan obtained permission to take over the care of the two younger children, Sulima had a difficult choice between joining her Muslim family, and accepting a more traditional female role, or staying in England, with the disapproval of all her relatives. Only her father in prison remained in this country and she would pay for independence with extreme loneliness. She elected to return to her birth country and we have heard no more of her.

Children in similar situations would do better if all were parented rather than one of the group being asked to act on behalf of the others, far beyond age and competence and in a situation bound to create great personal conflict and uncertainty.

Children may be bound together only by the disaster. Where there has been more than one marriage, some children may be deprived of a mother, others of a step-mother and, if the family has been riven by conflict before the killing, attachments between half-siblings may not be strong. However, finding out about these matters may take second place to the claims of blood ties, as when, as described in Chapter 2, one child went back to his birth mother and his step-sister to an adoptive home. It is difficult afterwards to evaluate the effects of this second loss upon siblings.

On other occasions, priority has been given to keeping children together in children's homes or other temporary arrangements, irrespective of their attachment needs. Sulima's dilemma is one outcome of such a decision; other more difficult problems may arise where a group of younger children turn towards each other for parenting.

One set of four brothers and sisters, aged between 5 and 10, became like a closed system, allowing their foster-mother and foster-father to provide only practical help and care. The foster-parents became more and more baffled. To them it seemed that the children cared only for each other and were cold and rejecting towards them and to the outside world in general. The foster-mother became very alarmed at her own anger which she felt towards these children; she felt that her own two were suffering from the tension in the home. Such children may remind their caregivers of the *Midwich Cuckoos* in the novel by John Wyndham, alien children implanted in an English village community. The children nurtured and cared for each other, and used the community as a cuckoo does when placed as an egg in another bird's nest.

Decisions made in emergencies may affect the children's lives for years to come. The children are in crisis, in most cases their families have not been known to caring agencies, and at this stage the difficult task of assessing whether they have been suffering from the effects of previous long-term violence must be attempted. The priority is to deal with immediate problems rather than to work out the children's attachment to each other, their problems of behaviour and learning or even whether they are blood-related. It may take some time to discover their nearest relations.

> One girl of 15, asked who could help in the emergency, thought first of her mother's best friend who lived two streets away. The girl joined this family 'for a couple of days' and was still living there a year later. Her half-brother, son of mother's first husband, went to his father's family and the two children next met at the funeral planned by mother's kin.
>
> The dead mother's friend coped until her protégée was 18 years old, successfully seeing her through A levels and university entrance, both daughter and foster-family being upheld by the determination that this is what the dead woman would have wanted for her child. The foster-mother, however, confided to one of our team that her own daughter had suffered badly during this period from being angry, jealous, hostile and falling back in her school studies. The foster-mother was full of regret at her own inability, as she saw it, to care for her dead friend's daughter and to look after her own family. Ten years later there is still anger between the foster-parents, with the foster-father blaming the foster-mother that their own child has been disadvantaged in life through the unsolicited and sudden stress which befell the family.

The problems of follow-up are discussed in Chapter 12. We do however have some indications about the practical results of decisions made. Half of the children we are concerned with have been placed with relatives and half with non-relatives and problems have been equally likely to crop up over time in both groups. The assumption that relatives, because they are familiar with the children, are the best people to offer support, is not necessarily borne out in practice. A balancing act is needed between the advantages and disadvantages of living with relatives or non-relatives, in the light of the previous life experience of the children (for example, how well they knew the available relatives and how they got on with them before) and the ability of relatives to cope with their own and the children's grief and anger.

Alliances and loyalties may become exaggerated. Those who stay with mother's kin are almost inevitably less likely to see their father, since mother's relatives will not want this and may well be horrified at the thought of visiting a prison or psychiatric hospital. Indeed, four out of five of children placed with mother's relatives said that they did not want access and most of them had not seen their father since the killing. Conversely, every single one of the children staying with father's relatives was said to want to see him; the obvious inference is that they were supported and advised to do this by the relatives. Children may find it hard to say nice things or have good memories about their father in the maternal relatives' home, or about their mother in the paternal relatives' home.

As we have indicated earlier, if father receives a short sentence, his relatives may have in mind to care for the children only until his release, when he will resume his parental task. Children may not be encouraged to form reliable, secure attachments in their 'temporary' home. One set of paternal relatives cared for two children aged 4 and 2 years at the time of the killing and, when father was released from prison four years later (having pleaded guilty to manslaughter), invited him to share their home. Within a few weeks father had quarrelled with his relatives and taken the children with him to live in a rented flat. The children lost all contact with their uncle and aunt. We heard their story three years later when both were showing severe problems of behaviour in school.

Obvious and foreseeable problems about what to tell the children, funeral arrangements, visits to prison, finances, accommodation, effects on children already in the household and so on should be discussed and considered with the children's relatives or other caregivers at the time when they are making far-reaching decisions. If anything, immediately after the tragedy, children placed with relatives, whether maternal or paternal, showed overall fewer symptoms and disturbances than those placed with non-relatives. However, we have found that where children are placed with relatives, the families are resistant to change and more unwilling to recognise the children's distress. Many of the children living with non-relatives were there because earlier family placements had broken down. This group may have been doubly or trebly stressed over time. However, those placed from the outset with non-related carers were more likely to keep contact with both sides of the family. On the other hand, those placed with relatives of the victim were likely to have fewer changes of carer.

The father's sentence and his continuing parental involvement

Often, conflict between the families of the victim and the perpetrator continues over years[122] (see Chapter 6) and is not necessarily at its most severe just in the immediate aftermath of the killing. At that point usually the father is in custody in a remand prison or psychiatric hospital. In the UK, if he is found guilty of murder this leads to a mandatory sentence of life imprisonment and he is likely then to serve a minimum period in prison, determined by the court, and after discharge from prison will remain on licence, literally for life, to the Home Office. However, what regularly happens is that, after negotiation with his solicitor, the perpetrator is allowed to plead guilty to the lesser charge of manslaughter. In justifying this he has to demonstrate to a court that he was in some way provoked or that he was suffering from diminished responsibility. Under these circumstances it is usual for the killer father to denigrate and vilify his dead partner, stating that she had been unfaithful or incompetent or aggressive or that she in some other way provoked her own death and, as we have described elsewhere in this book, this is an additional burden on the mother's family and on her children. Father may adduce psychiatric evidence that he is depressed as a result of this suffering.

The American term 'plea bargaining' is not in use within the UK, but an equivalent practice happens regularly, in that acceptance of a manslaughter plea is economical to the court, since there is no longer the cost of a full trial, and indeed for the penal system, since instead of a life sentence the killer is sentenced at the discretion of the judge. In our experience, as our study has continued, we have found that the penalties range from referral to a psychiatric hospital within the terms of United Kingdom mental health legislation, to a non-custodial sentence (which is rare), to, more usually, a sentence of between three to seven years of which part will be remitted if behaviour while in prison is acceptable. This sentence takes account of time spent in prison prior to the criminal trial.

As a result, if a man kills his partner when a child is 3 years old, spends one year on remand awaiting trial (as is not uncommon) and then receives a three-year sentence, he may be free on parole when his child is still only 5 or 6 years old. If this happens there is no assessment and no formal recording of previous criminal violence and, unless the father was known to the Department of Social Services because of child abuse or neglect or previous assaults on the wife and children, there may be no knowledge other than in the minds of child victims as to whether or not there was previous domestic violence.

> Matt and Annie, aged 8 and 6 years and living in a foster-family, began to show, in the form of play and drawings, and through nightmares, that they had been through violence to both themselves and their mother for at least two years before their mother died of head-injuries caused by their father. Father, on remand in prison, said that none of this was true and that the foster-family and the children's therapist had put these ideas into the children's heads. His behaviour in prison was impeccable and he insisted that the attack on his wife had been a single, totally uncharacteristic event 'caused' by her unfaithfulness.

Wife killers in prison and in psychiatric hospital regularly, in our experience, show model behaviour and, if they do go to hospital because of depression or other psychiatric illness, are soon judged to have recovered sufficiently for discharge into the community. Recommendations for discharge or parole are related to the current mental state of the prisoner and his behaviour rather than to an assessment of any risk that a crime of violence in the family may be repeated.

Carrie, aged 14 – who had seen her mother repeatedly attacked by her step-father when he was drunk, had tried to protect her younger half-brother and sister from their father's violence and eventually had come home from school to see her mother's battered body upon the floor – learned that her step-father had been given parole at the earliest possible date, having presented no problems at all throughout his prison sentence. 'That's right', she said grimly. 'He only hits women and children.'

Prisoners who lack income have access to legal aid and, since under current UK law they retain their parental responsibility in relation to the children unless, rarely, the latter have been adopted, fathers continue to influence their children's lives by requiring information, requesting contact visits, making representations as to where the children may live and, commonly, insisting that children be returned to their care once release has been achieved. All of this is still happening to Matt and Annie. Their father has been released from prison and has moved in with his mother. Both he and the children's paternal grandmother insist that Matt and Annie will be better off living with them and moving away from the dead mother's sister who, according to the father, constantly 'reminds' the children of the past when it would be better that they should forget. The children's father says, 'We have all suffered enough.'

All this is very hard on the family of the victim who have heard their dead daughter, sister or mother denigrated and belittled in court, and are expected to negotiate with the killer and his family over money, contact and residence, often using their own savings if they are not eligible for legal aid. Perpetrators are discharged from hospital or prison without the victim's family being informed: Matt and Annie's aunt first learnt that her dead sister's husband was released from prison when he telephoned her from a local call-box saying, 'It is time the children and I all lived together again.' Herman comments that it is a regular event that 'perpetrators of violence are of the opinion that others, including victims, must put the traumatic events behind them'.[104]

As our study has progressed, we have learned again and again that mourning for the victim by her family, hindered by all the troubles here described, often begins anew and more intensely upon the release of the killer from prison. This explosion of grief and anger takes children and their caregivers by surprise. After what for many has been the catharsis of the release of the body for burial, a trial, a sentence and the passage of three or four years, families may have begun to think that the worst of their agony has abated. The shock is enormous when a prisoner is released into the community: the victim is still dead, the killer is free. To make things more complicated for caregivers, children as they have grown older, and little ones who had not yet learned or were barely able to speak at the time of their mother's death, are now able to ask questions and express their emotions. They may need repeated therapeutic help, suitable for their age, of the kind which Pynoos[176] describes as 'pulsed intervention'. This need is increased by the intense impingement upon their lives of a parent, newly released into the community, often absorbed in asserting his parental rights and denying or minimising the effects upon his children of his own actions, or supposing that, if he apologises, he is able to expect unconditional forgiveness.

It is not right that children should remain on ice, unable to establish and rely on secure, deeply-supported attachments, throughout their childhood both when the man who committed the crime is in prison and after his release, nor that they suffer for years from continuing inter-familial battles. In our experience, many fathers, like that of Matt and Annie, deny the suffering and loss that their children have gone through or claim that, as the surviving parent, they are best placed to repair the damage. Children may need protection from being expected to blame a parent for her own death and to offer support and unconditional forgiveness to the perpetrator.

Some fathers who have agreed, while on remand and awaiting imprisonment, to care orders being made on their children and fostering arrangements being established, on release from prison, immediately apply via a court for variations of the orders made or for the return of their children. One family of bereaved maternal grandparents cared for children aged 8 and 6 years. They had seen their father stab their mother to death four years earlier and they refused to visit him in prison during his sentence for manslaughter. As the time drew near for his release, he applied for the children's return to his care and, failing this, for an order that they visit him regularly in the home of his new wife and step-family. He had married while in prison and continued to insist that he was innocent of the crime of which he had been convicted. The grandparents, and indeed the children, were outraged that they were required to go back to court in order to explain yet again their refusal to meet their father. The younger child had a return of severe and frequent nightmares, the older was able to say how angry she was that her father could request an order (she hated the word order) that she should visit him. A guardian *ad litem* represented the children's views to the hearing and these were respected.

It continues to be a matter for debate that in some cases, with suitable support and supervision, the father *may* be able to parent the child again. It is more likely to happen if the father takes responsibility for his crime and is genuinely sorry for what he did, does not blame or denigrate the children's mother, and especially if he can act as a repository of good memories of the mother for the children, can take advice appropriately from professionals and where conflict with the mother's family has been resolved or is limited. Unfortunately we have encountered few cases where these factors have obtained. In our experience, problems have arisen when the teenager has become defiant and provocative, not willing to recognise the father's moral authority, or when the father has become over-possessive and even jealous in the face of the teenager's growing sexuality and independence.

As our study has continued, it has become more and more clear that therapeutic work and a carefully thought-out plan for the whole of a child's minority are essential to the child's health and stability, and that this plan should be reviewed according to the child's age, needs and understanding.

There is a body of legal research and practical knowledge on which those who have to help in finding the best homes for these vulnerable children may draw (see Appendices 1 and 2) and which will continue to grow as children are followed into adult life.

The children of prisoners: wider issues

Our group of children has very specific problems. In one sense, however, they represent the tip of an iceberg of unknown size. Each year, in England and Wales alone, at least 100,000 children are estimated to experience the imprisonment of their fathers.[203] More than 3,000 a year are likely to suffer the imprisonment of their mothers but, since many women prisoners conceal the fact that they have children lest they be taken into care, this number may be an underestimate.[257] We consider this wider context.

Children of prisoners are at risk in numerous ways. They tend to live in impoverished one-adult households, with insecure housing conditions and changes of school. Their mothers or substitute carers have to struggle with ostracism and stigma as well as with poverty, the likelihood of increasing debt and loneliness. They may not be able to deal with the maze of social security services. They may attempt to conceal the whereabouts of the father from family and neighbours; stories of him working away or being in hospital are not uncommon. So these children are at risk of learning disturbing and unpalatable truths from neighbours, school or family – as has happened to some of the children in our study.

In general, there is great pressure on families to provide a base for the man when discharged from prison. The probation service, with its brief to resettle an offender back into society, is often seen, if only because resources are limited, as more available to the offender than to the supporting family.

Facilities within prisons for children when visiting are usually dreary and unsuitable. Some prisons now try to make family visits more relaxed and pleasant, but often architectural limitations, overcrowding and low staffing make it impossible in older establishments. Relatives of prisoners may arrive at a distant prison, by awkward cross-country routes, plus children and their equipment, to find that the prisoner has been moved without notification. Even if they get to the right place at the right time, they may have to wait outdoors, exposed to the weather, or in waiting areas decorated only with lists of regulations, without play materials or other equipment for children and redolent with the odour of the cigarettes rapidly and repeatedly inhaled by anxious people. Visits are limited in length, lack privacy for intimate discussion and again provide little in the way of occupation or distraction for very young children. Under such conditions, relatives repeatedly recount how they feel that they have to put on a brave front, that they cannot discuss their problems with the father who cannot deal with them and who will simply be left 'wound up' and distressed at the end of a short visit. Men in prison can earn very little indeed and they often ask for small comforts which are afforded with difficulty by relatives already stretched by having to care for the children.[145]

For the children of killers, their father's imprisonment may relieve them of a violent or abusive man, or one who has damaged the family finances. They may not want to visit a father in prison, especially if they witnessed the killing, and this may lead to applications through the court for contact orders, which may increase stress all round.

Children's law must attempt to balance continuing parental responsibility, even in the course of separation or divorce, against the rights and needs of children, but there is an inherent imbalance of power between the massive criminal justice system and the fragile civil rights of children.

There is surprisingly little research on psychiatric disorders or school difficulties among the children of prisoners.[19] The most relevant information comes from the study of children who have suffered the break-up of their families through divorce. Indeed, many children suffer from repeated spells of imprisonment of a parent and more than one divorce as well. Psychiatric disorder and delinquency are common sequels to such adversities.

Where mother is the criminal

When fathers go to prison most children remain with their mother. However, when the mother goes to prison children face far more disruption. Fathers rarely care for them and they are likely to have to change where they live, who looks after them and where they go to school.[50, 249]

About seventy babies each year in England and Wales are born to women serving prison sentences and usually the births take place in hospital with an accompanying prison officer. At least one-third of the 3,000 women in one study had children under 4 years of age,[257] and 61 per cent of all imprisoned women were either pregnant or had children under 18 years in a 1994 survey.[47]

Very few of these children will remain with their mother during the sentence. There are no prisons in Wales, Scotland or Northern Ireland which allow a mother to keep her child. In England there are four which do – Holloway in London, Styal in Cheshire, New Hall in Yorkshire, which are closed prisons, and Askham Grange open prison in Yorkshire. These prisons accept sixty-four babies in all and, in two of them, babies can stay only until 9 months of age. Askham Grange will accommodate children until they are 18 months old, as does Styal. So, only women serving a comparatively short sentence can expect to keep their child and, if a mother has a baby of 6 months and a child of 3 years old, the older child will have to be cared for by friends, relatives or by the state.[256]

The difficulties for children visiting their mothers in prison are similar to those described for visiting fathers, although Holloway prison for women has instituted a programme on two Sundays a month to allow children to stay all day with their mothers in the gym and education block. However, this is not available for prisoners on remand and the gap between visits is still too long for small children, although the service may be of great value to older brothers and sisters.

There is a serious dilemma as to whether children should be with their mothers in prison. It would be better to deal with an offender with dependent children wherever possible by not imprisoning her.[256] Where a mother has committed a crime of violence, and in particular where she has killed a partner, her fitness to take care of the child and to be a parent with moral authority has to be evaluated. This dilemma has been discussed further in Chapter 7.

In general, courts which contemplate a sentence of imprisonment where an offender of either sex has dependent children are in a moral quandary. Sometimes the sentence relieves the family of a burden, but more often they will lose material and emotional support and their hardship may be greater than that of the prisoner. Such families are entitled to welfare assistance and the social and probation services may try to tackle their emotional problems. But, however much the aim of a penal code may be to punish only the guilty, the reality is often that the innocent are indirectly punished as well.

Some jurisdictions do attempt a range of provisions. There may be advice that sentencing tariffs should be more personal and more sensitive to the individual, tailoring the punishment not just to the crime but to the criminal and his or her home circumstances. Imprisonment within the home setting, day prisons and a range of penalties which do not include imprisonment may allow justice to be done yet enable the offender to renew responsibility for the well-being of dependent children. This must be balanced against the risk for the child if he or she will be cared for by a parent who has been violent, especially if the child has witnessed it.

It might be thought that some at least of these problems are of little relevance to our families, where a major crime has been committed. But where a plea of manslaughter has been accepted, and mitigating circumstances are taken into account, a man or woman who has been on remand for a year awaiting trial may be released within two or three years of receiving sentence. Others, after sentence, are recommended for psychiatric treatment and are released either to psychiatric hospitals or directly into the community. Still others, particularly women, may be released on probation immediately after the trial. So our children are affected by all the issues mentioned above, in addition to the troubles related to their personal experience of violent crime.

Each civilised country should have a criminal justice system which minimises the damage done to children in the wake of criminal offences committed by their parents. A system of civil law should create a framework in which the needs of vulnerable children will be identified and met (see Appendix 2).

Chapter 10

Looking backward and looking forward

The consequences for adult life

Images burning their way
out of my unconscious
Into my mind
Are these my memories
Or those of others?
Why can't I remember.

They flash in front of me
And follow behind
They accompany me
Wherever I go
Yet there is a wall
Between them and me
And I can't remember.
(R. Gabriele S. Silten, 'High tower crumbling')

SUMMARY

Our study has, as yet, brought only a small number of contacts with adults who have survived this particular tragedy. We have been able to draw upon many stories of children in order to illustrate common themes and can draw on only a few adult experiences. Yet we estimate that fifty families a year, in the UK alone, launch children on their new life as survivors after a killing. This chapter delineates what is known.

In Henry James's novel *The Princess Casamassima* (1885)[112] an illegitimate child becomes parentless when his mother kills his father and is imprisoned for life. He is brought up by Miss Pynsent, a milliner who had been his mother's friend. The writer dwells on the dilemma in Miss Pynsent's mind about the conflict between her foster-child's 'lower class origins' and a dream that he would have riches and privileges were his father's family to recognise him. She tells the boy nothing of his background so that he grows up feeling mysteriously out of place in his surroundings yet asking no questions.

The novel opens when the child is perhaps 8 or 10 years old and Miss Pynsent has heard that his mother is dying in prison and asking to see him:

> It had been a terrible question with her, when once she had made up her mind, what she should tell him about the nature of their errand. She determined to tell him as little as possible, to say only that she was going to see a poor woman who was in prison because of a crime she had committed years before and who had sent for her and caused her to be told at the same time that if there was any child she could see, as children (if they were good) were bright and cheering – it would make her very happy that such a little visitor should come as well.
>
> (p. 30)

The child, called Hyacinth, is indeed taken to see his mother and there is a graphic description of his terror and bewilderment as he enters the prison. Still no explanation is given him and still he does not ask.

Much later, Hyacinth, now a young man, suddenly questions Miss Pynsent.

> 'Who was that woman you took me to see ever so long ago?' The expression of her white face, as she looked up at him, her fear of such an attack all dormant, after so many years, her strange, scared, sick glance was a thing he could never forget, any more than the tone, with her breath failing, in which she repeated, 'that woman?'
>
> 'That woman, in prison, years ago – how old was I? – who was crying and who kissed me so – as I never have been kissed, as I never shall again. Who was she? Who was she?'
>
> The strangeness of the matter to himself was that the germ of his curiosity should have developed so slowly; that the haunting wonder which now, as he looked back, appeared to fill his whole childhood, should only after so long have crept up to the air.
>
> (pp. 126–7)

Hyacinth grows up an articulate, intelligent, self-reliant and apparently resilient young man and Henry James uses him to delineate and contrast aspects of the class system in nineteenth-century London. But Hyacinth dies young, suddenly and inexplicably, to those around him, shooting himself. There are indeed immediate griefs and rejections in the life of the young man, but James leaves his reader to explore the connections between the bereaved, dislocated child and the man brought up on secrets and half-truths.

All societies must contain many young men and women whose lives were changed when one parent killed the other. Some may have been placed for adoption and do not know of their history. Others, like Hyacinth, may have asked, suddenly, in adult life as buried memories 'crept up to the air'. Some will have been involved in discussions or indeed battles as to whether a father or mother, newly discharged from prison, could resume the role of a parent. We have seen situations where this worked very badly indeed, leading to further grief and trauma for all concerned (though by the nature of our work these are the situations of which we are more likely to be made aware).

Other children have grown up into adulthood knowing that a parent was hanged, or is serving a life sentence, perhaps being discharged from prison when the young man or woman is becoming independent; a few will have parents in secure psychiatric hospitals. They must decide whether to keep such knowledge private or when or how to share it with friends and their own prospective future partners. Often they may live with fears that they may become violent or psychiatrically ill. There are small genetic risks of inheriting a limited number of psychiatric disorders.[54, 266] But the greatest fear is well expressed by King Lear's cry, 'O let me not be mad, not mad, sweet heaven / Keep me in temper: I would not be mad.'

The wonder is that so many survivors of disaster recover and learn from their experiences – a theme to which we will return.

Psychiatric disorder in adult life: risk and resilience

Although inevitably the children in our study show mixed reactions to disaster, we can outline four main categories of response.

Children who grow up despairing: depression, anxiety and psychosomatic illness

We think these may be many but they are also less easy to identify since their problems are private. There are known links between depression in adult life and the death of a parent in childhood, whatever the cause of that death. Depressive disorders are also linked with stressful events at any time of life. Loss of mother by death or separation before the age of 11 years leaves a child vulnerable to depressive illness if further disturbing life events occur,[43] and there is a recognised link between adult depression and disturbed parent/child relationships.[266] It is particularly likely that the traumatic death of a parent would be followed by a whole series of further disadvantages. We are not yet in a position to know to what extent good alternative parenting can protect traumatised and bereaved children and whether appropriate early psychiatric intervention and treatment may help them to form attachments and reduce later psychological problems.

Children who grow up angry: conduct disorder and crime

Some, though by no means all, children who experience violence at first hand grow up to be violent. There is some evidence for this: for example, 2,000 cases of child abuse and neglect, obtained from official records, were compared with a group of children who had not suffered in this way.[245, 246] These children were followed into adult life, over twenty years. Experiences of being victims in childhood were linked in a significant way to adult arrest records, and children who had been abused or neglected had higher rates of adult violent crime, the relationship being stronger for males. The author comments that this is not the only outcome of childhood abuse since many children show 'non-criminal' problems such as severe anxiety, depression and withdrawal, but the study does indicate that these children can end up hurting others. Some of the therapists working with children in our study have encountered terrifying levels of rage and are concerned that vengeance may be wreaked in future, either directly upon the parent who killed, or on unknown others.

Children who trust no one: disorders of personality, self-injury and aggression

It is likely that children whose lives were already violent and unpredictable, who have experienced recurrent or multiple traumas and whose lives are then dislocated in a final and dramatic way, will be the most vulnerable in our group. Such children are more likely to behave badly and be mistrusting or hostile wherever they are placed and those arrangements are likely in turn to break down. It is probable that a very serious pattern of anti-social behaviour combined with inability to relate to adults will ensue.

A 15-year-old, brought up in a violent and aggressive family, with many separations between the parents, whose mother heavily depended upon him to protect her from his father, lived for a while after his mother's death in a foster-home offered by friends of the family. Within three months he had attacked his pregnant foster-mother. He was moved at short notice to a children's home and then to relatives of his father. There, he got caught up in a frightening family feud involving brothers of his imprisoned father. He was asked to take sides in this feud yet was gripped also by a desire to avenge his mother's death. This duty, he felt, would fall upon him as he entered manhood, at the time when his father would be discharged from prison. This young man has lost all contact with any child protection or health services and indeed his whereabouts are unknown. To find out what happens to him would involve intrusive, even illegal, enquiries into his health, social security, employment and criminal record, so we can only guess at what his future will be, whether he will beat his wife if he marries and how he will fulfil the duties of a parent.

In research on adolescents who murder,[11] twenty children, between 11 and 18 years of age, were studied who came from families with high levels of violence and mental illness. In particular, fathers were violent and had behaved inconsistently towards the teenager throughout early childhood. A third of the children in this group had suffered sexual abuse. The young people, when compared with those in other studies, had also been violent many times before the killing of which they were now accused. In particular they were violent and disruptive in school and many had seen a psychiatrist, although this tended to have been only once, without any follow-up. As in other studies, many of these young people were influenced by alcohol when they killed. They tended to know their victims. So this small study showed that violence can be learned and repeated in the next generation.

Children who trust nothing: are there links with psychotic illness?

Chapter 1 outlined the life-view of traumatised children.[222] For some, this perception of events will become long term. They are different from those who despair, who may show clinical depression or chronic anxiety in adult life, and different from those who are angry or mistrusting of adults. Their difficulties are more profound and more all-embracing than any yet described. The debate about what psychotic illness is and how it arises is wide-ranging, and there is no doubt that there are genetic and other components. Yet it is possible that unrecognised or unacknowledged long-term trauma may be at the root of at least some psychotic illnesses. Denial of stress, cutting off from others, 'psychic numbing', losing touch with feelings and with what one experiences, together with vivid re-experiencing of trauma in the form of flashbacks, may create a constellation of symptoms which lead either the sufferer, or those attempting to assess the suffering, to think in terms of psychotic illness.[222] Sufferers may be, again in the words of Lear, 'more sinned against than sinning' (III, ii), 'yet the tempest in my life / Doth from my senses take all feeling . . . / Save what beats there' (III, iii).

Many adults in mental hospitals, including those with unstable personality, are victims of repeated childhood trauma and we underestimate the need to assess such incidents when taking their histories. Patients themselves may not be aware of the extent to which their conditions are trauma-related and physicians need to be alert to these possibilities and to ask more frequent and more carefully designed questions related to abuse, neglect, personal injury, threats to life and traumatic separations and bereavements. Some experiences may be inaccessible during the taking of a case history but often traumatic experiences are remembered but not linked, in the mind of the sufferer, with present troubles.

Therapeutic help

As yet there has been little or no use of medication for children who have suffered terrible traumas but over the next decade it is likely that this will change. The need is not for tranquillisers or sedatives to which children or adults may become habituated. However, trauma affects the way the nervous system works and there are now a number of medications which are being used, particularly for sleep disturbance and the symptoms of high arousal (thumping heart, sweating, dry mouth, bowel and bladder disturbances, suddenly feeling as though the whole experience were being relived) and flashbacks. Reduction of these symptoms may stop the trauma getting worse and make it easier to offer other kinds of therapeutic help. As yet most research has been on adults and in relation to war veterans; also the number of studies is small with lack of controls or comparisons. Also, we need to know much more about the natural history of traumatic stress disorders in children and adolescents. We need to know a lot more about what medicine to give, to what children, in what quantities and for how long in order to help with the immediate physical effects of being traumatised. Newman (1997)[161] reviews the current state of knowledge.

Bereavement counselling is discussed in Chapter 3, and Chapter 8 briefly describes help offered through cognitive/behavioural therapies, social skills training and Eye Movement Desensitisation and Reprocessing (EMDR).

The effects of psychotherapeutic help for children, backed by a growing body of knowledge, are real and may be measured.[128] There are two ways of promoting help. First, as outlined in Chapter 8, there may be direct psychotherapeutic work with the children, their families and those who care for them.[21, 68] Second, research and clinical knowledge enable teachers, doctors and social workers to support and work alongside parents and other caregivers in providing nurture and education tailored to the needs of children in trouble.[253, 262] This knowledge may enable therapeutic help to be obtained informally through friends, relatives and others with the right personality and natural therapeutic skills.

Children who grow up resilient

It seems likely that the ability of adult survivors to cope is influenced by a variety of factors. Those sustained by loving affectional links before the tragedy may well do better than those who suffered repeated earlier trauma: ''Tis better to have loved and lost/Than never to have loved at all' (Tennyson, *In Memoriam*). Those who witness the killing have different experiences and outcomes from those who do not. For all survivors, the quality and reliability of subsequent relationships will be crucial to their future well-being and adjustment. Emergency and planned longer-term therapeutic help may be of great value; there is a lot of work to do here to decide what is helpful or necessary. It is best to grow up as adults who have been informed, who can speak of their experiences and who have a factual knowledge of earlier events. Those who half know yet dare not ask may suffer most and longest. Those traumatised in childhood who are able to recollect in tranquillity appear to do best.[140]

Philippa, aged 23

Philippa was referred for therapy as a 23-year-old (p. 114). She told her therapist that things had been going well for her over the past few years. However, recently she had begun to feel very low and confused and she was concerned that she could not concentrate on her final exams at university.

Philippa said that she felt very confused about her four-year relationship with Jim and that she was fearful of losing that relationship. This was distressing: it was hard to live with herself. She was also confused about her mother's death, particularly about the moment she died. She remembered being in the bedroom before the attack and leaving the bedroom afterwards. She presumed she must have stepped over her mother's body to get out of the room. She frequently thought about that night and spoke of wishing to regress to that age to help her understand what happened. Philippa talked of wanting to know more about her mother – what she looked like and what her personality was like.

Philippa had lost a lot of weight over the previous months and mentioned that she was terrified of being fat. She believed that when she ate, bad things happened. She was afraid that life 'can always turn around' and that something bad happened to her every four years.

Philippa admitted to feeling very lonely and isolated. She had only told Jim and one other friend about her background as she felt so ashamed about her father being a murderer. She felt that nobody really cared about her and she felt sad that she had no one to share her achievements and experiences.

Philippa was also worried about her 'attacks'. She described these as happening rarely and always in a situation when she felt out of control. For example, she recalled an incident when Jim persuaded her to go to a stranger's house with him. She did not want to go but felt pressurised. When she arrived, panic feelings welled up and she felt 'paralysed'. She screamed when Jim touched her and felt she had to remain absolutely still. She was unable to speak and felt like she was shrinking. If she moved her head an inch, she would die. Philippa found these attacks both frightening and embarrassing.

Over several sessions Philippa and the therapist gradually formulated her current difficulties and made links to her early childhood experiences. It became apparent that Philippa had not processed the traumatic experience of her mother's death, she was wracked with feelings of guilt. She believed she had done nothing to stop her father killing her mother. She strongly believed that she could have prevented her mother's death if she had made a noise to draw attention to herself. She could not forgive herself for 'cruelly' stepping over her mother's body, to leave the bedroom, without checking to see if she was OK. She also felt very guilty that she had hardly thought about her mother over the years and recalled that she had been pleased that her mother had died as she did not like her.

Philippa's need to find out more about her mother was very interesting. It was not only linked with the need to grieve for her mother and 'internalise' an image of her in her mind, but also with a deep fear that her father would try to kill her. It became apparent that Philippa held a deep-seated belief that one day her father would also kill her and that this was more likely if she looked or acted like her mother. When she came for therapy she was roughly the same age as her mother had been when she married her father. This was a source of great confusion for Philippa, as she desperately wanted to grieve, 'make amends', 'ask for forgiveness' and identify with her mother, and yet by doing so she felt she was at risk of being killed by her father. It became apparent that Philippa was terrified that she was more 'genetically' like her father. This meant to her that she might also be capable of murdering her partner. Her father was a very obese man and this shed some light on Philippa's need to be very thin and her distress when she put on weight. She was able to acknowledge that her need to control her weight was in part linked to a fear of being like her father. Thus her belief that bad things happened when she ate reflected her fear that she would act badly, as her father had, if she were fat.

Therapy sessions began with exploring what had actually happened on the night of her mother's death. Philippa recalled what she could remember of that night. She was annoyed with herself for not being able to remember 'the most important bits' and she found it difficult to forgive herself for not doing anything to stop her father. It was clear that Philippa viewed the event through the eyes of an adult and not as a 4-year-old. She and the therapist set about understanding the world of 4-year-olds and Philippa tried to observe the behaviour of other small children she knew. Gradually she began to realise how powerless she would have been in that situation, aged only 4 years. She slowly began to forgive herself for not intervening and began to accept that there was nothing she could have done. This process was greatly aided by a bizarre incident in which one day Philippa arrived at her session saying she had been knocked down on a zebra-crossing. Although not physically hurt, the experience had been enlightening for her as only moments after the accident she could not remember exactly what had happened and whose fault it was. She used this experience to realise that if she could not remember what exactly had happened only moments after the accident, it was extremely unlikely that she would have been able to remember exactly what had happened on the night her mother died, given that she was only 4 years old. Philippa and her therapist also resolved the mystery of her 'attacks' as it became apparent that they were 'emotional' flashbacks to the night of the murder. Philippa realised that she must have been lying under the bedclothes, terrified to move an inch in case her father killed her too.

These remarkable insights led to an equally remarkable resolution of Philippa's guilt and cleared the emotional blocks which had been preventing Philippa's emotional processing of the event.

Philippa then began to grieve properly for her mother. She set about trying to find out what her mother was like and to find some photographs of her. Philippa desperately wanted to tell her mother how much she loved her and how sorry she was that she had initially been pleased that she was dead. Philippa decided to write a letter to her mother to tell her how she really felt and to ask for her forgiveness. She also found out where her mother was buried and planned to make a visit to the grave.

Philippa reported that she felt very much better and really felt that she had resolved some very deep issues around her mother's death. After fifteen sessions Philippa felt that she was ready to stop coming to regular therapy. The therapist was, understandably, extremely pleased at the considerable progress Philippa had made in such a short space of time; however, the therapist felt it was a measure of Philippa's strength of character that she was able to utilise her therapy so well. Given all that Philippa has suffered in her life and the pain and despair that she has often felt, it is remarkable and heartening that she also shows profound inner strength, compassion, love, intelligence and insight.

Two other young women referred for therapy had developed severe anorexia nervosa during their later adolescence. One knew that her mother had been strangled by her father, having heard a sound 'like a cat mewing' which she later guessed to have been the moment of her mother's death. She was a teenager when this happened and had been aware for many months of frequent violent quarrels between her parents. She describes a rootless life with relatives and in a boarding school and the pride with which, at 16 years old, she began to starve herself. Another girl became aware, at 16, that she was involved in violent arguments with her father very like those in which her mother had been killed ten years earlier. Each of these young women in therapy proved highly creative, one writing a diary, the other painting. By the time of this second edition, each is doing well in higher education.

Because we work with families in trouble we hear most about misery, anger and mistrust. There is, however, another side to the coin. All experiences, however traumatic, may be harvested so as to enrich and develop the suffering personality. There is a quality of resilience in childhood about which we need to know more. There is also great variability in the ways children survive life's disasters. We need to study this and to learn how to aid and enhance the capacity for survival and recovery.

A study of adult survivors of the Greek Civil War,[56] historical surveys such as that on children in the American Civil War,[238] literature such as de Bernières' account of the Greek island of Cephallonia from the 1930s to the 1990s,[60] and studies specifically of resilience,[239, 240] all enhance the range of current research concerning the effects of psychological trauma outlined in our first chapter. These are only examples of an increasingly fruitful and life-enhancing field of knowledge.

Adult survivors of childhood trauma may not know that they are unusual, valuable people able to contribute to others. As children, resilient adults tend to have been easy, affectionate people without distressing difficulties with eating or sleeping, likeable and with friends. Intelligence helps, as does an upbringing which has enabled a child to be independent and autonomous. Resilient people tend to oppose injustice and, as they grow older, they wish to choose their own education and way of life and they question attempts to indoctrinate them. Resilient children tend to grow up feeling that they can be in charge of their own affairs and plan their own lives, to be active and energetic with a good capacity for work and study. They tend to persevere in the face of difficulties.

The most detailed study to date[56] also indicates the importance of good-quality alternative care. The children in this study were separated from their mothers through civil war, when the mothers, often partisans, were in prison. The most important features were the continuity and reliability of substitute care. Many of the children who survived best also had significant other adults who supported and helped them in a variety of ways.

As our study has progressed, we have been struck, repeatedly and increasingly, as we have got to know more troubled children and families, by the way qualities of resilience, adaptability and ability to love and care for each other may be enhanced and dramatised by family tragedy. We need to learn from survivors of family violence what services they need and how to move towards a less violent and threatening society.

Survivors, now adult, write

Two young women survivors give their own accounts of their experiences of growing up with the effects of family tragedy to overcome.

Donna

by Donna Shears

The writer was 11 years old when her father killed her mother.

So strong is the need to feel normal, accepted and OK as a child growing up with a father who has killed a mother, so complete is the resentment that you have towards your parent's cock-up having an effect on you, that, at the age of 11 and for many years afterwards, I avoided the stigma by lying about my parent's death. When asked where they lived or what they did it was always 'a car crash'. (It was easier that way.) Even now, many years later, I have this need to make sure people know who *I* am before knowing what has happened to me. I hate their embarrassment and I have often thought, 'Just what will they think of me?' A lot of people now know. It was my choice to say, 'Hey, I survived this experience', but it has been a gradual process and people's reactions don't always match your expectations (some make you feel good about yourself and some quite often don't).

I have older brothers and sisters. Recognising that your siblings' or relatives' needs are vastly different from your own is perhaps the most difficult task. Their coping strategies have often made me experience a subsequent sense of loss. (I can remember being more upset because the family broke up and went in different directions, and didn't see how my initial loss had guided that intensity of loss the second time round.) Gradually the wider picture became clearer, and I can see the shocked and hurt children, bereaved of their mother and let down by their dad.

As an adult looking back now I don't feel quite so powerless. Most of the time I am able to meet my own needs. When I don't and I feel lost and alone, I am usually able to isolate the reasons why a lot quicker than I have ever done. I started feeling the loss and strain when I was in a safe environment at university. I think the biggest favour I ever did myself was allowing myself to grieve or be angry with life around me. I often did it away from those closest to me, scared I'd drive them away. It was frightening for me watching my previous coping strategies seem to fall apart. But I found new ones . . . I learnt to reach out and not hit back if the reaction I got wasn't the one I'd like. I learnt to say, 'Yes, there are support networks out there.' For me, friends have been a constant reminder of who I am. My family too, their struggles, successes, sorrows. We are closer now and I think we all share a pride that we got through it. There was so much distrust, anger, resentment and hurt there (and some things have changed so much) that I thought things would never feel safe again.

It helped me being brought up with my sister. Having contact with my family has enabled me to learn about what happened, also I am under no illusions. Both Mum and Dad were human and made mistakes. That doesn't mean to say I don't blame Dad. I do. I am perfectly aware that he felt justified in his needs coming first and, as such, I ceased contact with him when I was 13. For me he had changed. He was no longer the father I knew and he had selfishly taken the life of our mother. I knew I loved them both before they went. I just knew that contact with Dad would not have made up for my losses.

As a person I have seen much beauty and suffering in the world. I also know there will be good times and bad times ahead of me. I have educated myself through university and am now working on an MA and a diploma in social work. Learning about myself and the way I have coped with the past has helped my sense of awareness now and hopefully in the future, and being able to talk about these experiences has finally let me see I was normal anyway – I didn't need to try!

Esther

Esther was 5 when her father killed her mother. She witnessed the killing which took place in her bedroom, where her mother had taken to sleeping. When she was 7 she returned to her father's care and suffered at his hands. Now in her twenties, living independently, intelligent and gifted but still very troubled, Esther here reflects on the effect her mother's traumatic death at her father's hands has had on her during her childhood and now.

I look back on my experiences

by Esther Levy

> I will not look at things, I will not suffer
> things to look at me. Put out the torches!
> Hide the moon! Hide the stars! Let us hide
> ourselves in our palace, Herodias, I begin to be afraid.
> (From *Salome*, Oscar Wilde)

As far back as I can remember, it seems as though my life had not properly begun, not assumed significance until my mother's death. That event, my father ending her life, ironically catapulted me into mine. Most of what I have learnt and most of what I have lived, stems from her tragedy, and although she was my mother for only five years, it is her life, her chancing to meet my father, their relationship and her death by his hands, which have shaped the way I think and absorbed me entirely.

I always expect the unexpected, maybe I always expect the worst.

What could be more unexpected to a child than that after her father had sung to her their bedtime song as she sat on his knee, after she had gone to bed with her mother, that he should later creep into their room, with a hammer and a knife and kill her mother? That her own father whom she loved, should ambush her, take her off-guard, so that she would wake up when he was in the throes of it, wake up moments too late, because she was only a child and slept soundly.

What could be more unexpected than this?

It was bewildering to emerge from that room after I had woken up, to find the house in darkness. Everyone seemed to be hiding from each other; it is almost comic on reflection. My father was nowhere to be seen and my brothers remained behind the closed door of their bedroom.

I looked around on the upstairs landing and, when I couldn't find anyone, I began to descend the stairs, and discovered that someone was already coming up them. I remember that although I did not recognise the face, I was relieved to find this stranger in my house.

A wide-eyed child is the only witness. The other witness, the perpetrator, is too absorbed in the physicality of it to notice his wife's expression; he forgets to watch her die. She is accompanied only by the child, who has woken up sufficiently to see and hear everything, to be utterly transfixed, glued to her vantage point and too absorbed and afraid to move.

There is a real inevitability about it; things are only inevitable though, afterwards. On reflection, had I tried to prevent him, would this have been in her best interests or even in mine?

Although he had stolen from her whatever moments, whatever potentiality she had remaining, it is her death too and the manner in which it occurred which falls within this potential. In a sense then, I feel like I was a privileged witness to this, a person's most intimate moment.

And now I feel as though I am keeper of the riddle, guardian of her last moments. I cannot speak of what happened, I have forgotten it, I cannot recount it to you at will. It allows itself to be remembered only as a last resort. I used to feel very clumsy about forgetting, it was as if I had lost something important, or worst, that I had forgotten it because I didn't care. It seems to me now though, that inside me I can remember very well what went on and how it made me feel. But it has been both my secret and my shield over the years. Forgetting becomes a way of protecting yourself from knowledge and the danger that comes with it. So it withheld itself from me, until the time came when I was ready to know the truth; it would reveal itself to protect me and warn me of the imminent danger I was in from my father. The memory was my mother's last and lasting gift to me, and my gift to her that I would never share it with anyone.

Because of this, the way she was as she died has remained a private affair; others cannot speak of it. They cannot say if she permitted it, if she expected it, or if she struggled.

The length of time it takes to kill someone is hugely disproportionate to its ramifications. A few moments of someone else's madness become eternally transfigured and transformed, live on in the child like an infinite point of wonder, and become an endless source of creativity and inspiration. But it is difficult for a child to keep such a secret, even when everyone is too stupid to see that she has it, and is in fact madly waving it about for all to see.

Immediately, I became unable to sleep through the night, and would wake hearing strange voices when everyone else was asleep, strange internal voices which I thought were bidding me to do bad things. Visits to my father in prison were always followed by vomiting, partly out of a deep sense of pity and regret for my incarcerated prince. In later years, I would faint in difficult situations. The only way for me to overcome the racing of my heart and the pain in my head was to remain perfectly still and alone. Indeed I had a dread of being moved when in this state, and it was many years before it dawned on me that I had been re-experiencing those moments years before, when I had perceived that the only way to remain undetected was to keep still and hold my breath as I watched. This may have saved me then, and forgetting what I had seen saved me years later when I had to feign ignorance of it in my father's house. It is no coincidence then that I now make my living by keeping still for long periods of time as an artists' model.

And so my mother did not die alone; something in me died with her, whilst something living in her came to live with me. Where else did her remainder go? For she did not merely die, she left a trail of things unfinished, which had nowhere to go. These unfulfilled dreams, aspirations, plans she may have had, remain unknown, are taken with the spirit when it goes. But the gravity of their loss to her should not remain unknown, unconsidered.

And everyone was so preoccupied with putting it behind them, 'burying the past', getting over it like it was the 'flu', that the task fell to me to preserve something of this loss and find a medium for its expression. For years I hated everyone because of this: that although I was perceived to be the least aware of the facts because I was a child, and although I had no special relationship with my mother, some-how no one else shouldered the responsibility of remembrance and preservation. No one screamed for her, and everyone misinterpreted it, used it to foster an already-existing hatred between two families.

I felt as though I had killed her, this was the only way I could explain my tremendous guilt: the burden of feeling was with me, not because I was sensitive or could harness it positively one day, but because I was culpable. I was not a witness but an accomplice. Not an innocent child, but a sinister watchful child who hated her mother and watched gleefully in the wings while her avenger slayed the Witch. A powerful child who only had to wish for things to come true.

Today though, I feel honoured to sit and write this; to be the recorder of what has always gone on behind closed doors.

After being charged with manslaughter (or is it man's laughter?), my father spent two years in prison. He claimed that my mother had been having an affair and no doubt knew that she would be leaving him soon anyway. In order to ensure that she did not also take us with her, he killed her and got off very lightly. Soon we went to live with our father in a new flat; I remember very clearly how it felt being alone with him that first night. I was 8: I shut my bedroom door and hung my dressing-gown on the back of it. I felt terrible. I knew then that we were different; it felt wrong for two children to live alone with a man, it felt unsafe. But I consoled myself with the fact that my bedroom door had this handy hook that I could hang my dressing-gown on.

I lived with him in that flat for eight years, eight interminable years which yawned before me the whole time I was growing up, like the seemingly vast landscapes separating the characters in Thomas Hardy's stories from the destinies which beckon them. I thought I would never escape and worst, that I would never have the courage to leave.

I felt so sorry for him. He had no friends, no wife to talk to, he was largely treated with suspicion and wariness by the community, and he had trouble finding employment due to his criminal record. On top of all this, he had two children to look after, feed and clothe, be there for when they had measles and send on holidays.

No, we were not insensitive children, we were attentive to all his ups and downs. So we acted the parts he wanted us to play, and became skilful at concealing our true feelings for him. To this day I can appear intrigued by something which thoroughly bores me.

I spent most of my life tiptoeing around the huge bulk which became my father. I was like a spy, spending my time in my bedroom listening to the sounds that emanated from him; learning his habits, his movements, his rituals, the exact moment he awoke in the morning, his facial expressions, his body language; the sound his car made when he arrived home in anger, and the sound his keys made in the door when he'd had a bad day.

It was like living in a panopticon: the knowledge of his presence in the house was enough to control us, and when he wasn't there, we could only wait for him to return and hope that he wouldn't. I thought that life would always be like this, I could not predict my own freedom. I worried about this all the time. How could we escape this inevitability, this cycle of powerlessness?

At school we were taught that each Friday night, two angels, one good and one bad, would accompany the men as they walked home from the Synagogue. If, as they entered the house, all was in readiness for the Sabbath and there was a peaceful atmosphere, the good angel would declare: 'And so shall it be next Sabbath', and the bad angel would be bound to repeat the promise. If, on the other hand, the house was in disarray and the members of the family quarrelling among themselves, the bad angel would say: 'May it be so next week', and the good angel would be forced to agree. In my estimation, we were forced to relive bad Sabbath after bad, never freeing ourselves of the angels' curse.

And yet there were so many signs for all to see that something was wrong. My brother's school report went back unsigned by my father but covered in a spray of my brother's blood which he was forced to miserably Tippex out. My own school report was returned by my father with the worrying annotation that he would appreciate in future being notified at the time of my misbehaviour, so as to discipline me more effectively. There were marks all over the walls in our house, drawn there by my father, as he uttered threats in Arabic, each mark standing for one of our misdemeanours, lest we forget our crimes against him.

The truth is that my mother's murder pales into insignificance, contrasted against the events that followed. That my father would routinely punish me by cutting off all my hair is for me a much more heinous crime, for it was directed against me and I cannot think of any justification for it.

As children we are solipsistic: murder, death, upsets our routines, our games, causes us to be uprooted, up-ended, we are scorned or pitied, we no longer feel equal. And as adults perhaps we are just the same, we simply learn to disguise the inconvenience: we call it by the name of 'grief'. The death of another always leaves the mourner removed, that is removed from the person who has died, and removed from their experience of dying, which no one can ever expect to share with anyone else. This, their ultimate moment of 'authenticity', of complete aloneness cannot be conveyed to the grievers. Death therefore always alienates us from the person we have known.

My mother's death, though unexpected and, on reflection, untimely, seems to me not as unjust as the theft of my hair. I can understand that my father may have had a momentary lapse, or that he could not control his jealousy. I can even understand that he may have planned the whole thing; he had to pick up that knife and pick up that hammer, he had to climb the stairs, open the bedroom door, consider the form of his sleeping daughter; there was plenty of time to reconsider, to pause. The truth is we kill because we want to, it is something we are all capable of. Both victim and murderer somehow find themselves in a situation they cannot control, and yet it is not wholly unexpected, there must be a build up. And somehow they are thrown together in this state of enmity and at a certain point it becomes too difficult to determine who is killing who in the ensuing struggle.

What separates my father from me? The fear of being caught? Compassion? Social awareness? Luck?

I could not cause such pain, such mess, such chaos.

And yet something in him relinquished all of these taboos and allowed him to take those weapons in his hands and wield them dispassionately, and believe he had committed the beautiful-sounding *crime passionnel*: the thinking man's murder. He doesn't kill indiscriminately, only those he loves.

As I have said, the crime itself is over in moments, it is fleeting, and ultimately the victim's misery both in life and death is ended swiftly, and if it is tragic at all, it is only tragic for her; it is not my tragedy, I have no claims on it, it has no right to ruin me. But it's the small things, the mundane things which gnaw away at me, the crimes against me as a child and the change which came over my father, the madness that had taken him over, which must have been fuelled by a kind of guilt.

Let us imagine that he felt genuine remorse, and that he wished to be helped or fittingly punished, that the absence of both of these left him in a state of confusion and anger towards society for being so forgiving. The lengths he had gone to, to make himself stand out and still no one acknowledged what a big and dangerous man he was, a powerful, unnerving man who might at any moment lunge at someone and kill them, drench them in scarlet. It must have been maddening for him when the world didn't recognise just how terrifying he could be. As children, we *know* that murder is wrong; as adults perhaps we don't see things so clearly. He could rely on our being afraid of how far he could go but it seemed to us, and maybe to him, as though society had sanctioned his deed by allowing him to look after us.

Was I the thorn in his side, the worrying presence of the child who may or may not have seen and heard everything? Was he afraid of me?

There is something so naïve and almost childish in killing your wife and trying to deny it. It is so obvious who the perpetrator is and yet they look you straight in the eye, with big wide eyes and pin the crime on their wife's lover. You are caught with chocolate all round your mouth and your hand jammed in the cookie jar and still you deny you have been stealing cookies.

Lies. It is all lies, and worst, implausible lies. My house was full of them. And I also lied to him implausibly. I was so creative and elaborate in my lies. A good lie could save my skin: I cannot tell you how many times I dreamt up the most inconceivable lies which fooled him entirely.

How can I tell you that I hid in the toilet of a restaurant which I had flown into, in order to escape the sudden and unexpected arrival of my father into the vicinity of my night out? How can I tell you how I cowered in there, guarded by a couple of friends, hounded by angry waiters who had witnessed my trespass? How can you understand how rigid with fear I became when it was reported to me that my father had entered that very restaurant and calmly sat down to order a meal? I thought my life was at an end. I cannot tell you what a miracle it was when he inexplicably got up, refrained from ordering and simply left, not knowing or perhaps knowing all too well that his 16-year-old daughter was hiding from him in that place.

The following day he was brazen enough to ask me if I had ever been to that restaurant and I was brazen enough to say no. So he had known all along and had entered merely to outsmart me, to catch me in the act, like I caught him years earlier: but the fool had outsmarted himself, for it was my fear of him which prevented me from fearing the angry waiters and the indignant manager. Fear of him which meant that I would not, could not, give myself up. For I was hiding a multiplicity of sins: my clothes, my hair, my demeanour, my identity.

How can I tell you this? How could you ever understand it?

And so I was drawn into those lies. He knew that I knew he had been there, and I knew that he knew I had been there, but neither was in a position to confess or accuse the other. We lived with the lie and a thousand others. I was forced to play him at his own game, to become better at his game than he was because I had more at stake: I was only just beginning.

And somehow I always feel tainted because of this; that feeling of being an accomplice is inescapable, that knowledge that you have shared bad, unspeakable things, a part of me was irretrievably corrupted.

And yet . . . and yet . . . if you were to see him today, you would not believe me. He is no longer so striking. Indeed, the huge bulk which so impressed me as a child now makes him appear vulnerable and ineffective. If you saw him today you wouldn't know him at all. He leads a normal dull existence characterised by routine and punctuated with meals. He has become a cliché of middle-class values and it is difficult to believe that he was once the magnificent orchestrator of a fabulous tragedy, greater even than anything the Greeks wrote. And now, now he is no longer omnipotent but impotent. He is a shadow of himself. My tragic hero sits in his house as I write this, with his feet up in front of the television, eating pistachio nuts.

> I opened to my beloved; but my beloved had turned away and
>   was gone:
> my soul failed me when he spoke:
> I sought him, but I could not find him:
> I called him, but he gave me no answer.
>
> (The Song of Songs)

Where did all his power go? The truth is he had no power; it had always been an illusion seen through a child's eyes. And now that we are apart he wields nothing over me. And it is only this way because I have made it so. He did not bestow upon me my freedom, I created it out of nothing.

As I have already said, the buried memories are there to give practical assistance when the time is right; it reappears when you are ready to relive it and only then. Until I reached that point I had always been undecided, ambivalent about leaving. My heart would surge with pity for him, I would conjure up images of his loneliness: in my mind I envisaged his pain. And this love for him, which was childlike in its gentleness, always held me back, bewitched. But it was only a matter of time until I cultivated enough loathing for my father, and in much the same way, I took this hate and eyed it mercifully, but with myself in mind this time. I held on to this contempt like a raft and I abandoned ship.

We have not spoken of love until now. Of course I loved my father, of course I still love him. He is mine and I have no other. Despite this, I know now that I don't need his love in return, and I no longer seek it out. The more I sought his love, the more he failed me, he couldn't give me what I wanted. And eventually I realised that I had to stop asking from him what he could not give. And so we become less disappointed in ourselves, we let go of our wistfulness.

And now we are two strangers in the world, he and I. It is as though we had never even known each other. We are as far apart as we can be, but perhaps that is still not far enough for me. I wish he was dead, I wish I was as mad as him, I wish I could kill him.

But it is not yet the end. When will it be the end? It can never end. The saga still breathes, the mouth still speaks, recites. The further I get towards a form of expression, the more inadequate that voice seems. How to express years of expressionlessness? Strange things go round in my head, you and I are not alike. I feel strange, abstracted, maybe even powerful. And yet we all carry around our sack of sorrows, though mine is no longer very heavy, in fact I miss the burden of it. Good things happen and bad things happen, but we are neither good nor bad. But usually when bad things happen it is so that good can follow.

I know that the worst has passed, life will only improve, and it is better for me that I suffered as a child; nothing like that could ever happen to me again. However, it is dangerous to interpret the past as a bad chapter, a mistake, something which should never have happened. I am glad of the tragedy, I would not change it. I repeat: I would not change it, it was simply a double-edged gift, like all the best, most magical gifts. For although something precious was taken from me, I was given a lifetime's worth of thoughts in return, and it is the paradoxes that make life meaningful.

But from day to day, life wavers between the two extremes of the paradox; it feels marvellous to be alive for no particular reason and yet, it all seems to lack significance and everything is too easy. It becomes mundane and then I don't want that freedom I fought for, what did I want it for? For this? Was it worth it? It all seems so pointless now.

And it is as though I have a sign on my back which reads, 'Whatever it is you want from me, I cannot give it, my father killed my mother', and there is another sign on my front which says, 'Go on ask me, I can take it, my father killed my mother, I can do anything.' And it depends which way I am looking at the time which determines your impression of me.

And now, now I am no longer a Rapunzel, I have exited mythology and the point of my being here becomes the same as yours: to find a way of moving around in the world, to find a way of being, a way of coping with those little ups and downs. Only for me this must always take place in the light of what has happened. For me, everything always somehow relates back to that first moment when life's unpredictability became revealed, and that is always my first and most helpful reference point.

And in a way I will always be in its shadow, I will always remain 'in the shadows' as I did on that night, dwarfed by its intensity. I can never supersede or overcome it, because it is not there to be forgotten or named, or overcome. It is the unnameable, the unmentionable, the unthinkable and therefore it cannot be consigned to what is merely historical or accidental. Life will never be that precious or interesting again, and I miss that as much as I miss her.

Chapter 11

The legal system

Hear me for my cause.
(Shakespeare, *Julius Caesar*, III, ii)

SUMMARY

Children have legal rights and obligations which should be identified and upheld.

Who speaks for the child?

On the whole, children have been passive recipients of legal interventions in their lives and the law is slow. Moreover, criminal hearings are out of synchronisation with civil hearings. When a man goes to prison his children need secure, reliable care immediately, and they cannot remain on ice until months later, when father's case comes to trial. This may seem unjust, yet civil law concerning children is quite clear; their welfare is paramount. Sadly, legal disputes, adjournments and limited resources – numbers of judges, magistrates and supporting court staff, the lack of a framework to ensure that cases are heard according to the age and needs of the children, shortages of guardians and court welfare officers who can help the court by making careful enquiries into the needs of the children – may hinder fair and speedy decision-making.[157] Departments of social services with limited resources – under great pressure to provide adequate child protection services, to co-operate with health authorities regarding the care of the mentally ill and to provide packages of care in the community for people with disabilities, handicaps and chronic illnesses – are not well placed to pick up complex cases involving the civil rights of children, to deal with the emergency and then to follow up over months and years.

Moreover, not all children receive legal advice: many about whom we have been consulted have had all decisions made for them by adults who, however well-meaning, may have difficulty in acting fairly and impartially.

Don and Dan, aged 8 and 6

Two brothers Don and Dan were moved 200 miles, to the home of their mother's sister and her husband, whom they had seen once in the previous year. They travelled with a stranger, a social worker, since their aunt had two children of her own, one 3 years old and one a new baby. Three days earlier the boys' mother had been strangled by their father. That day, they had been met from school by a policewoman, who, together with their headteacher, took them to a children's home. Their father's body was later found in woodland; he had connected a hose-pipe to the car exhaust. The news had been broken to mother's sister by local police and she had agreed to take care of the children.

Some months after the killing, the uncle and aunt were put in contact with a local fostering and adoption service, for advice which they refused to take. They insisted that their nephews knew nothing of what had happened to their parents. They had been told that both parents were killed in a car crash and that is all they ever would be told. Their aunt said that they were far from their old home and they would see nothing of their father's relatives, so they could never find out. The aunt and uncle stressed that they intended to take full and disinterested care of their two nephews and had arranged that all monies from the sale of their parents' house and from insurance policies would be placed in an independent trust fund.

Since they refused to allow the boys to be interviewed, it was not possible to verify that the belief of the aunt and uncle about the children's knowledge of the events was correct, yet it was difficult to accept their certainty that the boys knew nothing, given that the double tragedy had been a *cause célèbre* in the village where the children had lived for three days after the killing and that the facts were known to teachers, school friends and to all the wider family. It seemed even more unlikely that the boys could be protected indefinitely. Yet no one wished to upset a home where they seemed well cared for while they were doing well and making friends at their new school. They were lucky to have guardians who cared for them; the risk was of a troubled adolescence.

There is a sensitive account of psychotherapy with a 6-year-old boy who, at 9 months, witnessed the killing of his mother by his father, but this was not acknowledged by his adoptive parents.[12] The material brought to therapy by this disturbed boy clearly shows that he witnessed the killing and that it was affecting his behaviour. Again the therapy was terminated prematurely when the parents realised that the secret might have to become overt.

Sometimes children do express their wishes but are not taken seriously. Or there may be a discrepancy between what they say and how they behave which is not recognised by those making decisions on their behalf.

Jonathan, aged 14

Jonathan was claimed by his father after he had spent three years in prison, having pleaded guilty to the manslaughter of Jonathan's mother. A psychiatrist reported that father was depressed at the time of his wife's death and had now recovered. Jonathan had regularly visited his father in prison and in the flat where he was now living. Father always referred to the death as an accident; he told Jonathan that his mother had caused the depression because she was an unfaithful wife. Newspaper reports, which Jonathan had read, described the boy's mother as having 'taunted' her husband just before she was killed. This was what father had said in court at the time when his case was adjourned for the preparation of a psychiatric report; there was, of course, no one in court to speak for Jonathan's mother.

Jonathan had to choose between a home with his father, with the unspoken expectation that he would go along with father's version of events, or a home with his mother's younger sister and her boyfriend. They were bitterly unforgiving, as were all mother's family, about her death.

Jonathan was a ward of court and the welfare report, which recommended to the judge that he should live with his father, considered only the risk to Jonathan of violence from his father, which was thought negligible. Jonathan did indeed say that he would like to live with his father but he developed a severe, persistent, involuntary blinking tic soon afterwards.

One of us told the court that Jonathan seemed likely to be giving a mixed message and, although his spoken wishes were respected, we continued to feel concern about him.

Children such as these, caught up in family tensions, may be protected from all knowledge and responsibility, or asked to make decisions far beyond what is appropriate, with no real option available. Sometimes this involves losing one-half of their relatives and years of denial or distortion of their memories.

Wardship is currently available only to private individuals and no longer to local authorities. The reasoning is that in England and Wales the Children Act 1989 has provided, since implemented in 1991, a just, yet equally flexible, package of provisions for children in trouble and that it is not appropriate that a local authority should have access to the wide powers of the High Court in cases where it may not be able to prove grounds for intervention (see Appendix 2 and Glossary).

The Children Act 1989 has been described as 'the most fundamental change of child law this century'.[244] It demonstrates that there has been a gradual shift from the perception of children as objects to a view of them as young people deserving of civil rights in their own account, in all cases, ranging from divorce hearings to child protection issues. The law now attempts to encourage greater partnership between parents and statutory authorities (local authorities, the NSPCC, police, health authorities) and to promote voluntary agreements rather than legal enforcement of child protection. It increases the ability of children to be parties separate from their parents in legal proceedings concerning them and provides a welfare checklist to which courts must have regard when they are making decisions concerning children.

Although this Act applies only to one jurisdiction, that of England and Wales, it is wide in scope and will have major implications for the practice of all who work with children. It changes the standing of children in law, creates new concepts regarding the responsibility of adults and develops the structure and functioning of civil courts in ways which are discussed later in this chapter. In place of wardship, it provides a new range of orders which relate to the care of children in private law (where disputes are between individuals, such as divorcing parents) and in situations where the state intervenes on behalf of the child.

Thus, Jonathan would not now be a ward of court, but a care order could be made to his local authority which could act in partnership with Jonathan and his relatives to plan where he would live, how he would be educated and how he would keep in contact with key adults in his life. Within this framework, a plan could be made that Jonathan live either with his mother's sister or with his father. Alternatively, a residence order could be made which would allow Jonathan to live with his maternal aunt, if she were to apply for such an order. If no order were made, Jonathan would continue in the guardianship of his father. No question of legal intervention in this arrangement would then arise unless new problems ensued.

This happened, for example, in the case of Anela, described in Chapter 5. She had been cared for by her paternal uncle and then by her father after his discharge from prison. When she was found asleep on a railway bench, and told her story to the policeman who discovered her there, she was made the subject of a care order. Until then no one had known her history other than her family. A local authority social worker sought advice from our service about how best to plan the future. There were important issues about where Anela would live, how she would continue her education, whether she should be upheld in her decision that she did not want at that time to meet her father, and how she could be helped to retain contact with her step-mother and younger sister whom she loved very much.

Whatever the legal system in which children bereaved through violence find themselves, we think that they have the right to independent representation and advocacy which considers their interests and protects them from powerful needs to deny, repress or distort agonising realities. This also offers indirect relief to relatives with similar burdens. We regret that the concept of *parens patriae* is not now available to children like Don, Dan and Jonathan. It is unlikely that anyone would have wanted to remove Don and Dan from the loving care of their family but, had they been wards of court or the subjects of care proceedings, it would have been possible for an independent inquiry to be made into their welfare, the question of whether they really were ignorant of their parents' murder and suicide, and their financial situation. This could have been helpful to the uncle and aunt, heavily burdened by this large and sudden task of parenthood, if offered tactfully and over time.

Jonathan, under the present law, might not receive legal help. To achieve a care order his local authority would have to apply to a court and prove that, unless the order were made, Jonathan would suffer significant harm. While there are now legal decisions which establish that the killing of one parent by the other is about as significant a harm as any child may undergo, the court still has to consider whether or not making an order is better than not making one. This may depend on external factors such as the availability of specialist social work, whether some alternative home is available and whether or not the court and the social workers decide that relatives are prepared to work in partnership to plan the child's future. It is quite likely in reality that no intervention would take place, no order would be made and a child such as Jonathan would continue in the guardianship of his father. Moreover, if Jonathan's tic continued, his school work fell off, or other stress symptoms showed themselves, only father, who still wanted to deny that Jonathan had any problems, would be available to ask for help on behalf of his son.

If courts act flexibly and sensitively so that children like this do not wait many months before decisions are made about them, it is still necessary to be aware that there is a gap between the resources available and the spirit of the law. It may be that in cases such as we describe legislation is somewhat optimistic, since the principle that there should be partnership between parents and social workers rather than the making of legal orders may be unrealistic where there is family violence. It is to be hoped that the overriding concept, that the welfare of the child is paramount, will create a spirit of continuing enquiry on behalf of children so that their needs will be met, as used to happen within the framework of wardship. A useful perspective has been provided on the gradual evolution of a family justice system better tailored to the needs of children.[234]

Children and money

As well as understanding, communication and advocacy, children need financial help and advice.

Thomas and Jane, aged 6 and 4

Thomas and Jane were in the care of their mother's sister (a common outcome when a mother is killed by her husband). For a year their aunt received no financial help. She and her husband, with three children of their own, found this very worrying. The children's father was on remand in prison, awaiting trial and denying that he had killed his wife. From prison he attempted to control each detail of the children's lives. The family home was locked, the key in the possession of the father's mother. The children had not been in their own home since their mother's death. The paternal grandmother had provided their clothes and personal possessions but insisted that mother's sister should travel fifty miles to collect them, refusing to visit her. Father demanded, through his solicitor, that the aunt should take the children to their grandmother's house so that they could then travel to the prison for a visit. Their aunt refused to agree to this.

The aunt thought that their former home should be sold and that the children should have the use of their inheritance. Their grandmother was planning to rent the house, use the income for the children's maintenance and keep the family home for the use of her son. Neither parent had made a will. Mother had an insurance policy payable on death to her next of kin, but no death certificate had yet been issued. The children had no legal advisor, nor did their mother's relatives, because legal aid is only granted to people on low incomes and the uncle and aunt did not qualify. Their salary was adequate for the mortgage and, just about, for the five children in the household, but there was no money to spare for legal advice. The local authority had not offered a fostering allowance or other emergency help to the family, nor had they instituted care proceedings. So the children were not legally aided to instigate direct financial claims against their father or to the Criminal Injuries Compensation Authority.

After consultation with our service, care proceedings were instituted and a solicitor instructed on behalf of the children. By the time this had happened, eighteen months after father's imprisonment, the precarious family arrangements were too much for the uncle and aunt and Thomas and Jane moved to a foster home.

Compensation claims

Whether or not there is family money to argue about, the children may be eligible for compensation through the Criminal Injuries Compensation Authority (London and Glasgow, UK).

The Official Solicitor acted on behalf of Paul, aged 14, Timothy, aged 5, and 1-year-old Elizabeth. He obtained a sum calculated according to the length of time each child, before reaching the age of 18, would have been deprived of the mother's care (so that the baby received the most substantial award). It could be argued, however, that Timothy, who can describe in vivid action replay the bathroom scene in which his father dismembered his mother, deserves compensation for having developed post-traumatic stress disorder. It could be argued too that Paul, who is terrified of his violent dreams, in some of which he kills his father, may suffer most and longest and deserves compensation for these sufferings.

If it is a principle of our society that victims of violent crime should receive compensation, this must apply to all. Claims to the Criminal Injuries Compensation Authority on behalf of minors may be made by guardians or legal representatives, including local authorities. Action must be taken within three years of the injury, but young people on whose behalf no such action has been taken may still claim within three years of their majority, or may claim against a local authority which has failed to act on their behalf. There need have been no criminal trial, but the perpetrator may not benefit from his crime. So Jonathan, who went to live with his father, would not be eligible unless the money were invested to protect his interests. Victims may also claim compensation from the perpetrator of the crime.[24] Compensation is calculated according to a tariff and psychological or psychiatric reports may help with this process.

Perhaps more important than compensation is the recognition that fathers, wherever possible, should support their children. Much can be done through the release of family assets for their benefit. Once the fathers are released they should pay maintenance.

It is important that legal precedents are considered and case law established to help children who are suffering as the result of criminal violence, as devastating as any major disaster. We have commented already that money cannot compensate for bereavement and trauma. Yet maintenance from fathers and tough-minded financial compensation, for trauma, subsequent stress disorder, bereavement, loss of security and loss of parenting for the rest of their childhood, will benefit the children. The families who take on their long-term care may require other help such as fostering allowances, and may be eligible for emergency help on behalf of the children, from departments of social services and the Department of Social Security.

To summarise, children need advocates who pay careful attention to what they say and do and to the tragedy through which they have lived and the family life which preceded it. They need advocates who will speak on their behalf about where they will live, which relatives they will see, what information they will be given, how they will be maintained, their legal rights and the financial compensation which may be made available to them. Families and foster carers, already under great strain, should not carry such great burdens alone. Independent listeners and advocacy will relieve their burden rather than impose further stresses on them.

Who listens to the child

Helping children to be witnesses

Media concern, therapeutic evaluation and the legal duties of a child witness have in substance been ignored for children who witness other forms of crime. Morgan and Zedner[151] carried out the first detailed survey of child witnesses to crimes such as violence, theft and homicide in the UK.

Most of our children are witnesses in the sense that they are interviewed by guardians *ad litem* or welfare officers when plans are to be made about their future, or by social workers seeking information about their earlier life. Since most parental homicides are 'crimes of passion' committed openly, the perpetrator is usually arrested either at the scene of the crime or soon afterwards. It is unusual for the aggressor to try to conceal his or her action and when this does happen the attempt tends to be ineffective.

However, we have encountered situations where children would have been able, had they been asked, to provide valuable circumstantial evidence to scene of crime investigators. For example, one father was found guilty of negligence, insisting that his wife's death was a tragic accident. His children, unquestioned at the time of the criminal investigation, later told an expert witness in care proceedings that their mother had been beaten several times and was often threatened with violence. They heard her screaming in response to threats from their father, prior to the death which father insisted arose out of a game which went wrong, during which the couple were laughing and joking.

It does happen that a child may be the only eyewitness to a homicide which has not been solved and may then have to take part in criminal proceedings. Some of our children have also expected, for periods of up to one year, to give evidence when their parent is charged with murder but has pleaded guilty to the lesser charge of manslaughter, which is being disputed by the prosecution.

If there is no arrest, anxiety is exacerbated and this, or prolonged delays, with increased anxiety at times of interim court hearings, may be linked with new re-enactments of the trauma and disturbing dreams. However, taking part in the legal process can help children to cope. There can be an initial difficulty for them: because the police are responsible for accumulating evidence and if necessary preventing witnesses from communicating, their prepared procedure would be to keep the children apart from each other after a killing. If this happens, and the child is also abruptly separated both from his dead or dying parent and from the arrested father, it is an additional source of stress and may interfere with the aim of the police, which is to get a clear account of what has happened.

Fatigued children are poor witnesses and, if they are young, and are asked initially about their name, age, school, etc., they may misinterpret these questions and fear they are under suspicion or have been arrested.[178] Those collecting evidence want to take the child step by step through a series of events. But it may be more meaningful for the child to talk first about the worst moment and to choose how to tell the story. In frustration, those exploring a crime may not recognise that young children, though mute, may be able to re-enact, play or draw events they have experienced. Another problem, more evident in older children, is the conflict of loyalties that may occur when they suddenly find themselves giving evidence about a loved parent who will then be branded a criminal.

Other children have been disturbed by being made accomplices to crimes. Frank, aged 15, spent a year in the expectation that he would appear as a police witness at his father's trial. He had been asked by his paternal grandmother with whom he lived to testify that his father was away from home at the time of his mother's death, and this Frank would not do. He was relieved of this burden when father pleaded guilty to manslaughter and his plea was accepted. But Frank suffered nightmares for many months before this happened.

Children can be helped to be witnesses. In proceedings concerned with planning a child's future, the judge has power to offer the child a private interview, although this is a limited power to help discover the child's wishes and not to gather evidence about what has happened in the past. In general, judges and magistrates prefer to rely on court welfare officers and guardians *ad litem* to do this work. Civil hearings in which children give evidence are heard in private.

Children should be taken to a court before they are witnesses, shown the layout and where they will stand (or preferably sit). Plans must be made that the child, however small, can see and hear, yet should not be required to look at or be seen by the person on trial. A screen may be used. (The use of video evidence is considered later.) A trusted adult should be available and after the hearing the child should be given the opportunity for debriefing, just as after any other stressful event. Children's evidence should not be rehearsed. But they can be helped by lawyers, as indeed are adult witnesses, to understand and prepare for the questions that will be asked of them. It is comparatively recently that planning such as this has been thought appropriate in courts of law.

The legal system

Children have not been thought to be accurate witnesses by lawyers, doctors and scientists. We know that human beings, whatever their age, vary widely in their ability to observe, recall and describe their experiences, to be truthful and not make up stories and to resist pressures from others to change, deny or exaggerate what has happened to them. When a court listens to a witness, the age of the person concerned is only one factor to be considered. Recent research into children's ability to remember, clinical work with children who have been involved in disasters, crimes or accidents, and attempts to create legal hearings a little more tailored to children's needs have shown that their ability to give evidence has been underestimated. After crime or catastrophe involving children, adults – particularly those involved in the violent events, or those such as relatives and social workers responsible for trying to sort out the child's world – have not wanted to question the child, or to listen to what they have to say.

Dogmatic and unfounded statements have been made which suggest that in any case it is not worth doing this. For example, an English lawyer (quoted in[208]) wrote in 1984 as follows:

> First, a child's powers of observation and memory are less reliable than an adult's. Secondly, children are prone to live in a make believe world, so that they magnify incidents which happen to them or invent them completely. Thirdly, they are also very egocentric, so that details seemingly unrelated to their own world are quickly forgotten by them. Fourthly, because of their immaturity they are suggestible and can easily be influenced by adults and other children. One lying child may influence others to lie; anxious parents may take a child through a story again and again so that it becomes drilled in untruths. Most dangerously, a policeman taking a statement from a child may without ill will ask leading questions so that the child tends to confuse what actually happened with the answers suggested implicitly by the question. The fifth danger is that children may have little notion of the duty to speak the truth, and they may fail to realise how important their evidence is in a case and how important it is for it to be accurate. Finally, children sometimes behave in a way evil beyond their years. They may consent to sexual offences against themselves and then deny consent. They may completely invent sexual offences. Some children know that the adult world regards such matters in a serious and peculiar way, and they enjoy investigating this mystery or defending themselves by making false accusations.
>
> (p. 162)

None of these statements applies to children as a class, although all may be applied to some people of any age some of the time. The allegation that children invent sexual offences against them has little substance and interviewing techniques have been developed which enable interviewers to make sensible assessments of allegations.[103, 117, 118, 242]

Memory

Recently, attempts have been made to assess the memory of children who have lived through frightening and dramatic events which threatened their lives or the lives of those they loved. For example, workers at the University of Glasgow interviewed fifty-four of the children of Lockerbie, for the purpose of insurance claims, one year after the disaster in which, in December 1988, a terrorist bomb caused the explosion of a Pan American jet over this small Scottish town, killing all the passengers and crew and eleven people on the ground, with much damage to the town. Six children were over 16, eighteen between 11 and 15, twenty-seven between 6 and 10 and eight under five.[170]

All children could give detailed stories of the crash, apart from an infant of fifteen months. Most described a loud rumbling noise, a big bang, an orange fireball in the sky and the sight and smell of burning debris; one boy said the heat was like being 'inside a furnace'. Those near the main crash craters recalled the terrifying experience of their houses shaking, fires and people screaming. Several children and parents came close to death or injury. Forty-five children were indoors at home with their families and nine were out of their houses in the vicinity.

The children were effective witnesses of facts and feelings, one year after the tragedy.

Children who had been on the *Herald of Free Enterprise*, the Channel ferry which capsized off Zeebrugge in Belgium in March 1987, were interviewed as part of an assessment for compensation.[264] Twenty-two children under 16 survived the disaster of whom thirteen were interviewed.

Like other workers, Yule and Williams comment that they were unprepared for the degree of distress shown by the children when they were interviewed away from parents and teachers (as discussed in Chapter 1). The records show that these children were also extremely clear witnesses. Children who have been debriefed, so that they are not hindered by intrusive, unbidden traumatic memories, and who have been prepared for court, can draw on their memories to give reliable evidence.

Egocentricity

All of us, at whatever age, remember better and are able more accurately to describe events which touch us nearly. Indeed, the main danger of egocentricity, when children are required as witnesses, is that 'the adults will be too self-centred to put themselves in the shoes of the child and appreciate the child's viewpoint'.[208]

Suggestibility

All human beings are suggestible to some extent and it is for this reason that doctors and lawyers are taught not to ask leading questions. (For example, doctors ask, 'Is there a pain?', rather than 'Where is the pain?') However, lawyers set aside this principle in cross-examination, when leading questions may be asked of witnesses of all ages. This may distort the information obtained and be very distressing to young witnesses, who think they are being accused of lying, or that they may be found guilty of a crime. Courts are alarming places and all witnesses need help, whatever their age, to give evidence that is truthful and accurate. The need is for clear, simply-worded questions with time taken to ensure that they are understood and that the child has been prepared for the task of a witness.

Fantasy and lies

All children fantasise and day-dream and so do adults. Children may, for example, when reliving the attack on their mother, fantasise a happy ending. It does not follow that they are unable to tell the difference between fact and fantasy when describing a real event.[215] It is a matter of good practice to ask young children questions which establish whether they can distinguish truth from falsehood, stories from real life. We have found that, by asking clear, simple, non-leading questions during therapeutic sessions with children traumatised by witnessing the death of a parent, we can get detailed, valuable accounts of the tragedies.

Children as witnesses: current law (UK)

Until 1992, before being allowed to give evidence a child would be given a 'competency examination' by the judge, who had to form an opinion on whether the child did or did not understand the difference between truth and falsehood and the importance of telling the truth. Until recently, it was rare for a court to hear from any child under the age of 7.

The Criminal Justice Act 1991 (Section 52), drafted in response to improved knowledge and decreased prejudice about the competence of children, makes any child who is able to communicate in an intelligible way competent to give evidence in a criminal case. All children under 14 will now be asked to give evidence unsworn. This has the disadvantage that more younger children may be subjected to this ordeal, which must be balanced against their potential contribution to just decisions.

Ironically, the higher criminal courts are now likely to be more flexible, in theory at least, towards children as witnesses than are the civil courts. Thus the Children Act 1989, used in civil proceedings, while allowing young children to give unsworn evidence, does not get rid of the 'competency examination' described above.

In theory, a child could be compelled to be a witness either in civil or criminal proceedings. But in practice this is rare in civil hearings, since the rules of evidence would not allow pressure to be put upon a child. Under the ever-important principle that the best interests of the child are paramount, the court would refuse a witness summons or set it aside if it seemed more likely to harass or distress the child than to help the process of law. Judges or magistrates must decide whether a child may give evidence.

Reviews of recent research[52, 58, 75, 204] describe the study of accounts by children of events which, although benign in intent, are likely to be perceived as stressful or threatening, such as medical examinations or inoculations. Accounts remain accurate up to one year and, moreover, when children are asked leading questions designed to suggest that they may have been abused, these are resisted. The children stick to their own accounts. The necessary modification of law and courtroom procedure for the facilitation of children as witnesses will require the development of consistent codes of practice supported by regular staff training.[59]

When an adult may speak for the child

A child may speak indirectly to a court, through a private interview with the judge, or, more usually, by speaking to a guardian *ad litem*, psychiatrist, welfare officer or solicitor. An account of what the child has said to an adult – hearsay evidence – may be used in child protection and other hearings if a court decides that the hearing of this evidence is necessary to a child's welfare and safety. A child may be in more difficulty in criminal courts where there is a rule against hearsay since, where there may be a finding of guilt and the awarding of legal penalties, the law states that evidence must be heard and the witness, irrespective of age, must be available for cross-examination by a lawyer acting on behalf of the accused. This has made it particularly difficult to obtain convictions upon the evidence of children since, until 1988, the judge was obliged to advise a jury that a conviction could not be made on the unsworn evidence of a child or children in the absence of corroborative evidence;[208] this, in the case of many crimes of violence and sexual crimes within the home, was of course not available. Now, if the offence is a sexual one the court still has an obligation to warn the jury that there is danger in believing the uncorroborated evidence of a complainant (whatever their age). But a jury may now convict despite this warning if they are convinced by the evidence.

Children also have rights as to who may not hear their evidence. Civil hearings will be *in camera*, heard in private with no member of the public present and no reporters allowed. A court may remove from the hearing anyone who is likely to upset the child during the giving of evidence.

Video evidence

An increasing concern that children have rights to be heard in court has led to the establishment of an advisory group on video-recorded evidence chaired by Judge Pigot.[172] It has recommended that the evidence of children in criminal cases should be obtained in private by skilled interviewers, informally, ahead of trial and videotaped. These examinations would include a cross-examination on videotape which would replace the live appearance of the child in court.

Only part of this advice has been accepted. Video evidence from children is now admissible but there is a strict condition that the witness must attend court for live cross-examination. Although this may be by a live video-link or, where this is not available, the child may be protected from sight of the accused by a screen, there are great disadvantages. First, protection of this nature is at the discretion of the court and is not a right of the child. Second, such resources are not available in all courts and, however much the child is protected, there will be a considerable ordeal. Moreover, given current delays in criminal justice procedures, the examination in chief and the interview with the child, which should take place, according to Pigot, as soon as possible after the alleged crime, may be separated by a period of months from the court hearing at which cross-examination will take place. However, one advantage of the Criminal Justice Act is that, where formerly children in criminal cases might have to give evidence twice over (at the committal proceedings and then at the trial), they may now give evidence in the form of written transcripts of tapes of interviews at the earlier hearing, appearing in court for cross-examination only at the trial.

Police, social workers and other professionals are now collaborating to develop ways of interviewing child witnesses, and of recording those interviews, taking account of the rules of evidence. An overview of the pitfalls and difficulties which face child witnesses to criminal acts is available.[76]

A Royal College of Psychiatrists working party,[193] including Dame Elisabeth Butler-Sloss, Lady Justice of Appeal, when considering the evidence of children in criminal cases, made the following recommendations in 1996:

1   The use, where appropriate, of initial talks with the child and a careful written record of what is said. The adult hearing information in the first instance has the task of listening as uncritically as possible, reassuring the child that, despite inevitable misgivings, disclosure is the best course, and bearing in mind that a formal interview will have to be carried out. It is essential that an adult at this stage should not mistakenly assure a child that what they say will be held in confidence, while acknowledging the child's misgivings and fears.
2   The Committee recommend that the recommendations of the Pigot Committee, outlined earlier in this chapter, should be carried out in full.
3   Procedures must be improved to provide for early and full liaison between the agencies responsible in individual cases for the investigation and evaluation of allegations so that, in particular, children are interviewed appropriately.
4   The Committee consider that the earlier recommendation of the 1992 Memorandum[109] on video-recorded interviews should be modified. That Memorandum recommends that not more than one formal interview be carried out. Psychiatrists and lawyers accustomed to working with children, while recognising that those who compiled the Memorandum were concerned about repeated and intrusive interviews, now think that the pendulum has swung too far in the other direction and that it is not realistic to expect that children who have witnessed or been subjected to criminal acts will necessarily be able to talk about it in just one session.
5   The Committee consider that, where appropriate circumstances arise, specially-trained child mental health professionals should be permitted to interview children in the course of criminal investigations.
6   They recommend formal training, particularly in respect of age-appropriate communication with children, for those involved in criminal cases involving child witnesses.

In future we can hope that children will be treated more respectfully and interviewed more competently, and also that clear and audible videotapes will be made of critical interviews. Children may be helpful to criminal proceedings regarding the crimes they have witnessed, and should be able to contribute, according to their age and understanding, as the law requires, to the civil hearings at which their future will be planned. The recommendations of the Royal College of Psychiatrists are also relevant to the latter circumstances.

In a better legal world, children will be seen and heard. Due note will be taken of their skills as witnesses, of their knowledge, feelings and wishes. They will not be harassed or brow-beaten by those defending alleged criminal adults (as indeed may happen, alas, with adult witnesses). The principle should rather be that all witnesses, whatever their age, should be treated with respect and courtesy. In civil cases, children should contribute but decisions beyond their capacity should not be laid upon their shoulders. The paradox is that children should be protected by adults yet listened to by adults. Their capacities should be recognised and valued, yet undue burdens should not be laid upon then. There is a long way to go but English law is currently moving slowly in the right direction.

In short, we should listen to children, record what they say, take them seriously as witnesses and provide independent legal advisors who will speak on their behalf.

Part III

Learning from experience

Chapter 12

Research findings

Order gave each thing view.
(Shakespeare, *King Henry VIII*, I, i)

Introduction

Since the beginning of our project in 1986 up to 1993, when the first edition of this book appeared, we had personally seen 111 children from 53 families in which one parent killed the other. We had offered consultation to professionals dealing with children, families and other carers in 9 other cases involving 19 children. Overall, therefore, we had heard the stories of, and turned our minds to the difficulties for, 130 children from 62 families devastated by the loss of their parents in this cruel way. In 6 cases the mother killed the father; in the rest (56 cases) it was the father that was the assailant, the mother the victim.

We have now seen 425 children who have been affected by one parent's death at the hands of the other; most commonly, the father caused the mother's death; in only 22 families with 44 children altogether (around 10 per cent) did the mother kill the father.

The research described in this chapter is in two parts. The first, completed in 1993, is an attempt at quantifying the information on the circumstances of the children we had seen by that time and the impressions we gained from our clinical interviews. We did not use standardised tests or measures; we did not have a 'control group' with which to compare the children we have seen. The group of children was clearly heterogeneous, referred for different reasons (from crisis intervention, through assessment and treatment, to advice on where the child should live and what sort of contact there should be with the surviving parent). They were seen hours, days or years after their parent's death and with variable regularity thereafter. The children differ in age (see Table 12.1). Each child and each family is unique in their history and circumstances, in the particular set of relationships that shape their family. And yet the data do tell a story; patterns begin to become discernible.

For technical reasons we computer-analysed the data on 97 of the 111 children referred before 1993. This represented the findings from 45 of the 53 families seen. (In a few families some of the children had grown up and were not directly assessed by us. For this and other reasons our data are incomplete and percentages quoted do not always add up to 100.)

In the second project, we describe the findings, three years later, of a follow-up questionnaire survey of the referrers of the children included in the first study, to get some idea of how the children were doing in the longer term.

STUDY I

Results

The sample: sex and age

The group analysed consisted of 56 boys and 41 girls. Thirty-eight children (40 per cent) were aged 5 or under, about the same number were between 6 and 11, and close on 18 per cent (17 children) were in their teens when one of their parents died at the hands of the other (see Table 12.1). Out of the 45 families, 28 had a child under the age of 5 in it at the time of the killing. This is in keeping with the finding that marital satisfaction is at its lowest when there is a child of under 5 in the household, which is probably reciprocally related to the well-known finding that the more children under 5 there are in the family, the greater the risk of clinical depression in the mother.[43] A further hypothesis is that, as a group, the parents were fairly young, or at least early in their marriages when the killing took place. The age of the children when referred to us is presented in Table 12.2. (Patterns similar to those in Tables 12.1 and 12.2 are seen in figures drawn from a larger sample at a later stage in our work: see Tables 12.20, 12.21 and 12.22 at the end of this chapter.)

Parental authority/responsibility

(For definition of terms and discussion see Chapter 11, Appendix 2 and Glossary.)

For a third of the children, their surviving parent still had parental authority (13 per cent) or shared this authority with the local Social Services (21 per cent) at the time of referral to us. In two-thirds of cases, this right to make decisions on behalf of the child had been withdrawn from the surviving parent and was vested in the High Court (60 per cent) or in the local Social Services (69 per cent).

Table 12.1 Age at time of mother's death

Age	No. of children	% of children
< 5	38	40
6–11	39	41
> 12	17	18

Table 12.2 Age at referral

Age in years	No. of children
1	1
2	0
3	5
4	7
5	10
6	6
7	8
8	11
9	3
10	7
11	5
12	5
13	3
14	4
15	4
16	1
17	0
18	2
19	2

Note
This equates to 27% aged 5 or under, 48% between 6 and 11, and 25% between 12 and 19.

Ethnicity and religion

In one out of ten cases the parents differed from each other in their ethnic origins and in one out of twenty there were differences in religion between the parents. Sixteen per cent of fathers and 16 per cent of mothers were Asian; 18 per cent of fathers and 11 per cent of mothers were from other ethnic minorities. This compares with figures of 2.4 per cent Asians and 2.3 per cent other ethnic minorities in the general population.[102] In other words, Asians and other ethnic groups were over-represented sixfold in our sample. With regard to religion, 20 per cent of fathers and 15 per cent of mothers were Muslim. In the general population 4.5 per cent are Muslim (source: Muslim Cultural Society, personal communication.) Thus, as a proportion, there were four times as many Muslim families referred to us as would be expected. In half the families headed by an Asian Muslim man, the parents were first cousins. Our speculations regarding these findings are presented in Chapter 2.

Family constitution

In one in four families, the parents had been separated for more than a month at the time of the killing. A smaller number (16 per cent) had separated but for a shorter time. Where the parents had separated, the estranged parent (usually the father) managed to maintain regular contact in half the cases; in a quarter contact was irregular or non-existent; and for the other quarter we were not able to ascertain whether there had been contact or not. Perhaps surprisingly, 60 per cent of families were intact at the time of the killing. This is, however, in keeping with the observation that until recently relatively few women in violent relationships have left their partners.[233]

Family conflict and violence

There was long-standing conflict between the parents in two-thirds of the families, with the children likely to have witnessed violence between the parents in nearly half the cases. This is almost certainly an underestimate; in a quarter of the cases we did not know whether or not the children had previously seen one parent being violent to the other. We established that in only thirteen cases was there any evidence of physical abuse of the child. This finding is discrepant with findings from research on battered wives where the violence did not end in homicide (for example Jaffe *et al.*, 1990[111]), which shows a considerable overlap between the husband's violence to his wife and his violence to his children or at least to one of the children. It is not clear to us at this stage whether this has heuristic value, which should generate new hypotheses. It may imply, indeed, that, contrary to our expectations, the children we have seen have less in common with the children of mothers who are beaten but not killed. Perhaps, however, it is a distortion produced by seeking the information from the child and in the context of one parent having killed the other. Children, out of shame or because they blame themselves, will often hide the fact that they have been beaten by a parent.

Alliances

Only one in ten of the children were closer to the father than the mother before the killing. Given that most children were quite young at the time of the death, this is perhaps not surprising; younger children tend to be closer to their mothers. Indeed half were closer to their mother; some (7 per cent) had been close to both. In 30 per cent we could not establish clearly what the child's relationship with their parents had been like.

Of the 95 children, 40 had maternal grandparents closely involved with the family even before the homicide; 25 felt close to both sets of grandparents; 10 felt close to neither; and only for 5 children were the paternal grandparents those they felt closer to. This had implications for placement of the children after the loss of their parents and with regard to their vulnerability to further stresses. (A close confiding relationship with at least one adult outside of the immediate family (usually a grandparent) has been found to protect children against the stress of marital discord, separation and divorce.)[113]

Factors associated with the homicide

As in other similar studies, sexual jealousy, whether based on actual or imagined infidelity, was the motivation most commonly associated with the homicide (36 per cent). Other cited and sometimes overlapping factors include escalation of chronic violence (32 per cent), the partner's threat to leave (23 per cent), and alcohol abuse (20 per cent). Definite evidence of formal mental illness, as indicated by the sentence at their trial, was a factor in 14 per cent only (6 cases).

Whereabouts of surviving parent

At the time of our assessment, 13 of the surviving parents were still on remand, 10 were serving sentences for murder, 11 for manslaughter; 9 had served time for manslaughter but had already been released, one had committed suicide and one was detained in a psychiatric hospital. The verdict of manslaughter was twice as common as that of murder.

Witnessing of the killing

Twenty-four of the 95 children actually saw their parent being killed; a further 9 heard but did not see the final violence. Forty-six children (nearly half of all the children) either were not present at, were asleep during, or did not acknowledge their awareness of the killing. In the cases of 16 children, whether the child had witnessed the killing could not be established.

Crisis intervention

Within weeks of the killing, only one in five children had been offered a crisis intervention, which according to our then definition meant a 'critical incident debriefing' (see Chapter 2).[150] In most cases we relied on others to say whether and to what extent this had occurred. In three cases in which we did the de-briefing ourselves, none went on to develop post-traumatic stress disorder in spite of witnessing the full horror of their mother's death. However, this effect of crisis intervention in preventing PTSD could not be demonstrated statistically on the figures available for the sample as a whole. Even when entered into a regression equation with age of the child at the time of the killing and whether the child witnessed the killing, it was not a significant influence on whether PTSD was present at the time of the assessment. Perhaps the crisis interventions made were not sufficiently skilled or intensive. Perhaps in part this lack of an association statistically could be attributed to the relatively small number of children offered a crisis intervention and to the fact that the time of assessment after the killing was variable and was not taken into account in a controlled way. More of the 40 per cent seen later than a year after the killing had not had a crisis intervention and did not have symptoms of post-traumatic stress compared with those seen earlier. This requires further statistical analysis and additional data. In fact the only proper way to evaluate the protective and/or ameliorative effect of crisis intervention debriefing is in a controlled prospective study. So far no satisfactory study has been done. The methodological and other issues involved in trying to demonstrate the efficacy of this treatment have been reviewed by McFarlane[147] and by Raphael, Meldrum and McFarlane[187] and this process must be continued.

What and whether the child was told

We were not always clear what the child had been told about the killing and by whom. Twenty-nine were presumed by their carers to know what had happened; 36 were told within a week (usually by a social worker), 9 were told later (often by a member of a child psychiatry team) and 13 had still not been told that their father had killed their mother, at the time of our assessment. Only very rarely was the child given this information by a relative. Our enquiries revealed that for nearly half of the children discussion or questions about the death of their mother at their father's hands were explicitly or implicitly forbidden or at least discouraged by surrogate parents. One in three had neither participated in any of the funeral rites nor had they visited the grave of the deceased parent. In only one in ten was mourning recognised and actively supported.

Conflict between kin

In a third of cases the two sides of the family, maternal and paternal kin, were actively hostile to each other. In fact this probably represents the majority of the families in which there was contact between the maternal and the paternal kin. In only very few of the families where contact continued had they come to terms with the events in a way that did not expose the children to what was tantamount to a continuation of the marital conflict by proxy (see Chapter 6). In one case this was achieved by the maternal grandparents coming to the father's defence and agreeing that their daughter's behaviour had been extremely provocative, even as a teenager while living at home.

Placement: where the child went to live

More than half of the children went to live with relatives straight after the killing: 35 per cent to someone from the deceased mother's family (usually the maternal grandparents), 17 per cent to the father's family (again, usually the grandparents). About a third went to foster-parents, the occasional child went to a friend of the family or a neighbour, and ten children from three families were found places in children's homes (see Table 12.3). (The more children there are in any one family, the more difficult it becomes to place them all together other than in a children's home.) At least three-quarters moved on from their first placement within the first year. Most of these moves were planned in the child's interests, although in one in six cases the children were moved because the placement broke down. Some of the most severely affected, and hence the more difficult-to-look-after, children ended up in children's homes. It is not clear from the data whether it is cause or effect that determines the greater difficulties of

Table 12.3 Placement of children

Immediate placement	No. of children	% of children
Maternal relative	33	35
Paternal relative	16	17
Friend	8	9
Foster-parent	26	28
Children's home	10	11

those who ended up in children's homes, especially when compared with those who were living with mother's family (significantly different at the $p = 0.04$ level).

At the time of our assessment, at varying lengths of time after the death, 40 per cent of the children were staying with kin, 26 per cent with mother's family and 14 per cent with father's. Almost 40 per cent were with foster-parents and 20 per cent were in children's homes, other placements being unavailable or having broken down (see Table 12.4). For most children, where they were living at the time of the assessment was the place that had been home to them for the longest time since their parent's death. Just over 40 per cent had had the one placement only; about the same number had had two moves to deal with (in most of these cases to an emergency placement and then to a planned placement). However, when analysing these figures it is important to bear in mind that the assessment took place at various times after the killing. That children seen relatively soon after the killing had had just one placement or perhaps two is not remarkable but it does introduce a bias, which makes the early picture too optimistic. Nevertheless thirteen children had already had three or more moves of home, which in itself is high but especially so for children already traumatised and who were vulnerable and needing stability more than most.

Table 12.4 Placement at time of assessment

Placement at time of assessment	No. of children	% of children
Maternal relative	24	26
Paternal relative	13	14
Foster-parent	34	37
Children's home	18	20

Contact with the surviving parent

Only half of the children had seen the surviving parent by the time of our first meeting. Again the timing of the first assessment in relation to the killing needs to be borne in mind. Nearly half did not wish to see the surviving parent, and for only a third was contact regular. One in five children had seen their remaining parent, usually the father, in prison but had discontinued this. Children were most likely to have seen their surviving parent in prison if they were living with foster-parents; this was least likely if they were living with maternal kin (p = 0.02). Children with PTSD were less likely to be in regular contact with the surviving parent (p = 0.04). This may reflect their abhorrence or fear of the parent, since children who witnessed the killing were much more likely to develop PTSD (see later), or it may be a distortion of the picture since the children with PTSD were more likely to have been seen within a year of the killing before regular contact could be established. Certainly, having been exposed to chronic violence between the parents did not lead to the child seeing the incarcerated parent less. Statistically, if anything, the opposite was true (p = 0.05), leading to the speculation that children who witness violence between their parents may over time adapt by taking on the parental role. Taking care of their parents' needs, even to the exclusion of their own, and seeing their surviving parent more often than other children, if indeed this is the case, may be a learned compulsion to protect and care for the parent(s).

Psychiatric sequelae for the child

Quantifying the mental health costs of these events for the indirect victims, the children, is complex, depending not only on the direct effect of the traumas and losses but also on pre-existing vulnerability or psychopathology (about which we had very little information in most cases), and on the effects of their current circumstances and relationships on their ways of coping. To simplify the analysis, we used problem or symptom categories rather than isolated symptoms, or formal psychiatric diagnosis. Because some problems tend to occur early (for example symptoms of post-traumatic stress disorder) and some later (for example identity problems), the timing of the assessment influences the rate of recorded symptoms. Symptoms that occur early and then recede and symptoms that only emerge later on will be underestimated. Because there was no suitable control group, the comparisons between different affected groups lend themselves better to inferences than to conclusions. Except for the relationship between crisis intervention and PTSD, we are not able to measure the effects of our other interventions; to do so would require a 'no treatment' comparison group, something that seems to us clearly unethical. The analysis we can do relies on 'naturally occurring experiments' only. The results convey only impressions, glimpses of the overall picture.

PTSD

So far what we have recorded is that a quarter of the children showed moderate or severe symptoms of PTSD, another quarter had mild or few symptoms only, often with traumatic nightmares as a single symptom especially in younger children, and just under a half had no residual symptoms of PTSD or had not had PTSD at all (see Table 12.5). Children who had witnessed the killing were much more likely to develop PTSD (p = 0.001) (Table 12.6); the child's age, sex and whether they had a crisis intervention did not add to the prediction.

Table 12.5 Children showing PTSD

Children showing PTSD	No. of children	% of children
Severe	5	5
Moderate	19	21
Mild	20	22
None	41	45

Table 12.6 The relationship between the child witnessing the killing and the development of PTSD symptoms (p = 0.001)

	PTSD	No PTSD
Witnessed killing	26	7
Did not witness killing	18	28

Externalising and internalising behaviour and emotionality

Nearly 60 per cent had behavioural problems (externalising behaviours), around 40 per cent in the moderate or severe range (see Table 12.7). Children in foster-placements were less likely to have behavioural disturbance while children in children's homes had significantly more (p = 0.015) when compared with children living with relatives of their mother. Which relatives the children lived with (the father's or mother's) seemed to make little difference on this criterion (see Table 12.8). This was statistically significant also when entered into a regression equation with age, sex and exposure to previous family violence, none of which added to the prediction. Neurotic symptoms, like phobias or obsessions, or mood disorder ('internalising symptoms'), with a moderate or severe extent, were present in 40 per cent of the children (Table 12.9), with two-thirds judged to be moderately or highly emotional and a quarter thought to be over-controlled or constricted in their emotional range. Less than one in ten were thought to have emotions which were normal in both expression and range (see Table 12.10). Although almost as many boys as girls were thought of as being more emotional than the average child, there were relatively fewer girls with normal emotional expression (Table 12.11). Thus, overall, girls are more likely to be highly emotional (p = 0.02). There was a slight trend in this direction too for children with 'internalising symptoms' (p = 0.1) (Table 12.12). Children with these neurotic symptoms were also more likely to have been exposed to previous

Table 12.7 Externalising behaviour

Externalising behaviour	No. of children	% of children
Severe	10	11
Moderate	23	26
Mild	19	22
None	36	41

Table 12.8 The relationship between the placement of the child and behavioural disturbance ('externalising') (p = 0.015)

Present placement	No. of children showing externalising behaviour	No. of children not showing externalising behaviour
Maternal kin	11	13
Paternal kin	8	5
Foster-parents	14	20
Children's home	16	2

Table 12.9 Internalising behaviour

Internalising behaviour	No. of children	% of children	
Severe	6	7	40%
Moderate	30	33	
Mild	29	32	52%
None	18	20	

Table 12.10 Emotionality

Emotionality	No. of children	% of children
Highly emotional	21	23
Moderately emotional	39	43
Constricted and over-controlled	21	23
Low emotionality	6	7
None	3	3

Table 12.11 The relationship between the sex of the child and emotionality (p = 0.02)

	More emotional than average child	Not more emotional than average child
Females	32	7
Males	28	20

Table 12.12 The relationship between the sex of the child and 'internalising' behaviour problems (p = 0.1)

	Internalising behaviour	No internalising behaviour
Females	29	10
Males	36	20

Table 12.13 The relationship between exposure to previous violence in the family and later 'internalising' behaviour problems

	Internalising behaviour	No internalising behaviour
Family violence	31	17
No family violence	14	3

Table 12.14 The relationship between internalising behaviour problems and discouragement from speaking about the mother's death (p = 0.1)

Mother's killing	Internalising behaviour	No internalising behaviour
Taboo	17	10
Not taboo	38	20

inter-parental violence (again a slight trend only: see Table 12.13), and to feel that talking about their mother's death was discouraged (p = 0.1) (Table 12.14).

Academic performance

More than half of our cases had had a noticeable deterioration in their school performance. Only thirteen children (15 per cent) continued to do as well after the loss of their parents. One-third of the children had either not started school or could not be assessed because we had insufficient information (see Table 12.15).

Table 12.15 Academic deterioration

Academic deterioration	No. of children	% of children
None	13	15
Some	38	43
Marked	8	9

General health

A quarter had health problems which were thought to be psychosomatic.

Identity problems

Nearly half of the children tended to be victimised in their peer-groups, with only 15 per cent showing persistent aggression or bullying of any significance. Very few showed sexual identity problems but we would not have expected to elicit any acknowledgement of such problems in an initial assessment interview. In any event it is a problem which would tend to arise later. Nearly one in ten were thought to be false or excessively superficial in their relationships. Although more children who were regarded as excessively passive in their interpersonal relationships came from families in which there had been long-standing violence between the parents, this did not achieve statistical significance ($p = 0.17$). Boys were as likely to be regarded as passive as girls. Children who were regarded as bullying were no more likely to come from families in which there had been chronic violence, but there were four times as many male bullies as female bullies ($p = 0.01$).

Attachment problems

A quarter of the children were known to have a significant degree of difficulty in their relationships with their attachment figures, indeed in their capacity to attach at all. Over 30 per cent were under-attached to both their foster-mother and foster-father, although for some this may have related more to the brevity of their association than to a more enduring incapacity to form meaningful and secure attachments. Surprisingly few showed anxious, insecure patterns of attachment; 40 per cent had no discernible attachment problems. Aided mourning (a concept used mainly at the time of assessment implying that the child had participated in funeral rites and/or visited the grave) did not by itself reduce the risk of attachment problems.

Comment

Most of the associations analysed were not statistically significant. That is not to say that the factors we examined were insignificant. Perhaps the most important thing the statistics tell us is that individual children were in the main more different than they were alike. This is frustrating for the empirical researcher, but for the clinician it is confirmation that sound practice should continue to be rooted in attention to the uniqueness of the child and the particular circumstances, within the wider common context.

STUDY II

Method

Every professional referrer (in most cases, the allocated social worker) of the forty-five families in the original cohort was sent a twelve-item questionnaire for each child in the family we had originally assessed. A reminder letter was sent out after three months, in some cases followed by a telephone call. Data was analysed using the statistical package of the SPSS with chi-squared analysis of association.

All children had had their initial assessment with our service more than eighteen months before follow-up (the median was three-and-a-half years but with a range of nineteen months to fifteen years). This meant that many of the children had not yet reached adolescence.

Results

Response rate

About three-quarters (74 per cent) of the referrers returned our questionnaires. The follow-up information we requested was not always available to the respondents and we ended up with useful but incomplete data on 61 children from 33 families whom we had assessed, and in some cases treated.

Characteristics of non-responders

The children lost to follow-up (n = 34) were not significantly different from those we were able to follow up with regard to age or whether they had witnessed the killing. Most successfully followed up were the children who were at the time of the assessment living in children's homes or other residential institutions – questionnaires were returned on 15 children out of a total of 18 (83 per cent). We lost contact with 8/13 who had been staying with paternal relatives at the time of our original assessment (61 per cent), 10/24 who had been with maternal relatives (41 per cent) and 16/34 who had been with foster parents (47 per cent). It was not possible, from an examination of the case notes, to determine where six children in the follow-up sample were living at the time of the assessment.

Placements

At the time of assessment there were more children living with mother's relatives (26 per cent of the original sample) than with father's (14 per cent); 37 per cent were in foster-care and 20 per cent were in children's residential establishments. At the time of follow-up about one-third of children (N = 21) were living with their mother's relatives, 16 per cent were with father or his relatives (N = 6 and = 4 respectively), and nearly half were not living with relatives (26 per cent were in long-term foster-care (N = 16), 8 per cent (N = 5) had been adopted and 15 per cent (N = 9) were in a residential home or living independently).

Only about half the children (30), on whom follow-up data is available, were in the same placement as they had been in at the time of our original assessment. Fourteen children (about a quarter) had had more than one change of placement after the assessment. Twenty-nine children (that is nearly half of this sample) had had three or more placements after the homicide of their parent (see Table 12.16).

Table 12.16 Children with three or more placements since death of parent

No. of placements	No. of children	No. of families
3	15	8
4	6	4
5	6	3
6	2	2
Total:	**29**	**17**

Of the first placements that became permanent, 69 per cent were placements with the mother's kin. In all of these cases, the mother was the victim (see Table 12.17).

Table 12.17 Children who had had one placement only

	No. of children	No. of families
With mother's kin	16	9
With father's kin	1	1
With long-term foster-parents	6	2
Total:	**23**	**12**

Children who were in foster-care or in adoptive placements at follow-up had had more placements than others, although the only significant difference within this domain was between the number of placements of those in foster-care or adopted, and those in the mother's family. Our early involvement did not necessarily reduce the number of placements.

Contact with the thirty-one surviving parents (perpetrators)

One-third of the perpetrators were convicted of murder and one-half of manslaughter. Three were detained under the Mental Health Act and in two cases the outcome was not yet determined. One parent committed suicide. Of those convicted, one was released on appeal and one died in prison of a heart attack. All of those convicted of murder received the mandatory life sentence, but only four of those convicted of manslaughter received a sentence of more than six years. Those not receiving life sentences rarely served more than a few years before being released on licence. In two out of the three cases in our original cohort where the mother had killed the father, the mother was convicted of murder. Both had suffered chronic violence from the husbands they eventually killed. (Chapter 7 discusses additional cases.)

At the time of the follow-up, sixteen of the convicted parents had been released (all fathers). In three families, the children (N = 6) were now living with their father. Five of these six children were boys. In one other case, a daughter (living independently at follow-up) had lived with her father for a while but eventually had to be moved because of his violence. Of the other thirteen sibling groups whose fathers had been released, only two had regular contact with him, and both these sibling groups were living with long-term foster parents. The remaining eleven sibling groups had infrequent or no contact. Of these, seven were living with maternal kin, two in a children's home, one with foster-parents and one was living independently.

The overall pattern of contact with the perpetrator at follow-up (including with the parents still incarcerated) revealed that children with frequent contact were all living with long-term foster-parents. All the children living with maternal kin had no, or no regular, contact. For the two sibling groups (n = 4) living with paternal relatives, contact was infrequent or had ceased. (It must be said that this latter finding is at odds with what we found in our original study and subsequently with the much larger number of children we have seen, where the children living with paternal relatives are almost inevitably in contact with their fathers.)

Psychological outcome for the children

Our intervention was designed to clarify for the child what had happened to the parents, and, if they had witnessed the killing, either to intervene specifically to try to prevent the onset of post-traumatic stress disorder, or to begin therapy for established post-traumatic symptoms (usually along the lines suggested by Pynoos and Eth[180]). If the child did not witness the killing, we would begin the process of bereavement counselling as described in Chapter 3. We tried to arrange for this to be continued by local professionals if the child lived far from our clinic.

In the follow-up we wanted to get a rough idea about the children's adjustment in the longer term. We asked whether, in the referrer's view, the child/children had benefited from our brief intervention. They felt that more than half the children had shown some improvement (see Table 12.18). The intervention had made things worse for only one child.

Table 12.18 Referrer's view of outcome of brief intervention

Much improved	Improved	No change	Worse	Not known
18 (30%)	16 (26%)	17 (28%)	1 (2%)	9 (14%)

We were particularly interested to know whether the child felt freer to talk more openly to their carers about their parent's death following our brief intervention, and indeed this was the case in the majority where the referrer was able to form a view (56 per cent). Twenty-eight children (46 per cent) could talk more openly to carers about their parent's death, six (10 per cent) could not. In twenty-seven (44 per cent) the referrer had insufficient information to give an opinion. This was especially the case with the children living with their father (0/6), and to a lesser extent those living with mother's family (12/21.) If we take only those cases that the referrers could comment on, then it would seem that, through our intervention, four out of five children (82 per cent) were enabled to talk about their parent's death.

After our assessment we recommended specific psychiatric treatment in most cases, but, as far as we could establish, only half (twenty-nine children, 49 per cent) actually received further therapy. Our method of data collection did not allow us to ascertain whether those who did not have further intervention needed it as much as those who had received it. The children living with their father were the least likely to be in receipt of psychiatric or therapeutic follow-up (only one out of six).

Witnessing the killing

In our original study we had found that there was a strong correlation between witnessing the killing and the development of post-traumatic stress disorder in the child. Twenty-six of the 33 children who witnessed the killing developed PTSD, whilst only 18/46 who did not witness it developed PTSD. Many of the latter children who had PTSD at assessment had witnessed serious domestic violence before the killing occurred. Children who had witnessed the killings were more likely to have more treatment sessions with us. Nevertheless children who witnessed the killing of their parent had more persistent behavioural problems at follow-up ($p < 0.05$), according to the referrers (approximately 80 per cent item response rate). There was also a trend for such children to have more emotional problems ($p = 0.12$) (see Table 12.19).

Children who had post-traumatic stress symptoms at assessment were not more likely than their counterparts without post-traumatic stress symptoms to have overt emotional problems at follow-up, according to the referrers' observations. Children who had witnessed the killing of their parent were also not any more likely to be in receipt of psychiatric follow-up. Of the 33 children in the original sample who had witnessed the killing of a parent, 15 had more than three

Table 12.19 Continuing problems in children who witnessed killing

		Behaviour problems		Emotional problems	
		Yes	No	Yes	No
Witnessed killing:	Yes	10	13	8	13
	No	4	21	4	19
	Total:	**14**	**34**	**12**	**32**
		p < 0.05		p = 0.12	

sessions with us, which included a treatment component; whereas of the 53 who had not witnessed the killing, only 5 got more than three sessions (p = 0.06).

The effect of further local psychiatric intervention did not appear to make a significant difference to the outcome. The length of time that had elapsed between the homicide and the assessment did not appear to affect outcome in this small group.

Referrers thought that 'treatment' (that is, more than three sessions) positively affected the capacity of the children to speak freely about their parent's death to their carers. (p = 0.001). Overall, of those children in the follow-up sample on whom we have sufficient information regarding the original contact with our service (n = 44), 15 had three or more therapeutic sessions. Most of them (14/15) were rated by the referrer as having improved whereas only 16/29 children who had fewer than three sessions showed an improvement. Of the 13 who did not seem to improve following our intervention, 12 had had the assessment component only. Thus, those children who received an assessment interview plus a more formal therapy component were significantly more likely to show improvement discernible to the referrer, compared with children who received assessment only, even if that included a brief intervention.

Placement effects

We examined aspects of outcome for the children according to where they were living at the time of our initial assessment and, separately, at follow-up. In all three cases in which the mother had killed the father, the children were placed with non-related carers.

At follow-up we found that children who had, at assessment, been living with the perpetrator's family were doing proportionately worse, with regard to behavioural and emotional problems, than children in any other placement.

With regard to peer relationships, we identified children at either end of a spectrum – of pronounced bullying or victim behaviour – as having a poor outcome. On this dimension, the children who were in foster-families at the time of assessment were doing much worse than the other groups at follow-up (p = 0.05). Children living with their mother's family at assessment were rated as better socially adjusted with peers than children placed with their father's family, but this did not reach statistical significance. The children who were in children's homes when we first saw them had tended to come from large sibling groups who could not be placed together elsewhere. It may be that being kept together helped these children to get on with others better than the children in foster-care.

Children living with their mother's family at the time of follow-up had improved in their behaviour and emotions significantly more following our intervention than children living with their father's family (p = 0.0001), at least in the referrers' opinion. So had the children in foster or adoptive care (p = 0.005). This might call into question – at least in these unusual circumstances – the received wisdom embodied in the Children Act 1989 which assumes that, when children cannot live with their parents, it is better for them to be placed with family members than outside the family.

Children living with the victim's family (in all cases, the mother's family) at follow-up were doing much better with regard to peer relationships than children in foster-care, and both groups were doing better than children in the perpetrator's family, although this difference does not reach statistical significance. Children in adopted placements were doing better than children still in foster-care. If this finding is confirmed by further studies on our larger number of cases, then the results are important for long-term planning for these children.

Relationship to family violence

Only one of the children in our follow-up group for whom data was available had not been exposed previously to domestic violence. The analysis of the associations between exposure to family violence before the homicide and subsequent findings was therefore not possible. However, it is worth noting that only between one-quarter and one-third of these children, who were known to have been exposed to previous domestic violence, were seen to be having overt problems with regard to their behaviour, their emotions and their social identity formation. Most (that is between two-thirds and three-quarters) did not (N = 38). This argues for significant resilience, if the referrers were accurate and reliable in these observations.

Relationships with new carers

When one parent kills the other, the child loses both parents. In most cases this means the child becoming used to new surrogate parents. The child's assumptions about the availability and reliability of carers are disorganised by the violence and the sudden loss and disruption of their caring environment and relationships. We wished to evaluate how the traumatic bereavement had affected the child's care-eliciting and care-seeking (attachment) behaviour, as reflected by the child's capacity to form meaningful relationships. In our original assessments, we had histories and descriptions which pointed to the fact that 30 per cent of the children had not formed meaningful relationships following the killing. We speculated that for some that was possibly an effect of time – not being with their substitute carers long enough to attach. We asked the referrers to rate the children at follow-up on this criterion on a 10-point visual analog scale, with one end of the scale defined as 'forms meaningful relationships' and the other end as 'superficial detached relationships'. We regarded a rating of 7 or above as indicative of problems in this domain. In more than half of the cases, the referrers did not feel able to answer this question (although it was not clear whether this was to do with the subjectivity of the question, or whether the referrers did not know enough about the child's relationships).

Of the children on whom we have data (38), 5 were not rated as having attachment-related problems at assessment. Of these, 4 continued to have no problems at follow-up, and only one child having no problems initially was seen to have problems at follow-up. Of the other 18 children, considered to have had attachment problems of some kind when seen by us at assessment, about half continued to have some problems, while half were thought by the referrers to have no significant relationship problems. Of the children with attachment-related problems at assessment, those whom we thought showed elements of avoidant attachment[3] had the least favourable outcome. They were more liable to go on to develop problems of social identity formation (that is becoming victims or bullies).

On only 28 of the 61 children did we have information both on their attachment at assessment, and their peer relationships at follow-up. Six of the 10 children who appeared to be avoidant at assessment had peer-relationship problems at follow-up, while only 4 out of the remaining 18 were regarded as problematic ($p = 0.018$).

Where the children were living at the time of the original assessment did not seem to be associated with the children's capacity to form meaningful relationships. However, placement at follow-up did seem to have some correlation ($p = 0.01$). Compared with children in foster placements, children in the mother's family and children living with paternal relatives were doing significantly less well ($p = 0.05$). To try to increase accuracy on this scale, children doing very well (0–3 on the scale were compared with children doing poorly (7–10 on the scale), and an intermediate category (4–6 on the scale) was excluded from calculation. According to the referrer's view then, children in either of the placements with relatives did not seem to form meaningful relationships as easily as children in foster placements or adoptive placements, and there seemed to be no particular difference, at least at a statistical level, between children living with mother's family or with father's family.

Children who return to their father's care

In the small group that returned to the father's care after his release from prison, and were living with him at follow-up (6 children from 3 families), very little information was available from the referrers. In some cases they were relying on the fact that the children had not come to their attention again to presume that there were no problems. They were usually denied access to the child when a supervision order expired. Most of the children who were returned to their fathers were not particularly disturbed or poorly functioning in our original assessment, but we have no information on the children from the referrers after their return to father's care. We have limited clinical experience after children return to a perpetrator's care. Of the 16 fathers who have so far been released, only 3 resumed the care of their child/children.

Our *clinical* experience with children living with the surviving parent (and this now includes some mothers) is that they tend to be 'very good' during the primary school period, but their rebelliousness, sexuality and individuation during adolescence may be experienced as extremely challenging by their perpetrator parent. In two cases at least, daughters aroused their father's jealous anger when they started taking an interest in boys, thus recreating the pathological dynamic which had led to their mother's death. They were removed into care when their father became violent to them. In another case, a teenage daughter re-united with her father to whom she had remained loyal while in the care of her paternal aunt, ran away when she was reminded of her father's proclivity for violence during an argument with his new wife. She developed flashbacks, which had been repressed before apparently, became anorectic and was admitted to a psychiatric unit. She did not return to live with her father. In another case, an 8-year-old girl went back to her father on his release, but was removed at 13 because he was sexually abusing her. Two adolescents, returned to their father's care after living with their paternal grandmother during the imprisonment, developed extreme anxiety and the elder complained of assault. 'Once a violent man, always a violent man', said the younger. At 14 and 12 years, they insisted on moving to live with relatives of their dead mother, remaining defiant and hostile to their father.

Discussion

The original research was done *post hoc* on a clinical sample. The children were interviewed within a clinical framework, not a research one. We felt that it would be unethical to approach the children and their carers directly for follow-up information without careful preparation. This would, in all probability, have also introduced a selection bias, since the children and carers who would have given their permission for a follow-up research interview would have been more likely to be those who felt that the children had benefited from our initial intervention. Although there are clear limitations to the methodology we chose – that is, a questionnaire to the referrers – we thought that this would give us a wider and more balanced sample. With hindsight, we have some reservations about the form of some of the questions we posed to referrers and recognise that we did not test the questions for reliability nor indeed for validity. This of course applies especially to the psychological outcome data. We did not anonymise the responses and, even though the correspondence was done through a research assistant and our covering letter encouraged frankness, some referrers may still have erred on the side of politeness when asked to evaluate the effect of our intervention! It was noticeable that respondents answered with least frequency the questions that required the most in-depth knowledge about the children, that is, regarding their openness with their carers about their mother's death, and the extent to which they were able to form meaningful relationships. It seems likely that they would have had less contact with those children who did not seem problematic, and this may have omitted from the responses (as 'don't know') some children whose adjustment was satisfactory.

However, the information about the nature of the children's placements and their contact with their surviving parent could be regarded as relatively hard data. We were able to confirm that, in the long term, these children did indeed have a greater number of changes of placement than was desirable or expected. Placement within the victim's family appeared to have advantages over placement with that of the perpetrator's, and was the most stable placement type. Surprisingly, since in the original sample the children in the children's homes were the most disturbed, at follow-up they appeared to be doing reasonably well in terms of their social adjustment – at least as well as, or better than, children in foster-homes. One of course needs to question whether there might be a greater degree of tolerance and false optimism on the part of their carers towards these particularly disadvantaged children growing up in a children's home.

In the majority of cases, referrers felt that our intervention had done some good (56 per cent) or at least no harm (28 per cent). This was important information for us since our brief intervention sometimes produced distress at the time. In the majority of cases, the assessments were requested by a civil court to help with decisions about where the children should live and with whom they should have contact and the frequency of contact. In many of the cases referred, the children travelled great distances; this made it difficult for us to offer treatment ourselves. We often questioned whether a brief 'preventive' intervention, without the opportunity to review and extend treatment, might do more harm than good. This did not appear to be the case. However, there was more observable improvement in children who had a longer period of therapeutic work.

We would tentatively conclude from our findings that, especially for children who witnessed the killing who have a high risk of developing PTSD, a brief crisis intervention is not sufficient, and the children should be assessed for their treatment needs following any brief intervention. The children who did best in our study were those who received longer therapeutic input, even though one might have predicted that these children would have done worse. We treat these results with caution, as internalising symptoms are notoriously unreliably rated by untrained observers.[13, 127] The children's post-traumatic symptomatology may well have continued in some cases without this having come to the attention of the carer or referrer. It would be necessary for a clinician to examine children in order to elicit symptoms and signs of PTSD as children rarely volunteer them, and indeed may actively conceal them from their carers in order to protect them emotionally. It was not possible using our method of data collection to ascertain whether PTSD persisted. Our clinical experience, and that of others in this field, is that PTSD is a chronic, remitting and relapsing psychiatric disorder which is difficult to treat once established. There is controversy about whether an early intervention following a disastrous event can prevent it.[187]

About 10 per cent of our larger clinical group are children whose mothers killed their fathers (41 children). Most of them have not yet reached adolescence but our clinical impression so far is that these children do well during their pre-adolescent years, becoming very difficult and defiant when peri-pubertal.

The children placed with relatives of the perpetrator are more likely to return to their surviving parent's care when he is released from prison. Even if the relatives are horrified at the actions of the father, and form a firm intention to rear the child to adulthood, they find it very difficult to resist the pressure from father for the child's return, and the child is more likely to return to his care. Our clinical experience is that the children who do return to their surviving parent's care on the whole do badly. When that option seems the 'least detrimental'[87] then it may help to recommend some statutory supervision.

Our finding from this study, that there was a persistence of avoidant attachment, especially in young children living with relatives, is likely to have significance for later mental health. Insecure attachment patterns have been described as ways for a child to deal with particular abnormal parenting situations and, although they may represent the only adaptation possible, they are maladaptive in that they do not prepare the child for successful adjustment in the world outside their families, and they are risk factors which increase the likelihood of later psychiatric disorders.[265]

The effects on these children of their traumatic bereavements appear to be that they may not be able to talk freely about the dead parent, are less likely to receive the therapy they need, and they fail to make secure attachments following the homicide and are more prone to develop disorders of attachment. These problems are compounded by the high number of moves of home and changes of carer that many of them have and by the resurgence of grief and anger when a perpetrator is released from prison.

The findings from this limited study do not enable us to make any definitive recommendations for practice and it must continue to be good clinical practice to approach each case on its merits. The findings that children are less likely to move frequently when placed with the victim's rather than the perpetrator's family, and are less likely to develop psychological problems, may help in decision making when the advantages and disadvantages of placement are otherwise fairly balanced. For this rather unusual group of children, thankfully rare, we do question the assumption, embodied in the Children Act 1989, England and Wales, that it is better for children to live with relatives when they cannot live with their parents. It is clear that our adopted group did well, and the foster-children also seemed to do well on a number of ratings, especially, according to the referrers, with regard to forming meaningful relationships.

Congruent with our clinical view, the findings from this study confirmed that for many of the children psychological problems were persistent. It was disappointing, therefore, to find that fewer than half of the children received any further therapy after they left our clinic. In some cases (as when the children returned to the care of the perpetrator parent), treatment was refused, but in most cases the lack of local child psychiatric resources was the reason.

Summary

A postal questionnaire was sent to the referrers of 95 children where one parent had killed the other, on whom data had been collected at the time of referral. The response rate was 64 per cent with data on 61 children. The main findings were as follows:

This young group of children experienced many changes of home and carer. Half of the children were living at the time of follow-up with unrelated carers. Of those living with relatives, the fewest changes of carer occurred when they were initially placed with relatives of the victim, rather than the perpetrator.

Most children had little contact with the surviving parent. They were more likely to have maintained regular contact if they were in care.

Children who had treatment sessions as well as assessment interviews appeared to have fewer problems on follow-up than those whose contact was briefer. This included the children who had witnessed the killing. About half of the children who had had a brief intervention were rated as being able to talk more openly to carers about the death of their parent, especially if the carers were unrelated to them. Those who had been adopted were most able to talk freely about the dead parent.

Few children received further therapy in their locality, even though it had been recommended in most cases.

At least half of the children had continuing, overt emotional and/or behavioural problems. Children who witnessed the killing were more likely to develop post-traumatic stress disorder, and were more likely to receive treatment, but were also more likely to have persistent emotional and behavioural problems at follow-up.

Children placed with the perpetrator's family did worse on ratings of overt emotional, behavioural and peer problems than did those placed with the victim's family, and the latter did worse than children living in non-related households, except with regard to getting on with peers.

Most children had witnessed domestic violence before the killing, but the majority were not having problems at follow-up, in the referrer's opinion.

Children assessed clinically as having attachment-related problems with their new carers were more likely to be having similar problems at follow-up.

Children living with relatives at the time of follow-up seemed to be having more difficulty in forming attachments than children living with non-related carers.

Children living with relatives of the perpetrator were more likely to return to their surviving parent's care. The clinical evidence is that they behave well as children but may show disturbance in adolescence only. The numbers of those in our sample who returned to their parents' care were too small to either verify or disprove this.

We conclude that, whilst good practice requires that each child and family is assessed on their merits, placement of these children with the victim's family appears to lead to fewer changes of placement than placing with the perpetrator's family; and that the treatment needs of these children, who carry an enhanced risk of developing emotional and behavioural problems, attachment disorders and problems of peer relationships, need to be given more consideration.

The work continues: additional data

Table 12.20 Age at time of parent's death

Age in years	No. of children whose father killed mother	No. of children whose mother killed father	No. of children whose parent killed the other
1	31	6	37
2	20	1	21
3	21	5	26
4	17	4	21
5	16	3	19
6	17	2	19
7	19	3	22
8	12	1	13
9	13	2	15
10	12	2	14
11	12	2	14
12	11	2	13
13	4	2	6
14	4	0	4
15	7	0	7
16	1	0	1
17	1	0	1
18	0	0	0
Total:	**218**	**35**	**253**

Note
This equates to 49% aged 5 or under, 38% between 6 and 11 and 13% between 12 and 18.

Table 12.21 Time elapsed between the killing and assessment

Seen at clinic	No. of children whose father killed mother	No. of children whose mother killed father	No. of children whose parent killed the other
Within one month of the event	31	12	43
Within one year of the event	99	9	108
More than a year after the event	51	14	66
Total:	**181**	**35**	**216**

Chapter 13

Planning services for bereaved and traumatised children

Small service is true service
while it lasts.
    (Wordsworth, 'To a child: written in her album', 1835)

SUMMARY

The children of violent families require a range of services that ought to be available for children in trouble within any civilised and caring society, only they need them more urgently, more intensively and perhaps for longer.

Up to two-thirds of children with severe behaviour problems could suffer in later life from depression, criminality, marriage break-up and other problems. Professional help could make a difference.[196] There is a lack of awareness in society at large about the nature of emotional and behavioural disturbance among young children, even amongst those who are deeply concerned for the coming generation.

The knowledge that we in the child and mental health professions have we tend to assume as general knowledge and this is not so. There is still a very common assumption that the troubles of childhood would pass, that children are resilient, that they forget. The truth is that children's lives are continuous. The scars of early childhood do enormous emotional damage in the present to the child. Then, because of the effect the damage has on the capacity to make relationships, they affect the child's future, and they impinge on the welfare of others. Severely emotionally damaged children therefore need highly skilled treatment and they are treatable. There are, inevitably, differences of opinion among the professional groups, differences about diagnosis, about treatment, about professional boundaries, but this is far outweighed by the consensus that exists about the conditions that children need for healthy development. It also needs to be widely recognised that the problems of disturbed or disruptive children inadequately helped quickly become the problems of society. Drug and substance abuse, vandalism, joy riding, public disorder, crime, homelessness and prostitution are not disconnected phenomena. They are the end result of systems which have failed to protect properly, to nurture, to educate. Family disruption and unhappiness precipitate the need for help with troubled children and the nature of society's response is crucial to their recovery.

(pp. 6–7)[14]

We lack adequate services in three areas: training, the planning structure of services and the resources spent on them. At present, within the United Kingdom, services for troubled children are provided by:

1   the health service, with its limited network of child mental health services staffed by psychiatrists and psychologists, psychotherapists and some social workers seconded from departments of social services;
2   child protection and child placement services, funded and managed directly by departments of social services;
3   education welfare and education psychology services, intended to help troubled children in mainstream schools, along with a range of special needs teachers, to provide specialist help for them, funded and serviced by departments of education.

These limited, specialist, somewhat invisible services must compete with other priorities. For example, in England and Wales, the Education Reform Act of 1988 and the Education Act 1996 have devolved management and responsibility directly to schools, leaving education departments with very limited facilities and cash for the provision of services to children with special needs. The Education Act (England and Wales) 1996 contains a code of practice on special educational needs, with rights of appeal against an education authority, but funds and professional skills remain at a premium. Social services departments do try to give priority to child protection but are very limited in their resources for preventive work or, where children have fallen through the net, for specialist family placement services. Residential care in the form of specialist children's homes, special needs residential schooling or psychiatric in-patient units is expensive in cash and manpower and the effectiveness is difficult to evaluate. The family justice system, which attempts to provide clear, appropriate and timely assistance to children who need legal protection (see Appendix 2), is likewise under-funded and the support services lack structure, training and tools for evaluation of the work attempted.

Voluntary services should never be relied upon as substitutes for state provision but may complement and extend it. They can and do provide:

1   innovation;
2   flexible local and national responses to unmet need;

3 active community involvement in providing timely effective help in a specific disaster or emergency;
4 support and counselling for victims and their families and for offenders and their families;
5 self-help groups for survivors of traumatic events;
6 specialist services for children such as therapeutic family placements and residential care which may be monitored and evaluated.

Voluntary services can raise funds, promote public awareness of specialised or minority problems, gather relevant information, put people with comparable difficulties in touch with one another and promote research.

There is urgent need for a policy for children in which all concerned agencies contribute equally and fully. The provision should include:

1 good support services to families in early childhood;
2 support to schools via education psychology, education welfare and special needs teaching;
3 effective psychological/psychiatric health services for troubled children and their families (these services must, with the consent of all concerned to the sharing of information, take their place as part of a coherent, consistent network of services to children, adolescents and families);
4 well-staffed, carefully monitored residential facilities for the minority of children who need this form of provision.[14]

At present, education, health and social services departments and the family justice system work in considerable ignorance of each other's skills, strengths and weaknesses. There is need for central government initiatives at ministerial level, such as interdepartmental committees to improve services for troubled children.

For our children, who have been through private and personal disasters, it would be appropriate to apply what is known of disaster mental health programmes. A series of disasters, together with the Gulf War and continued fear of major terrorist action, has led to a reappraisal of national and local disaster planning.

In 1989 a Disasters Working Party was funded and set up by the Department of Health with members representing voluntary services, the Department and the range of local authorities. Its terms of reference were to consider lessons to be learned from recent major disasters and to consider:

1 what steps should be taken to provide social and psychological support in the aftermath of such disasters;
2 how best to achieve co-ordination among agencies in the arrangement of the necessary support;
3 how the lessons learned from recent disasters might be disseminated;
4 the setting up of information systems.

The report, *Disasters: Planning for a caring response* (the Allen Report),[64] provides valuable lessons for domestic as well as public disasters. Its guidelines for children are relevant to violence in the family. Workers involved in helping should keep the following in mind:

1   Children, especially young ones, should be protected from frightening sights and sounds which are distressing even to adults but which affect children even more deeply and adversely. (This is difficult to achieve, particularly where violence is unforeseen, but the aftermath of domestic violence – police sirens, flashing lights of cars and ambulances, forced entry to the home and the arrest of a parent – is among subsequent events which may be very frightening to children and this should be borne in mind by emergency services personnel.) *Notice the children* is good training advice.
2   All children, particularly those under 5, should be kept with familiar caregivers wherever possible. This of course is a difficulty where one family member has killed another but it may at least be possible to ensure that siblings are allowed contact with each other immediately after the crime, rather than separating them to prevent them discussing the evidence which they may give to police. Wherever possible, at least some familiar family member or neighbour should be sought to provide help through the emergency.
3   Where there is no available caregiver, a helper with some knowledge of child development should be allocated specifically to each child or family of children. This helper should try to keep the children informed and to answer or to anticipate the questions they may wish to ask.
4   All children involved in the disaster, including those not present but affected by death or injury or loss of familiar surroundings, should be screened for psychological problems immediately and over the next two or three months. Arrangements should be made for appropriate help.
5   Group or individual debriefing should be available but not insisted upon within hours of the disaster. Bereavement counselling should be available as necessary.
6   Group counselling for children may be appropriate.

One researcher has written:[171]

> There need to be disaster mental health programmes for children and adolescents with active involvement by psychiatrists and other mental health professionals who work with young people in the planning and delivery of preventive and treatment services. While disaster planning is relatively well advanced in developed countries, we have to remember that this is far from the case in the developing nations and regions of the third world, many of which are specially vulnerable to the effects of natural hazards and civil strife. Disasters themselves can never be eliminated, but their effects can be moderated by effective pre-disaster preparedness and well informed

post-disaster response, to both of which the providers of mental health services should be making a significant and growing contribution.

(p. 12)

If our society develops a range of educational, health and social services for troubled children and considers the impact of major disaster on children as well as on adults, a framework will be created in which a small but very important group of children, those who have experienced overwhelming domestic disaster, may have their needs identified and met more effectively than hitherto has been the case. In short, if we regard children within our society as a major resource and responsibility, our care of those in trouble will serve as a critical indicator of our progress towards civilisation. It was disappointing, therefore, to discover how few local authorities had taken cognisance of the Allen Report. A survey of the provision for psychological services for disasters made in 1993 found only three regional health authorities which had taken on board its recommendations.[2]

Specimen court reports

The primary report to a court should be that of the child's guardian *ad litem* which may be complemented and strengthened by reports from those with specialist knowledge of children's development and of social, educational and mental health needs. Reports should be prepared in the process of consultation between the relevant professionals (a child mental health service has skills in initiating this process). Reading, with permission from judge or magistrates, all the relevant material available to the court is complemented by interviews with children and key adults. The resulting report should help judges and magistrates in their task of making a decision after they have evaluated available options.

Each court report we prepare has a very clear framework.[24] We start by describing our qualifications and credentials, set out the reasons for the referral and list the documents which the court has allowed us to read by way of background information. Then we provide a lengthy and detailed account of the content of the assessment interviews. This is followed by a formulation which takes an overview of the history, the information given before the referral, the interviews and their outcome. We follow this with a recapitulation of the questions asked of us, our discussion of the options available, recommendations and a summary.

Each report is written on the understanding that it will be circulated to all the parties concerned, with permission of the court, and that the writer will be available at the court hearing. A decision may be made at this point by negotiation which sometimes takes place in the corridors and waiting-rooms adjacent to the court and includes all the parties and their representatives. The agreed plan is then presented to the court for evaluation and approval. Otherwise a judge or magistrates will hear all the available evidence, each party having the right to cross-examination of witnesses through their legal representatives. A framework for the preparation and writing of reports is available.[24]

The court must take into account the wishes and feelings of the child, ascertained according to age and understanding. The judge who makes the decision and everyone who presents evidence to the court must regard the welfare of the child as paramount.

The two reports that follow are not based on any individual child known to us but the stories told, and the opinions given, are likely to seem familiar to anyone involved with children who have lost one parent at the hands of the other. This is because the children, those who try to care for them, the courts who make decisions on their behalf and the professionals who attempt to help the courts in those decisions find themselves faced with common and recurrent dilemmas which create great anxiety and uncertainty for everyone concerned. The first report discusses a request for advice about the therapeutic and placement needs of children immediately after their loss. The second deals with a situation with which we are becoming increasingly familiar. The children, three years after their bereavement, are living with maternal relatives. Father has been discharged from prison after serving a sentence for manslaughter and wishes his son and daughter to return to his care.

Report 1: Psychiatric report on Susan, aged 7 years, and Andrew, aged 4 years

The father killed the mother and her female friend when the children were 6 and 4 years old. They are now living with Mr and Mrs K, foster-parents, in Loamshire.

We saw these children with their foster-parents and foster-sister Sandra (aged 8) and their social workers, Mr X and Mr Y, in March in order to prepare a report for the court. We were asked to determine the likely effect on the children in the long term of their remaining in their home area. We had a letter from the county solicitor which set out the circumstances of the children coming into care and being made wards of court by Mr and Mrs H, friends of the natural parents who are applying for care of the children. They were invited to meet us but we were told by the social worker that they had decided to withdraw from the case for the present.

We learned the circumstances of the deaths of the mother and her friend through the children's graphic drawings and descriptions. We understood from them that this was the first time that they had been asked to talk about their experiences and although they found it difficult it was clear that it was important to them to convey their experiences. Susan was able to draw, choosing a red pen, the position of her mother slumped by the chair and her mother's friend lying with a knife in her, and how she and Andrew had been outside the door after their father had left the house, and how she had run to a neighbour for help. Later, while in the waiting-room with one of our staff, Andrew had played a game in which some animals had torn tigers to bits while giraffes playing with their parents were hiding in different rooms, and had been able to talk about their bad memories of the frequent fights between their parents. Susan had been able to express some of her yearning and longing for a reunited family. We were also able to observe how Susan had to some extent assumed a mothering role with Andrew and how they were both able to turn very appropriately to Mrs K for some of their affectional needs.

Mr and Mrs K told us that the children had been staying with them for about six weeks and behaved like normal children. They were sleeping and eating well, although the children acknowledged that they had some bad dreams at times. Susan was making good progress at her school and was particularly close to their daughter Sandra. We noted that the Ks had a strong commitment to the children, and were thoughtful and sensitive people who were able to make use of the observations and advice that we offered to alter their handling of the children, in an impressive manner.

Both the foster-parents and the social worker had until now avoided talking with the children about their experiences, believing that it was better to leave it to the children to talk about it in their own time. However, we explained to them that the research evidence favoured helping children to express their feelings and to describe their experiences as soon as possible after the traumatic events, and that the work of Pynoos and others who had worked with children who had witnessed violence indicated that much of the post-traumatic stress disorder could be mitigated or prevented by such methods. We were able to demonstrate within the interview how getting the children to talk about their experiences was both possible and helpful for them.

Summary and recommendations

Susan and Andrew were present in the house when their father killed their mother and were in the same room as the mother's friend when she was killed. Although they had had a period of relative stability in the previous nine months, before that the family had led an unsettled existence with much marital violence and frequent separations. We had no details of the children's births and early development but they appeared to be developmentally within normal limits and we understand that Susan is progressing well at school. Their behaviour since they have been with the Ks has been normal and they do not appear to be symptomatic apart from some bad dreams.

However, it was clear that they had been given little opportunity to talk about their traumatic experiences or to begin the task of grieving for their dead mother. The funeral has not taken place, they are barred from entering their home and they have not retrieved any of their old possessions. It is unlikely that they will be able to start the task of mourning until they are securely placed in a permanent home. They need to express their grief and their anger (anger with their mother for leaving them and with their father for being the cause of their mother leaving them). These are painful and disrupting emotions that can only be expressed when the children are sure that the adults in their world can care for them, and that they can survive the pain. When it is made clear to them that the setting is a permanent one, then it will be both possible and necessary for them to receive help in remembering and coming to terms with their experiences. It is therefore urgently necessary for permanent planning for their future to be made. They were able to tell us of the many scenes of violence that they have witnessed between their parents. We cannot see it as being helpful to these children to return during their minority to the single-handed care of their father given those experiences and what his violence led to. We would therefore advise the court to consider planning for a permanent placement in substitute care and therefore to consider adoption in the long term as the least detrimental solution for the children.

We consider that it would be helpful for the children to be allowed to settle in their home area. This will ensure continuity of schooling, friendships and an opportunity to begin the work of recollecting and working through their experiences. In their area they are known to many people who cared about their mother and there is a fund of goodwill and community caring. This has been exemplified by the willingness of the Ks to come forward as foster-parents and assume their care. We recommend that their social worker begins to make a life story book for the children which they should help him to compile and that as soon as is possible the children are taken back to the house and encouraged to talk about the traumatic events and of the previous years they spent together with their parents. They need to revisit their old home and school and should be encouraged to express their sad and angry feelings, perhaps by a letter to their father and later a visit. We would advise however that the visit does not take place before they are in their permanent home. We recommend that the assessment procedures for approving Mr and Mrs K as foster-parents are completed as soon as possible so that the uncertainty in the children's minds and their minds can be removed and they can give the children a sense of security. We have encouraged their social worker and the foster-parents to make use of a child psychiatric consultation to help them to work with the children over their traumatic experiences.

We have not met Mr and Mrs H but would have marked reservations about placing the children with people who were their father's acknowledged best friends because of the conflict of loyalties that might arise for them when the father comes out of prison.

It has been expressed to us that keeping the children in the area which may remind them of the pain of their loss might be cruel and that it would be kinder to give them a fresh start in a new area. The research evidence is that children do best in the long term if they have an opportunity to express and work through their painful feelings and that this is aided by reminders of the events, providing that the experiences can be tempered by the presence of a trusted adult. There is therefore in our opinion no disadvantage to the children in remaining in their home area and there may be advantages. We would reiterate the need for permanency planning for these children during their minority and for some speed in effecting a permanent placement. We would be glad to remain available to their social workers and carers in any capacity they care to use.

Comments

This is a case where the father killed the mother and her friend in the children's presence. Although the two psychiatrists' brief was to advise about which area the children should reside in, it proved important to enable those caring for them to help the children to express grief and begin the task of mourning. This was started during the consultation and freed the foster-parents and social workers to broach the hitherto taboo subject.

Report 2: Psychiatric report on John, aged 14 years, and Jane, aged 12 years

Background information

John and Jane Doe were respectively 10 and 8 years old when their father strangled their mother with a scarf. On the day of the killing the children were on a weekend visit to their mother's mother, where they often spent Saturday and Sunday, and so they saw neither what happened to their mother nor her body after death. They heard of the killing from police who came to their grandmother's house. They were told that their father, having killed his wife, had sat alone with the body for two hours and then had gone to the police station to confess to the deed.

Their grandmother offered the children a permanent home. She was a 64-year-old widow in good health and her offer was seen by all to be the most suitable arrangement available, particularly as she lived quite near the home of her dead daughter, which meant that the two children could continue to attend their local schools.

Mr Doe, the children's father, was remanded in custody to await trial. He agreed that the children should live with his dead wife's mother. Although a social worker visited the home on a few occasions to see that all was going well, and the grandmother was approved as a foster-parent so that financial help could be given to her, no court order was made concerning the children. They remained in their father's guardianship.

The family had lived in a council house which was vacated; the children's personal clothes and possessions went to their grandmother's home. No claim was made for criminal injuries compensation. Mr Doe was charged with murder and denied this but later, on the advice of his solicitor, changed his plea to guilty to a charge of manslaughter. In his defence, he said that his wife had been having an affair and that he had become enraged by this. This was reported extensively in the local paper and greatly grieved the children's grandmother who said that there was no shred of truth in it. Mr Doe's plea of manslaughter was accepted and he was sentenced to five years in prison. John and Jane visited him every month. They were accompanied by father's brother, their paternal uncle. Their grandmother said that she could understand that the children wanted to see their father but that she could not bear to have anything to do with the arrangements or to discuss their visits with John and Jane.

Mr Doe was released on parole two and a half years after his wife's death. At this point a bitter battle developed. He said that he had always expected that as soon as he was free John and Jane would go back to live with him. Their grandmother said that she had offered the children a home until they were grown up and could choose for themselves and that it never entered her head that they should or could live again with the man who had killed their mother. Mr Doe said that John and Jane had often told him, when visiting the prison, that they longed for the day that they could all be together as a family and he was backed up in this by the children's uncle.

The local authority social worker, involved in working with the children's grandmother as a foster-parent, was concerned at this situation and consulted her legal department. Care proceedings were begun and a guardian *ad litem* and solicitor were appointed to represent John and Jane so that a decision could be made about their best interests. The guardian asked our service for an expert opinion about the issues to be considered.

By now Mr Doe had been living out of prison, in a rented flat, for nine months; John was 14 years old and Jane 12. The children were interviewed together with their grandmother, separately and also together with their father, on a separate occasion since their grandmother refused to be in the same building at the same time as Mr Doe. The children were asked in interview to describe the manner of their mother's death. They did not know it. Their father had never discussed this with them during their prison visits and their grandmother had assumed that the social worker would have told them. The social worker explained that she thought the children had discussed this most intimate matter with the people most closely concerned and she had not wished to intrude.

Mr Doe had not expressed any guilt or remorse over his wife's death. He spoke of it as 'something we all have to come to terms with and recover from', as though he and their children had been through a difficult experience together which was not of their making. He had never spoken to John and Jane about his defence in court, that their mother was said to be an unfaithful and irresponsible person, and the children had never asked him about this. Mr Doe had never talked to the children about the possible feelings of their mother's mother. She in turn had not spoken of her feelings to the children, deciding that it would be unfair on them to burden them with her grief and rage when they themselves were wishing to see their father as peacefully as possible.

The report (in part)

Under circumstances such as these the legal requirement that children's wishes should be ascertained according to their age and understanding becomes burdensome and unrealistic of achievement. Neither of these children is in possession of a coherent account of their mother's death and at no point have they been debriefed, helped to mourn or to express their anger, grief and bewilderment. Indeed, it has been a requirement of them that they do not speak of such feelings lest they disrupt the apparently peaceful bond between themselves and their mother's mother, which she has established out of the kindest good wishes, and in order to enable them to see their father. They have maintained this situation lest they further hurt, grieve and distress her. Their visits to their father have similarly been sustained at a level of apparent calm and affection, the content, as described by all concerned, being accounts of the children's day-to-day activities and their school work. The break-up of their family, its cause and effects have never been a matter for discussion.

There is evidence that the façade began to crumble as soon as Mr Doe came out of prison. It was an unexpected event for the mother's family and they were given no advance notice of this, for them, unexpected and bewildering decision of the parole board. Indeed, their first knowledge of it was a telephone call from Mr Doe who had taken up lodgings within walking distance of the children and their grandmother. Since that time the children's grandmother has grieved not just anew but in some ways for the first time. By her own account her initial grieving was set aside in the service of the children and she made strenuous efforts to control and mask what she was feeling. This must have been additionally difficult given that her much loved husband had died suddenly and unexpectedly just one year before her daughter's unlawful killing. At the time of our interview with her, the grandmother was sleepless night after night, weeping in the small hours of the morning, seeing in her mind's eye her dead daughter and finding it difficult to concentrate on day-to-day tasks. She had lost about ten pounds in weight in the course of a few weeks. She said that the release of her daughter's killer from prison had re-awakened agonising grief and she repeated to herself again and again that he was alive and free whereas her daughter was dead.

Mr Doe, in complete contrast, describes himself as having put the past behind him and being ready to love and care for his children as he always did before. He says that he was a family man who worked only for his wife and children and that his sole wish now is to give John and Jane the good home which he knows would be in their best interests. His brother, the children's uncle, supports Mr Doe in this position and further presses his brother's claim to resume the care of John and Jane by pointing out that their mother was never a competent or suitable person to bring up children.

The lines are therefore drawn for a situation in which John and Jane cannot make choices and are likely to suffer severely. Indeed they are showing this stress.

John, formerly a very compliant, friendly and 'easy-going' boy has lately been very difficult in school, according to his grandmother and his class teachers. He has truanted several times, sometimes does not come home from school after hours and on one occasion did not return until midnight. He regularly goes to visit his father without first telling his grandmother where he is. His grandmother often guesses that this is where John is but is unwilling to make telephone calls to Mr Doe in order to check it out and worries greatly about John's whereabouts. Asked whether he wants to live with his father or with his grandmother John says he wants to live with his father. Several times lately he has shouted and sworn at his grandmother. In anger she has said that perhaps with his father is where he should be and that John and his father are two of a kind.

Jane says she wants to live with her grandmother. She too seems depressed. She has been eating too much and has put on quite a lot of weight and her school work has deteriorated. Her teachers say that she is quiet and unresponsive in class and not overtly a nuisance. She too goes to visit her father and Mr Doe claims that on these occasions Jane is much brighter and more cheerful and says that she wishes she could stay with him always.

Our service was asked by the children's guardian *ad litem* whether care orders should be made in respect of John and Jane, the balance of advantage in their living with their maternal grandmother or their father, whether they should be placed separately or together, what arrangements should be made for contact with the relative with whom they did not live and whether there was need for therapeutic intervention in their lives.

Formulation

These children are in an impossible position. For the three years since the death of their mother they have not been helped to grieve; this normal process has been repressed or denied out of mutual generous protective wishes to avoid painful shows of feeling between themselves and their grandmother. They have also done little or no work on comprehending the manner of their mother's death, the relationship between their parents which led up to that death, and their own unexplored feelings about their part in that process as children of a troubled marriage (perhaps as children who blamed themselves that they did not see or understand any of what was happening). This avoidance has been to the short-term advantage of Mr Doe, who has been able to deny or set aside responsibility and remorse when dealing with his children, but to the disadvantage of John and Jane who in colluding with their father have avoided dealing with the traumatic stress as well as grief.

Mr Doe asserts that he is not and never would be a danger to his children. This is an untested proposition. Because his plea of guilty to manslaughter was accepted, there was no forensic evaluation of the crime or its precursors nor of Mr Doe's personality. In denying responsibility for his late wife's death, expressing no guilt or remorse and minimising its effects upon the children, he unwittingly creates a situation in which, in order to accommodate him, the children must accommodate also a denial of their feelings regarding their mother's death. In effect, they must join him, silently, in belittling her, denigrating her and setting aside her worth as a human being.

Their difficulties have been intensified by the delayed but entirely appropriate grief now shown by their grandmother. In this household there is for the first time some communication about the loss sustained and the anger aroused by that loss.

In circumstances such as these there are a number of features to be considered by those making decisions on behalf of the children:

1 Delayed or denied mourning links with personality deficits in the maturing child so that attachments tend to be insecure and the ability to trust distorted or diminished.
2 If, under such circumstances, the children of the destroyed marriage live with the person responsible for the killing they must deny or mask feelings of fear or anxiety regarding their own dependent relationship with that person. These feelings may not be overt or indeed conscious and their necessity may be denied by all concerned but it is likely that they will persist none the less. Under such circumstances it may be that children will be inappropriately placating or compliant. Alternatively, opposition may trigger memories of parental quarrels. This is likely to be a particularly delicate situation for the adolescent daughter of a dead mother. Both children must come to terms with their roles as the children of a killer.
3 The children are also in an impossible position regarding the half of the family with whom they do not live. Currently, John is acting out this dilemma by spending time with his grandmother, with whom he is angry and disruptive, and then going without leave or discussion to

his father who says he is co-operative and compliant – though this involves a denial of his disobedience to the grandmother.

In these circumstances it is not realistic to expect children such as John and Jane to express consistent, coherent or sustained wishes. They are likely to act out their confusion and ambivalence, as indeed John is doing, or to lapse into depression and limited communication, as seems to be happening to Jane.

Opinion and recommendations

It is in the children's interests in these circumstances that a care order is made. These children lack clear, consistent, reliable and independent parental guidance and in our view there would have been a strong case for the making of a care order at the time of their mother's death. This would have allowed independent assessment of their needs including the probability that therapeutic input at that time would have been beneficial to all concerned. It would also have allowed a claim to be made on their behalf to the Criminal Injuries Compensation Authority. A care order at this time will remedy some of these deficiencies. The claim could still be made and independent therapeutic help be sought for these troubled and confused young people, each of whom is of an age and understanding to make good use of this.

With regard to where the children should live we recommend that the decision should be made by the court and not by John and Jane. The least detrimental solution available, one that she herself strongly wishes, is that they should remain in the care and control of their grandmother. It would be appropriate that they are told that this is a decision of the court so that they may be released from their responsibility to please both father and grandmother.

In these circumstances each of them still wishes to see father and this should not in our view be opposed. But we advise that Mr Doe seek some independent counselling about his wife's death and its effect on the children. It is not in our view helpful to them that he continues to make so little of this tragedy for which he is responsible. Contact arrangements between John and Jane and their father should as before be arranged by some person other than their grandmother, for whom this would be an intolerable burden. But we hope that their feelings about these visits can be discussed between them and their grandmother rather than being avoided lest anyone's feelings be wounded.

Since this family lives in another part of the country it is not appropriate that our service attempt to offer direct therapeutic help to John and Jane. But we will be happy to be available for consultation and review if this is requested and we will welcome the opportunity to hear more of the children and how the decisions made affect their well-being and education.

In summary: our recommendation is that care orders be made, that legal advice should continue to be available to the children, for example in respect of compensation, that their living arrangements with their maternal grandmother continue but that therapeutic help be made available to the children and their grandmother. We recommend that contact with Mr Doe, their father, should be arranged without immediate stress upon their grandmother and hope that Mr Doe will also accept some therapeutic help and advice towards accepting responsibility for his action. The writer of the report will be available for attendance at court as a witness if required.

Outcome

John and Jane have continued to live with their grandmother under the terms of a care order. They are old enough to make direct arrangements with their father for meetings and outings and their grandmother has agreed to this arrangement, which she prefers, in the knowledge that the children's social worker is available to help sort out difficulties. The legal department of the local authority responsible for the care order has applied on behalf of the children to the Criminal Injuries Compensation Authority, has approved the children's grandmother as a foster-parent and has arranged maintenance payments by Mr Doe. Father says he does not need counselling but the children and their grandmother have accepted referral to a child mental health service which has offered family and individual appointments. John continues to be rude and disobedient to his grandmother but her health and that of Jane is improving.

Mr Doe has agreed that the children should continue to live with their grandmother until adulthood.

As a result of discussion of the reports these arrangements were agreed by negotiation between the lawyers representing children, father and grandparents and approved by a judge, thus sparing all concerned a lengthy and distressing court hearing. Should future problems arise, guidance from the court may be sought and further reports submitted to the judge.

Interviewing the traumatised child

Part I: Circumstances of the homicide

This is our framework for an initial interview followed by more detailed gathering of information about each child who is referred to us.

Where referral takes place immediately or soon after the homicide, we administer a semi-structured interview specifically related to these events and based on Pynoos.[180]

This should take precedence over the wider assessment (see Part II), particularly where the child has been or may have been a witness to the homicide. It is a matter of clinical and forensic judgement as to whether children should be interviewed separately or together if involved in the same tragedy.

1   Have the child draw or tell a story about a picture of his choice (he will often spontaneously draw the traumatic experience).
2   Explore fully the child's experience of the traumatic event, paying attention to physical (including sensory) and affective experience:

> physical mutilation;
> the issue of human accountability/impulse control;
> post-traumatic incidents;
> ask the child to draw or play or act the central event;
> consider fantasies of revenge;
> any other significant element.

3   Closure: review the child's present and future life concerns:

> consider and support the child's mourning work;
> review the matters discussed in the interview;
> invite the child to return for another interview;
> take leave.

Arrange to be available to child and family during criminal/civil proceedings. Consider formal psychiatric evaluation and treatment.

Part II: Later assessment

Semi-structured interview(s) where referral is *not* immediately related to trauma, for example later referrals for bereavement counselling/therapy, placement or advice about contact, court reports. NB: record where information is *not* available or not known to current carers or social workers (for example, whether children saw the body or attended the funeral).

   More than one session may be required. Some information may be obtained from previous records.

1 Name of child / d.o.b. / sex / religion / address / legal status / general practitioner.
2 Name(s) of caregivers, current and former social workers, guardian *ad litem*, divorce court welfare officer, solicitor, other relevant workers.
3 Name of father, age, religion, ethnic origin, language of origin, language spoken, occupation, whether married to mother, current address when known, legal status, e.g. sought by police, on remand, convicted.
4 Name of mother, note where religion, ethnic origin, etc. differ from father's. Languages spoken. Whereabouts of mother's body. Inquest completed? Body released for burial? Has funeral taken place?
     NB: Father accused of homicide may be step-, adoptive, or putative father or father substitute to some children in the household. Some children bereaved of parents with whom they were living may have legal parents elsewhere. Also children may be bereaved of a parent with whom they were not living at the time of the murder. Record as appropriate for each child.
5 What do children know of the homicide and its aftermath? Were they witness to the killing? Have they seen the body, attended the funeral? Are there plans for them to do so?
     NB: It is important to consider seeing caregivers/social workers prior to interviewing the children, to ascertain what the children have been told about the killing.
6 Key maternal relatives – where living, access to children before and subsequent to the homicide, offers to care for the children, contact with father and/or father's family.
7 Key paternal relatives – where living, access to children before and after the homicide, offers of care for the children, contact with father and/or mother's relatives.
     NB: Note blood relationships between father's and mother's family, e.g. where mother and father were first cousins. Also note friendships, e.g. between sets of in-laws, rivalries, disagreements.
8 Were family known to social or court welfare or psychiatric services prior to the homicide? Record details.

9 Placement and contact. Where did the children live at the time of their bereavement and with whom? Immediately afterwards? Subsequent placements? Were placements planned or made *ad hoc* in response to breakdown of earlier arrangements?

What are the legal arrangements?

no order, placement with relatives;
child protection order;
interim care order;
wardship;
care order;
freeing for adoption;
adoption disputed/undisputed;
guardianship.

What are the arrangements about contact with key relatives and other significant adults and children? What are the children's wishes?

10 Compensation claims: are these being considered? Who will act on behalf of the child? Has referral been made to the Criminal Injuries Compensation Authority? Should there be a claim for compensation made against the surviving parent?

Part III: Issues relevant to therapy

Record the following separately for each child:

Present in house at time of mother's death?
May have witnessed the killing?
Heard the killing?
Realised retrospectively that they had heard or seen matters relevant to the killing?
Had the child heard or witnessed previous marital violence, experienced personal abuse or that of siblings?

Record also:

Who found the body?
Did the child seek help?
Has the child seen the body/attended the funeral/visited the grave/taken part in the memorial service?
What religious rites were used? (This may be a source of family conflict.)
What did father do after the killing? E.g. leave/lock up children/suicide?
What did he tell the child?
If children not at home or not aware of the killing who told them what?
How soon after the killing?
Have children been told that their father committed or is alleged to have committed the crime?

Part IV: For each child

School: record/educational attainment/current school arrangements. Note gaps in knowledge.
Assessment of psychiatric disorder.
ICD-10[260] classification/*DSMIV*[7] classification.

Formulation. Prognosis. Recommendations.

See also: Joseph *et al.* (1997)[120] for an understanding of the role of psychosocial factors in the development and persistence of post-traumatic stress disorder; and Raine *et al.* (1996)[183] for an account of the physiological and biological changes which may persist in victims of violence.

Principles and practice in child law

The principles listed below are clear-cut and should be borne in mind by all who are concerned with children and young people under 18 years of age. They were used by UK legislators in revising of the law (Children Act 1989, England and Wales).

1   The welfare of children must be the paramount consideration of courts in making decisions.
2   The concept of 'parental responsibility' is introduced to replace that of 'parental rights'.
3   This law confers certain duties and powers on local authorities to provide services for children and families.
4   Local authorities are charged with the duty to safeguard and promote the welfare of children in need. Need is specified in broad terms and local authorities are charged with the identification of the children in need.
5   The Act provides a checklist of factors to be considered by the courts before making decisions. The list includes:
    a   the ascertainable wishes and feelings of the child concerned (considered in the light of his age and understanding);
    b   his physical, emotional and educational needs;
    c   the likely effect on him of any change in his circumstances;
    d   his age, sex, background and any characteristics that the court considers relevant;
    e   any harm which he has suffered or is at risk of suffering;
    f   how capable are each of his parents, and any other persons in relation to whom the court considers the question to be relevant, of meeting his needs;
    g   the range of powers available to the court under this Act in the proceedings in question.
6   Courts should not make an order unless this is shown to be better for the child in each case than not making an order. (The idea is that as much as possible should be arranged by agreement rather than imposed upon children and families.)

7   Any delay in deciding questions relating to the upbringing of the child is
    identified as likely to prejudice the child's welfare. (This is an important
    principle which may help local authorities to make plans for children during
    what may be a long period of uncertainty pending a criminal trial of their
    father or mother.)
8   The Act makes it easier for children to be parties separate from their parents
    in legal proceedings concerning them. (Thus, there is a distinct and increas-
    ingly clear guidance within this framework that children have civil rights
    and are not simply the property of adults or of the state.)

This is but one example of legislation which creates a framework for the civil
rights of children (see[101] for a wider discussion). The aim is to bring together
private law, which is concerned with disputes between individuals, and public
law, which requires or enables the state to be responsible for the care and protection
of children, to identify the rights of children in law, to encourage greater partnership between statutory authorities and parents, and to balance on the one hand the
duties of adults to protect children and, on the other, parents' ability when need
be to challenge state intervention in the upbringing of their children.

Criminal and civil justice systems have taken little account of the rights of
children but, in a rapidly changing world, this is being remedied. To sustain,
evaluate and enforce a revised body of law will require resources, training and
careful monitoring. Our children are but one small group of those who need such
services.

Living away from birth parents: fostering and adoption

When children cannot live with their birth parents, they may need to be fostered
or adopted by others. In general these are some of the most valuable services
which adults may give to children in our society. The services provided, and the
planning of them, come within the area of public law since decisions involve the
state and not just private individuals. State involvement in the case of fostering
continues long term, with payments to foster-parents and defined legal duties.
Thus, foster-parents are required to share their task with the state, usually
through a social worker who is allocated to maintain links with significant people
in the children's lives. If the child is adopted, the duty of the state ends at the
point where the adoption order is made. Then the child has legal rights as a
member of the new family, including those of inheritance.

The term fostering covers a range of services and it is essential that the task
defined be identified and agreed by all concerned. Short-term or emergency
fostering should be just that, a breathing space in which children are kept safe
and provided with basic care and nurture when their birth family are unable to
provide this for whatever reason. Social workers use the term 'drift' to describe
what happens when children are placed as an emergency without a clear plan

being made and the placement gradually becomes longer and longer without anybody having decided what would be best for the child.[142]

Fostering may be planned from the start for specific purposes: for example, where children need a bridge placement while work is done with their original family to allow them to return safely, or where the plan is that they move on to a long-term substitute family. Foster-parents may provide a valuable service to abused, neglected or traumatised children in caring for them and providing a specialist assessment of their needs. Another shorter-term goal may be to provide a base for troubled teenagers who do not get on with their family of origin and are not yet ready to live independently.[202]

For many children these functions are served by the wider family, some of whom become formal 'foster-parents' so that financial help may be given to them by a local authority. In many cases, however, children will be placed with unrelated foster-parents, identified and approved by the local authority and available for emergency or planned longer-term care. There is a great need for the provision of sufficient numbers of professional foster-parents who, whether related or unrelated to the children concerned, will take on very difficult and disturbed young people, receiving realistic recompense for the job and working closely with social workers, health-care workers and schools.

Adoption used to be a service for childless couples who were 'matched' with babies, and the original adoption laws were designed with this kind of arrangement in mind. For the past twenty years the numbers of babies so placed have decreased, since it has become more acceptable for women or men to become single parents (although financial difficulties may be very great), and since the concept of illegitimacy has disappeared.

Children who require permanent, legally secure homes can now benefit from two decades of work in which homes have been found for a whole range of children who once would have been thought unsuitable for adoption.[191] Families may now offer permanent homes to older children, those damaged by neglect or abuse, with mental and physical handicap[134, 255] or life-threatening illness, and those who, because of their skin colour or for other reasons, do not look like the prospective adoptive parents.[224] To this may now be added children traumatised by a violent death within their original family. Adoptive families should have available as a right, to be asked for when needed, financial and specialist help from a range of services. It is already possible for families to receive adoption allowances so that they can offer children legal security with less financial penalty than formerly – when all financial help was lost after a child moved from foster to adoptive status – although this is only a discretionary allowance, unlike allowances to non-related, approved foster-carers.

All such children are likely to have important memories of their birth families and may have relationships which they want to sustain or relatives who wish to keep in contact with them.[8] Adoption law in various jurisdictions is currently being reviewed to consider issues such as how children may keep in contact with members of their birth families, under what circumstances it is best to place a group of siblings together, and how, if they are separated because their parenting needs are so great or varied, they may be kept in contact.[8, 105] There is also a body of knowledge on how to put together, for each child in care, an archive of information about the original family, places in which they have lived, key events in the family, plus the child's personal health and education record. It is essential that traumatic bereavement does not leave a child with a past unknown and unrecorded, as though he or she has entered the future leaving a disappearing wake of previous knowledge.[100]

When children, such as those we are describing, cannot live with their parents, their needs (for protection, for a permanent home, for counselling, etc.) are so great that we believe that in every case there should be a legal framework of protection for them, even when the child-care arrangements appear to be satisfactory. With the coming of the Children Act 1989, some local authority social service departments have been reluctant to invoke child protection procedures, arguing that the child has a suitable home and no 'significant harm' (see Glossary) can be proved. We have argued successfully that there may be future significant harm if a child is, by default, not protected from having to return to a parent who has killed the other parent without there having been an opportunity to consider whether that is in the child's interests, and legal precedent has established that the concept is applicable to any child so bereaved. It is essential that local authorities are enabled and resourced to protect children so that the intention of the Children Act will be realised. For an overview of the network of services involved in the provision of legal services to children and those who care for them see Walsh (1998).[234]

Appendix 3

The classification of post-traumatic stress disorder

The 1978 *International Classification of Diseases*, published by the World Health Organization (*ICD-9*)[259] did not include post-traumatic stress disorder as an illness of adult life. *Acute reaction to stress* was defined as: 'a very transient disorder – in response to exceptional physical or mental stress, such as natural catastrophe or battle. Such reactions usually subside within hours or days.' (One may question whether it is at all normal for reactions to battle or natural catastrophe to subside quite so quickly.) Another harmless sounding term, *adjustment reaction*, is applied to 'mild or transient disorders, generally reversible and usually lasting only a few months'. However, in 1980, the American *Diagnostic and Statistical Manual*, published by the American Psychiatric Association[5] did provide a classification scheme for post-traumatic stress disorder. This, plus a further decade of research on the effects of stress in children and adults, has led to a revision of the World Health Organization classification which now (*ICD-10*)[260] takes more serious and coherent account of this condition.

In 1980, when work began on this concept, the American classification for post-traumatic stress disorder was as follows:

1 Existence of a recognised stressor that would evoke significant symptoms of stress in almost anyone.
2 Re-experiencing of the trauma as evidenced by at least one of the following:

   a Recurrent and intrusive recollections of the event.
   b Recurrent dreams of the event.
   c Suddenly acting or feeling as if the traumatic event were recurring because of an association with an environmental or an ideational stimulus. (The sufferer hears, sees, smells, touches or suddenly remembers a thing which acts as a trigger: the trauma is then re-experienced rather than remembered.)

3 Numbing of responsiveness to or reduced involvement with the external world, beginning some time after the trauma, was shown by at least one of the following: markedly diminished interest in one or more significant activities, feelings of detachment or estrangement from others, constricted

affect. [*Comment*: numb, compliant children may be rather a relief to adults struggling with the aftermath of a disaster so this behaviour is supported rather than discouraged.]

4   At least two of the following symptoms which were not present before the trauma: hyper-alertness or exaggerated startle response, sleep disturbance, guilt about surviving when others have not or about behaviour required for survival, memory impairment or trouble concentrating, avoidance of activities which arouse recollection of the traumatic event, intensification of symptoms by exposure to events that symbolise or resemble the traumatic event.

A subsequent edition[6] developed this classification, which is now agreed to be valuable to anyone involved with traumatised children. In this revision, symptoms must be present for twenty-eight days before the diagnosis is made, thus distinguishing between symptoms of traumatic stress which may appear immediately after the disaster and a state of illness which is likely to persist over time.

PTSD in children so young that they have little or no language

Scheeringa and colleagues (1995)[198] have modified the American *Diagnostic and Statistical Manual* (1994) (*DSMIV*)[7] classification to take account of the youngest child victims.

The first criterion is that the child 'has experienced, witnessed or been confronted with an event which involves actual or threatened death or serious injury or a threat to the physical integrity of the self or others'.

Re-experiencing: play may be compulsively repetitive, representing part of the trauma, is unimaginative and does not relieve the child's anxiety, or may re-enact the trauma. There may be recurrent memories of the trauma, nightmares, or it may be possible for observers to identify dissociative features or evidence that the child is experiencing flashbacks. The child may show *numbing* via play which is limited in scope, withdrawal socially, restricted range of emotions and loss of previously acquired skills.

Also there may be increased *arousal*, shown by night terror, difficulty in going to sleep, frequent waking, poor concentration (compared with what the child could achieve before the event), excessive alertness and ability to be startled. The child may show *fears* and *aggressive behaviour* not present before the trauma, for example being more clinging, more afraid of the dark or of being alone or even of events and situations not linked with the trauma. As in the *DSMIV* classification, these problems must have been present for one month to be recorded as PTSD.

Compensation for post-traumatic stress disorder

Recent UK cases, clarifying the concept of post-traumatic stress disorder and the use of the expert psychiatric witness, apply in the main to catastrophes. A discussion by a lawyer, with illustrative case histories in relation to the claims of adult passengers who survived the capsize of the *Herald of Free Enterprise*, off the coast of Belgium at Zeebrugge in 1987, can be found in[159, 160]. In their discussion, the arbitrators quoted the *Diagnostic and Statistical Manual*, revised third edition,[6] which classifies PTSD as a syndrome if it persists more than a month.

The main points made by the Zeebrugge arbitrators were as follows:

1 Post-traumatic stress disorder is a recognised psychiatric illness.
2 Many Zeebrugge victims suffered PTSD.
3 The *DSMIIIR* [now superseded by *DSMIV*] is a useful guide to diagnosis.
4 Pathological grief is a recognised psychiatric illness in excess of normal grief.
5 Some survivors suffer from other psychiatric illnesses such as depression and it is possible to suffer simultaneously from more than one psychiatric illness.
6 It may be reasonable for survivors to refuse to undergo psychiatric treatment and this should not affect compensation.
7 Account should be taken in individual cases of any vulnerability to future psychiatric illness.

Comparable case law concerning children, limited as yet, will be developed over time.

See also: Black, Harris-Hendriks and Wolkind (1998)[24] and Eastman (1997).[66]

Voluntary help: useful addresses

In England and Wales, Part III of the Children Act 1989 defines a duty of local authorities to safeguard and promote the welfare of children in need and to promote the upbringing of such children by providing 'an appropriate range and level of services'. This flexible definition certainly must encompass children and young people under 18 years of age who have lost one or, indirectly, both parents through family violence. Services should be available via police, social services and health care and should range from emergency protection to advice, guidance, counselling, debriefing and therapy. Children and their caregivers may need practical input such as day-care or home help. Others need accommodation (residential care planned in partnership with families), while a majority require legally secure state parenting. The reality is that local authorities and child health services lack resources for such a comprehensive range of services. There is a gap between the law, which 'enables' rather than 'requires' such provision, and what is available on the ground. Those who seek and those who attempt to provide services must act together to identify and cost unmet needs. Meanwhile, a number of charitable organisations provide invaluable help, undertake research and publish relevant information.

Aftermath
P.O. Box 414, Sheffield S4 7RT (0114 275 8520)
(offering support and counselling for families of perpetrators of serious offences)

British Agencies for Adoption and Fostering
Skyline House, 200 Union Street, London SE1 0LX (020 7593 2000)
(for children who may not be able to live with birth families)

Bridge Child Care Development Service
1st Floor, 34 Upper Street, London N1 0PN (020 7704 2386)

Compassionate Friends
53 North Street, Bristol BS3 1EN (0117 966 5202; Helpline 0117 953 9639)
(self-help for bereaved families)

CRUSE – Bereavement Care
126 Sheen Road, Richmond, Surrey TW9 1UR (020 8940 4818)

DAPHNE Initiative
The DAPHNE Initiative is a European Community programme (with 5 million euro of funding for 1999) which supports non-governmental organisations (NGOs) and voluntary organisations in measures aimed to prevent violence against children, young persons and women.

The European Commission is proposing the creation of a five-year programme (2000 – 2004) to continue the Initiative. A Call for Proposals for projects from NGOs is published in the European Community Official Journal normally in March each year. The deadline for the submission of proposals is normally mid-June for projects to start in December of the same year.

The co-ordinator of the DAPHNE Initiative is Anthony Simpson, Secretariat General, Task Force on Co-operation on Justice and Home Affairs, avenue des Nerviens, 9, 6 25a, 200 rue de la Loi, 1049 Brussels, Belgium. Fax: (+32 2) 295 0174 and e-mail: anthony.simpson@sg.cec.be.

Federation of Prisoners' Families Support Groups
c/o SCF, Cambridge House, Cambridge Grove, London W6 0LE (020 8741 4578)

National Association of Bereavement Services
20 Norton Folgate, London E1 6DB (020 7247 0617; Referral services 020 7247 1080)
(information about services for the bereaved)

National Association for the Care and Resettlement of Offenders (NACRO)
169 Clapham Road, London SW9 0PU (020 7582 6500)

National Association of Citizens Advice Bureaux
Myddleton House, 115–123 Pentonville Road, London N1 9LZ (020 7833 2181)

National Council for Family Proceedings
University of Bristol
Wills Memorial Building, Queens Road, Clifton, Bristol BS8 1RJ (0117 954 5381)

National Council for Voluntary Organisations
Regents Wharf, 8 All Saints Street, London N1 9RL (020 7713 6161)

Press Complaints Commission
1 Salisbury Square, London EC4Y 8JB (020 7353 1248)

Relate (Marriage Guidance)
Herbert Gray College, Little Church Street, Rugby, Warwickshire CV21 3AP (01788 573 241)

Samaritans
10 The Grove, Slough, Berks SL1 1QP (01753 216500; National Helpline 0345 909090)

Support After Murder and Manslaughter (SAMM)
Cranmer House, 39 Brixton Road, London SW9 6DZ (020 7735 3838)

Victim Support
(National Office), Cranmer House, 39 Brixton Road, London SW9 6DZ (020 7735 9166)
(for victims of crime)

Young Minds, Children's Mental Health Charity
102–108 Clerkenwell Road, London EC1M 5SA (020 7336 8445; Parents' information service 0800 0182138)

Principles for practice and signposts for future work

Impact

1   The children need immediate care in a place which feels safe to them. Care-
    givers need support and help, and emergency state care may be required.
    Everyone concerned with the immediate criminal act and its aftermath
    should pay particular attention to the children, and what they may have seen,
    heard, touched and smelled, who interacted with them and what attempt was
    made to explore and record their experiences at the time and immediately
    after the event. All concerned should remember that children can be material
    witnesses whose perceptions have often in the past been underestimated or
    ignored. There should be most careful observation of children too small
    to speak: their needs are often unrecognised or underestimated.

2   Emergency legal protection should be sought. Children commonly require
    independent representation and advocacy and the state should act on their
    behalf. Compensation and other financial issues should be given early and
    continuing thought.

3   Children should be protected from further trauma. Besides their being kept
    safe, warm and fed, this involves continuing awareness by carers and profes-
    sionals of traumatic events such as scene of crime investigations, emergency
    resuscitation procedures, removal of the corpse, media intrusion, reading
    newspaper accounts of the crime and seeing it reported on television. The
    principle should be *not* that children can be protected from all such events
    but that there should be sympathetic understanding of their impact, which
    should be kept to the minimum achievable, and evaluated.

4   Care services should be placed on alert to help the children, who will require
    psychological first aid, whether or not they saw the killing, and an evaluation
    concerning the risk that they may develop a post-traumatic stress disorder.
    Bereaved relatives also may require urgent help.

5   Possessions, including those of the lost person, family records and photo-
    graphs, pets and routines are important to dislocated children and thought
    must be give to how they may be helped in this respect.

6   Expert advice should be sought regarding the planning of contact between

children and other key relatives, particularly in relation to visits to prisons and hospitals. Viewing of the dead and ceremonies of grief and mourning are important and should be planned to take account of children's needs and wishes.

Aftermath

1   Planning for the children must begin at once and should not be delayed while the alleged perpetrator of the killing awaits the result of criminal proceedings. Children should not be placed with alleged perpetrators nor with their families other than rarely and with most careful evaluation and consultation.
2   Emergency arrangements should not be allowed to drift, without planning, into becoming long term. Principles for good practice are as outlined in Appendix 2.
3   Contact with the perpetrator and other key relatives is the right of the children and not of the adults concerned. Where conflict arises this must be the guiding concept of courts, professionals and carers.
4   Therapeutic help should be available to those who care for the children. Schoolteachers should be informed and consulted, with appropriate permission from the children and their families.

Signposts for future work

1   The criminal court case and relevant publicity arouse intense emotions in children and in the families of the alleged perpetrator and the victim.
2   Changes in carers necessarily impact upon the children: frequent changes in placement make the outlook worse.
3   Further disturbance in the child, which may be related to particular developmental stages – learning to talk, entering school, becoming adolescent, leaving home, etc. – may require renewed and specifically focused therapeutic help.
4   The release of the perpetrator from prison or hospital is commonly linked with a welling-up of grief and anger in the victim's family. There may be renewed conflicts about contact; laboriously achieved residence and contact arrangements may be under threat.
5   Children are particularly vulnerable to further family upheavals, particularly if these involve the illness or death of other significant members of their family.
6   Similarly, they are vulnerable to new traumatic events and these are more likely to happen in families who already are unhappy, dislocated and traumatised.

In the longer term

As our study has progressed, the following features have emerged as particularly unhelpful to children.

1   Placement with relatives who over time are not able to deal with their own grief and so have difficulty in meeting the children's emotional needs.
2   Forty per cent of the children whom we meet are under 5 years old at the time of the killing. We need to learn much more about the ways in which violent events affect language development, create long-term physiological problems and hinder attachment formation.
3   Placement with relatives who hold off from making attachments with the children, either because they have taken them on with reluctance or because they see themselves as short-term carers, perhaps because an emergency placement has continued longer than was intended or, on occasion, because the caregivers see their job as looking after the children until the perpetrator's release from prison.
4   Problems of communication between caregivers and children, and the non-availability or refusal of therapeutic help both worsen the outlook.
5   Frequent changes of caregivers and a lifestyle that is uncertain and un-predictable make things worse.
6   Children traumatised and dislocated have trouble in trusting and attaching to those who care for them and may precipitate or increase some of the problems listed above.

How to make things less bad

Children who are guided and helped through trauma and grief, who have independent advocacy, who are offered therapeutic help, who are cared for by adults who are able to meet the children's needs and who themselves have help and advice at hand are likely to do better. They need to be able put down roots in a stable environment, to continue their education supported by understanding teachers, to retain memories and records of their earlier life and contact with important friends and relatives. Children who are very young at the time of the tragedy need information appropriate to their understanding, as they grow older. They and those who look after them will need continuing support and advice concerning contact with the perpetrator and continuing family disputes which may include arguments about money and possessions. Our study has now gone on long enough for us to have learnt that children can and do survive such terrible events and so on to live successful and fulfilling lives. We salute and thank the children of this study from whom we have learnt so much.

Glossary

This glossary is based on the wording of the Children Act 1989 (England and Wales). A child is referred to as 'he' or 'him' throughout this legislation, as indeed is usual in other legal frameworks.

Adoption A court order vests parental responsibility in an adopter or adopters, extinguishing the parental rights or duties which belonged to any parent or guardian before the adoption order was made.

Attachment The process whereby affectional bonds are developed between members of a species, including humans.

Attachment behaviour The ways in which the development of attachment is demonstrated.

Care order A court order which places a child in the care of a named local authority. The authority then has parental responsibilities in respect of that child although the parent also has continuing parental responsibility which can only be abrogated by an order of the court.

Child For the purpose of legislation in England and Wales this is a person under the age of 18 years.

Concurrent jurisdiction Hearings concerning children may be held in the High Court, County Court or Magistrates Court (now known as family proceedings courts) as appropriate to the length and complexity of the case. The same law applies in each court.

Contact This term replaces the older concept of 'access' and refers to an order which requires, or informal arrangements which allow, a person with whom a child lives or is to live to arrange for a child to visit or stay with other important people in his life, such as the parent with whom he does not live, grandparents, other relatives, brothers and sisters and friends. A court may make directions about arrangements for contact.

Detachment The end product of a process whereby relationships which are broken, unreliable or insecure lead to a state of mind which is untrusting and unreliant on others.

Emergency protection order This court order is limited in the first place to eight days to ensure that a child will be safe when, if the order be not made, he is thought likely to suffer significant harm. The order can be made without a parent or guardian being present but those with parental responsibility have a right to apply to a court for a rehearing within seventy-two hours. The court can direct where the child will live, who has contact with him and whether he requires medical or psychiatric examination or other assessment. The child's wishes must be considered according to his age and understanding and his welfare is paramount. If the child is to remain in a place of safety, an interim care order must be made within eight days and there must be a full hearing of all the evidence before a decision is made about his future.

Guardian *ad litem* This man or woman with specialist social work skills is appointed by a court to safeguard the interests of a child during court proceedings. Guardians *ad litem* are organised in panels comprising probation officers, social workers and other people with appropriate knowledge and skills. The person representing the child must be quite independent of any department of social services or other specialist agency involved in the hearing. The guardian *ad litem* can instruct a solicitor on behalf of the child or the child can instruct the solicitor independently of the guardian if old enough to do this. The Official Solicitor (see below) acts as a guardian *ad litem* when he is involved in a case concerning a child.

Injunction/non-molestation order This court order requires a person to do something or refrain from doing something thought to be injurious to another party to the case. For example, a woman who fears marital violence may ask a court for an injunction to prevent her partner from entering the marital home or coming within an agreed distance of it. Infringement of an injunction is contempt of court and can be punished by a fine or imprisonment.

Interim care order This order places a child in the care of a local authority for an agreed period while the evidence for a full hearing is gathered.

Looked after This is an arrangement whereby children who are not in the care of a local authority may receive services such as accommodation in a foster-home or children's home in agreement with the child's parents or guardians.

Official Solicitor This is an office of the Department of the Lord Chancellor (analogous to a Minister of Justice) staffed by solicitors and senior civil servants. Its work includes acting for people with disabilities but in the main it provides services on behalf of children. The Official Solicitor is likely to act as guardian *ad litem* for wards of court, in adoption hearings, or for children in complex matrimonial disputes.

Parent This word applies to the mother and father of a child whether or not they are married to each other.

Parental responsibility This legal term covers all the rights, duties, powers and responsibilities which a parent has in law in relation to the child and the property of the child. If at the time of the birth mother and father are married both share parental responsibility. If they are not married only the mother has such responsibility but father may obtain it either by an agreement with the mother or by a legal contract. If a care order is made by a court, parental responsibility is shared with the local authority.

Parenting by default This occurs in the aftermath of private or public disaster concerning children when adults or older children take on the task of parents unexpectedly and without preparation.

Parties to a case This term is used for all the persons with an interest in court proceedings whose names appear in the title to the hearing. They have a right to attend the hearing, and to have legal representatives to present their case and to examine witnesses. The original parties may be the parents and, say, the local authority, but others may be added such as the grandparents, and the child, etc.

Regression This describes the behaviour and feelings of a person (child or adult) who returns partially or completely to an earlier stage of development.

Repression This term from psychoanalysis refers to the process whereby painful experiences become unavailable for conscious recall by the person who suffered them.

Residence order This court order replaces the older concept of 'custody' and determines where a child will live after divorce or other forms of family break-up.

Significant harm Section 31(9) of the Children Act 1989 defines this as ill-treatment or the impairment of health or development. Only one of the conditions needs to be proved for a care order to be granted.

Supervision order This is an order putting a child under the supervision of a named local authority or of the probation service. It can be used either when a child is in difficulties through family disharmony or for other reasons, or when a child himself has become involved in criminal behaviour.

Ward of court This term applies to a child under the protection of the High Court which acts in a parental role on his behalf. No important step may be taken in his life without the consent of the court. Wardship can be used by private individuals but not, since 1991, by local authorities which, if they wish to take on parental responsibility for a child, now must prove that a care order is required. The inherent jurisdiction of the High Court may however be used regarding controversial issues about the health, safety and well-being of a child. This means that, irrespective of the legal status of a child, this court has innate powers to arbitrate on controversial issues such as the right of a child to refuse treatment for a life-threatening illness, to have or refuse an abortion or to take other major decisions not approved by his parents or guardians.

This glossary draws on White (1998) (pp. 99–125)[243] and Black, Harris-Hendriks and Wolkind (1998) (pp. 203–8).[24]

References

1 Abrahams, C. (1994) *The Hidden Victims: Children and domestic violence*. NCH: Action for Children, London.

2 Adshead, G., Canterbury, C. and Rose, S. (1993) *Current Provision and Recommendations for the Management of Psychosocial Morbidity Following Disaster in England*, Institute of Psychiatry, University of London, London.

3 Ainsworth, M.D.S., Blehar, M.C, Walters, E. and Wall, S. (1978) *Patterns of Attachment: A psychological study of the strange situation*, Lawrence Erlbaum, Hillside, NJ.

4 Alessi, J.J. and Hearn, K. (1984) 'Group treatment for battered women', in *Battered Women and their Families*, edited by A.R. Roberts, Springer, New York.

5 American Psychiatric Association (1980) *Diagnostic and Statistical Manual of Mental Disorders*, 3rd edn, APA, Washington, DC.

6 American Psychiatric Association (1987) *Diagnostic and Statistical Manual of Mental Disorders (DSMIIIR)*, APA, Washington, DC.

7 American Psychiatric Association (1994) *Diagnostic and Statistical Manual of Mental Disorders*, 4th edn *(DSMIV)*, APA, Washington, DC.

8 Argent, H. (1988) *Keeping the Doors Open: A review of post-adoption services*, British Agencies for Adoption and Fostering, London.

9 Arnold, L.E. (1995) 'Some non-traditional (unconventional and/or innovative) psychosocial treatments for children and adolescents: critique and proposed screening principles', Review, *Journal of Abnormal Child Psychology*, 23(1): 125–40.

10 Ayalon, O. (1983) 'Coping with terrorism', in *Stress Reduction and Prevention*, edited by D. Herchenbaum and M.E. Jememki, Plenum Press, New York.

11 Bailey, S. (1991) 'Adolescents who murder: a study of 20 cases', Paper presented at 12th Conference of European Association of Child and Adolescent Psychiatrists, London.

12 Balbernie, R. (1999) 'Inadmissible evidence: an example of projective identification', *Clinical Child Psychology and Psychiatry*, 4(2): 215–24.

13 Barrett, M.L., Berney, T.P., Bhate, S., Famuyiwa, O., Fundudis, T., Kolvin, I., and Tyrer, S. (1991) 'Diagnosing childhood depression: who should be interviewed – parent or child?', The Newcastle Child Depression Project, *British Journal of Psychiatry*, 159 (supplement 11): 22–7.

14 Bennathan, M. (1992) 'The care and education of troubled children', *Young Minds Newsletter*, 10: 1–7.

15 Birtchnell, J. (1970) 'Early parent death and mental illness', *British Journal of Psychiatry*, 116: 281–8.

16 Birtchnell, J. (1970) 'The relationship between attempted suicide, depression and parent death', *British Journal of Psychiatry*, 116: 307–13.

17 Birtchnell, J. (1971) 'Early parent death in relation to size and constitution of sibship', *Acta Psychiatrica Scandinavica*, 47: 250–70.

18 Black, D. (1988) 'Imprisoned children', *The Medico-Legal Journal*, 56(3): 139–49.

19 Black, D. (1992) 'Children of imprisoned parents', *Archives of Disease in Childhood*, 67: 967–70.

20 Black, D. (1996) 'Childhood bereavement', Editorial, *British Medical Journal*, 312: 1496.

21 Black, D. (1997) 'Treatment of children and families', in *Psychological Trauma: A developmental approach*, edited by D. Black, M. Newman, J. Harris-Hendriks and G. Mezey, Gaskell/Royal College of Psychiatrists, London: pp. 281–93.

22 Black, D. (1998) 'Working with the effects of traumatic bereavement by uxoricide (spouse killing) on young children's attachment behaviour', *International Journal of Psychiatry in Clinical Practice*, 2: 245–9.

23 Black, D., Harris-Hendriks, J. and Kaplan, T. (1992) 'Father kills mother: PTSD in the children', *Psychotherapy and Psychosomatics*, 2: 152–7.

24 Black, D., Harris-Hendriks, J. and Wolkind, S. (eds) (1998) *Child Psychiatry and the Law*, 3rd edn, Gaskell/Royal College of Psychiatrists, London.

25 Black, D., Harris-Hendriks, J. and Wolkind S. (eds) (1998) 'Compensation claims', in *Child Psychiatry and the Law*, 3rd edn, Gaskell/Royal College of Psychiatrists, London.

26 Black, D. and Kaplan, T. (1988) 'Father kills mother: issues and problems encountered by a child psychiatric team', *British Journal of Psychiatry*, 153: 624–30.

27 Black, D., Kaplan, T. and Harris-Hendriks, J. (1992) 'Father kills mother: effects on the children', in *International Handbook of Traumatic Stress Syndromes*, edited by J. Wilson and B. Raphael, Plenum Press, New York.

28 Black, D., Kaplan, T. and Harris-Hendriks, J. (1992) 'Children who witness parental killing', in *Violence*, edited by C. Thompson and P. Cowen, Butterworth Heinemann, Oxford.

29 Black, D. and Newman, M. (1996) 'Children and domestic violence: a review', *Clinical Child Psychology and Psychiatry*, 1(1): 79–88.

30 Black, D., Newman M., Harris-Hendriks, J. and Mezey, G. (eds) (1997) *Psychological Trauma: A developmental approach*, Gaskell/Royal College of Psychiatrists, London.

31 Black, D. and Urbanowicz, A. (1985) 'Bereaved children – family intervention', in *Recent Research in Developmental Psychopathology*, edited by J.E. Stevenson, Pergamon, Oxford.

32 Black, D. and Urbanowicz, M.A. (1987) 'Family intervention with bereaved children', *Journal of Child Psychology and Psychiatry*, 28: 467–76.

33 Bohman, M. (1971) 'A comparative study of adopted children, foster children and children in their biological environment born after undesired pregnancies', *Acta Paediatrica Scandinavica*, suppl. 221.

34 Bohman, M. and Sigvardsson, S. (1980) 'A prospective, longitudinal study of children registered for adoption: a 15-year follow-up', *Acta Psychiatrica Scandinavica*, 61: 339–55.

35 Boston, M. and Szur, R. (1983) *Psychotherapy with Severely Deprived Children*, Routledge & Kegan Paul, London.

36 Bowden, P. (1990) 'Homicide', in *Principles and Practice of Forensic Psychiatry*, edited by R. Bluglass and P. Bowden, Churchill Livingstone, London.

37 Bowlby, J. (1969) *Attachment and Loss, Vol. 1*, Hogarth Press, London.

38 Bowlby, J. (1972) *Attachment and Loss, Vol. 2*, Hogarth Press, London.

39 Bowlby, J. (1980) *Attachment and Loss, Vol. 3*, Hogarth Press, London.

40 The Bridge Child Care Development Service (1991) *Sukina: An evaluation report of the circumstances leading to her death*, Bridge Child Care Development Service, London.

41 The Bridge Child Care Development Service/Islington A.C.P.C. (1996) *Neglect: A fifty year search for answers*, The Bridge/Islington A.C.P.C., London

42 Brinich, P.M. (1989) 'Love and anger in relatives who 'adopt' orphaned children: parents by default', *Bereavement Care*, 8(2): 14–16.

43 Brown, G. and Harris, T. (1978) *The Social Origins of Depression*, Tavistock, London.

44 Brown, G.W., Harris, T. and Copeland, J.R. (1971) 'Depression and loss', *British Journal of Psychiatry*, 130: 1–18.

45 Brown, R. and Kulik, J. (1977) 'Flashbulb memories', *Cognition*, 5: 73–99.

46 Butler Committee (1975) *Report of the Committee on the Mentally Abnormal Offender (The Butler Report)*, HMSO, London.

47 Caddle, D. and Crisp, D. (1997) *Imprisoned Women and Mothers. Home Office Research Study 162*, London.

48 Carlen, P. (1983) *Women's Imprisonment: A study in social control*, Routledge & Kegan Paul, London.

49 Carlson, V., Cicchetti, D. Barnett, D., and Braunwald, K.G. (1989) 'Disorganised/disoriented attachment relationships in maltreated infants', *Developmental Psychology*, 25(4): 525–31.

50 Catan, L. (1992) 'Infants with mothers in prison', in *Prisoners' Children: What are the issues?* edited by R. Shaw, Routledge, London.

51 Cathcart, F. (1988) 'Seeing the body after death', Editorial, *British Medical Journal*, 297: 997–8.

52 Ceci, S.J. and Bruck, M. (1995) *Jeopardy in the Courtroom: A scientific analysis of children's testimony*, American Psychological Association, Washington, DC.

53 Chimbos, P. (1978) *Marital Violence: A study of interspouse homicide*, R & E Associates, San Francisco.

54 Clarke, A.M. (1981) 'Adoption studies and human development', *Adoption and Fostering*, 10(4): 17–29.

55 Cooper, J., Brown, L. and Christie, R. (1988) *Victim Support: Families of murder victims project*, Victim Support, London.

56 Dalianis-Karanbatzakis, M. (1994) *Children in Turmoil During the Greek Civil War: Today's adults*, Karolinska Institute, Stockholm.

57 Danieli, Y. (1992) 'Child survivors as orphans, offspring and parents', unpublished.

58 Davies, G. (1991) 'Research on children's testimony: implications for interviewing practice', in *Clinical Approaches to Sex Offenders and their Victims*, edited by C.R. Hollin and K. Howells, Wiley, Chichester.

59 Davies, G. (1992) 'Protecting the child witness in the court room', *Child Abuse Review*, 1: 33–41.

60 de Bernières, L. (1994) *Captain Corelli's Mandolin*, Vantage, London.

61 Dent, R.J. (ed.) (1998) *Dangerous Care: Working to protect children*, The Bridge Child Care Development Service, London

62 Department of Health (1995) *Children and Young People on Child Protection Registers, Year Ending 31st March 1994*, Government Statistical Service, London.

63 Dillner, L. (1992) 'Keeping babies in prison', *British Medical Journal*, 304: 932–3.

64 The Disasters Working Party (1991) *Disasters: Planning for a caring response*, HMSO, London.

65 Dyregrov, A. and Raundalen, M. (1992) 'The impact of the Gulf war on children in Iraq', unpublished.

66 Eastman, N. (1997) 'Psychiatric assessment of stress disorders for legal purposes', in *Psychological Trauma: A developmental approach*, edited by D. Black, M. Newman, J. Harris-Hendriks and G. Mezey, Gaskell/Royal College of Psychiatrists, London.

67 Edwards, G., Hensman, C. and Peto, J. (1971) 'Drinking problems among recidivist prisoners', *Psychological Medicine*, 1: 388–99.

68 Emanuel, R. and Mendelsohn, A. (1997) 'Psychodynamic psychotherapy', in *Psychological Trauma: A developmental approach*, edited by D. Black, M. Newman, J. Harris-Hendriks and G. Mezey, Gaskell/Royal College of Psychiatrists, London.

69 Emery, R.E. (1982) 'Interparental conflict and the children of discord and divorce', *Psychological Bulletin*, 92: 310–30.

70 Eth, S. and Pynoos, R.S. (1985) 'Interaction of trauma and grief in childhood', in *Post-Traumatic Stress Disorder in Children*, edited by S. Eth and R.S. Pynoos, American Psychiatric Association, Washington, DC.

71 Eth, S., Silverstein, S. and Pynoos, R.S. (1985) 'Mental health consultation to a preschool following the murder of a mother and child', *Hospital and Community Psychiatry*, 36: 73–6.

72 Fabian, A. (1988) *The Daniel Diary*, Grafton, London.

73 Finkelhor, D., Gelles, R.J., Hotaling, G.T. and Straus, M.A. (1983) *The Dark Side of Families*, Sage, Beverly Hills, CA.

74 Finkelhor, D. and Yllo, K. (1982) 'Forced sex in marriage: a preliminary report', *Crime and Delinquency*, 28: 459–78.

75 Fivush, R. and Hudson, J. (eds) (1990) *Knowing and Remembering in Young Children*, Cambridge University Press, Cambridge.

76 Flin, R. and Spencer, J.R. (1995) 'Annotation: children as witnesses: legal and psychological perspectives', *Journal of Child Psychology and Psychiatry*, 36(2): 171–89.

77 Frederick, C.J. (1985) 'Children traumatized by catastrophic situations', in *Post Traumatic Stress Disorder in Children*, edited by S. Eth and R.S. Pynoos, American Psychiatric Association, Washington, DC.

78 Fristad, M., Jedel, R., Weller, R. and Weller, E. (1993) 'Psychological functioning in children after the death of a parent', *American Journal of Psychiatry*, 150(3): 511–13.

79 Furman, E. (1974) *A Child's Parent Dies*, Yale University Press, New Haven and London.

80 Garmezy, N. and Masten, A. (1994) 'Chronic adversities', in *Child and Adolescent Psychiatry: Modern approaches*, 3rd edn, edited by M. Rutter, E. Taylor and L. Hersov, Blackwell Scientific, Oxford: especially pp. 201–3.

81 Garmezy, N. and Rutter, M. (1985) 'Acute reactions to stress', in *Child and*

Adolescent Psychiatry: Modern approaches, 2nd edn, edited by M. Rutter and L. Hersov, Blackwell, Oxford.

82 Gayford, J. (1975) 'Wife-battering. A preliminary survey of 100 cases', *British Medical Journal*, i: 194–7.

83 Gelles, C. (1990) *Family Violence*, Sage, Newbury Park.

84 Gibson, E. (1975) *Homicide in England and Wales, 1967–1971. Home Office Research Studies No. 31*, HMSO, London.

85 Gillies, H. (1976) 'Homicide in the west of Scotland', *British Journal of Psychiatry*, 111: 1087–94.

86 Goldner, V., Penn, P., Sheinberg, M. and Walker, G. (1990) 'Love and violence: gender paradoxes in volatile attachments', *Family Process*, 29(4): 343–64.

87 Goldstein, J., Freud, A. and Solnit, A. (1980) *Beyond the Best Interests of the Child*, Burnett Books, London.

88 Goldstein, R.D., Wampler, N.S. and Wise, P.H. (1997) 'War experiences and distress symptoms of Bosnian children', *Pediatrics*, 100(5): 873–8.

89 Goodwin, J. (1985) 'Post-traumatic symptoms in incest victims', in *Post-Traumatic Stress Disorder in Children*, edited by S. Eth and R.S. Pynoos, American Psychiatric Association, Washington, DC.

90 Goodyer, I.M. (1990), 'Annotation: Recent life events and psychiatric disorder in school age children', *Journal of Child Psychology and Psychiatry*, 31(6): 839–48.

91 Gorst-Unsworth, C. and Goldenberg, E. (1998) 'Psychological sequelae of torture and organised violence suffered by refugees from Iraq: trauma related factors compared with social factors in exile', *British Journal of Psychiatry*, 172: 90–4.

92 Green, A.H. (1985) 'Children traumatised by physical abuse', in *Post-Traumatic Stress Disorder in Children*, edited by S. Eth and R.S. Pynoos, American Psychiatric Association, Washington, DC.

93 Green, B.L., Korol, M., Grace, M.C., Vary, M.G., Leonard, A.C., Gleser, G.C. and Smitsoncohen, S. (1991) 'Children and disaster – age, gender, and parental effects on PTSD symptoms', *Journal of the American Academy of Child and Adolescent Psychiatry*, 30: 945–51.

94 Greenblat, C.T. (1983) 'A hit is a hit is a hit . . . or is it? Approval and tolerance of the use of physical force by spouses', in *The Dark Side of Families*, edited by D. Finkelhor, R.J. Gelles, G.T. Hotaling and M.A. Straus, Sage, Beverly Hills, CA.

95 Greenland, C. (1990) 'Family violence: review of the literature', in *Principles and Practice of Forensic Psychiatry*, edited by R. Bluglass and P. Bowden, Churchill Livingstone, London.

96 Hafner, H. and Boker, W. (1973) 'Mentally disordered violent offenders', *Social Psychiatry*, 8: 220–9.

97 Hamilton, J. (1990) 'Manslaughter: assessment for court', in *Principles and Practice of Forensic Psychiatry*, edited by R. Bluglass and P. Bowden, Churchill Livingstone, London.

98 Hansard (1991) House of Commons Parliamentary Debates, *Hansard*, 196(157): 190–2.

99 Harris, T., Brown, G. and Bifulco, A. (1986) 'Loss of a parent in childhood and adult psychiatric disorder: the role of lack of adequate parental care', *Psychological Medicine*, 16: 641–59.

100 Harris-Hendriks, J. (1989) 'The health needs of children in care', *Adoption and Fostering*, 13: 43–50.

101 Harris-Hendriks, J. and Williams, R. (1992) 'Annotation: The Children Act 1989', *Newsletter of the Association of Child Psychology and Psychiatry*, 14(5): 213–20.

102 Haskey, J. (1991) 'Ethnic minority populations resident in private households. Estimates by County and Metropolitan Districts of England and Wales', in *Population Trends 63*, HMSO, London.

103 Heiman, M.L. (1992) 'Annotation – putting the puzzle together – validating allegations of child sexual abuse', *Journal of Child Psychology and Psychiatry*, 33(2): 311–29.

104 Herman, J.L. (1992) *Trauma and Recovery: The aftermath of violence – from domestic abuse to political terror*, HarperCollins, New York.

105 Hersov, L. (1990) 'The Seventh Jack Tizard Memorial Lecture. Aspects of adoption', *Journal of Child Psychology and Psychiatry*, 31: 493–510.

106 Hill, O.W. (1969) 'The association of childhood bereavement with suicidal attempt in depressive illness', *British Journal of Psychiatry*, 115: 301–4.

107 Home Office (1970) *Treatment of Women and Girls in Custody*, HMSO, London.

108 Home Office (1990) *Criminal Statistics England and Wales 1989*, HMSO, London.

109 Home Office and Department of Health (1992) *Memorandum of Good Practice on Video-recorded Interviews with Child Witnesses for Criminal Proceedings*, HMSO, London.

110 Hotaling, G.T. and Sugarman, D.B. (1989) 'Intrafamilial violence and crime and violence outside the family', in *Family Violence, Volume II: Crime and Justice: A review of research*, edited by L. Ohlin and M. Toury, University of Chicago Press, Chicago.

111 Jaffe, P.G., Wolfe, D.A. and Wilson, S.K. (1990) *Children of Battered Women*, Sage, Newbury Park.

112 James, H. (1885) *The Princess Casamassima*, reprinted 1988, Heron/Macmillan, London.

113 Jenkins, J.M. and Smith, M.A. (1991) 'Factors affecting children living in disharmonious homes: maternal reports', *Journal of the American Academy of Child and Adolescent Psychiatry*, 29: 160–8.

114 Jenkins, J.M. and Smith, M.A. (1991) 'Marital disharmony and children's behaviour problems – aspects of a poor marriage that affect children adversely', *Journal of Child Psychology and Psychiatry*, 32: 793–810.

115 Johnson, M.K. and Foley, M.A. (1984) 'Differentiating fact from fantasy: the reliability of children's memory', *Journal of Social Issues*, 40: 33–50.

116 Jones, A. (1991) *Women Who Kill*, Gollancz, London.

117 Jones, D.P.H. (1991) 'Working with the Children Act: tasks and responsibilities of the child and adolescent psychiatrist', in *Proceedings of the Children Act 1989 Course. Occasional Paper OP12*, edited by C. Lindsey, Royal College of Psychiatrists, London.

118 Jones, D.P.H. and McQuiston, M. (1988) *Interviewing the Sexually Abused Child*, Gaskell, London.

119 Jones, K.W. (1985) 'Support for grieving kids', *Home Health Care Nursing*, 3: 22–7.

120 Joseph, S., Williams, R. and Yule, W. (1997) *Understanding Post-Traumatic Stress: A psychosocial perspective on PTSD and treatment*, Wiley, Chichester and New York.

121 Kaplan, T. (1997) 'Psychological responses to interpersonal violence: children', in

Psychological Trauma: A developmental approach, edited by D. Black, M. Newman, J. Harris-Hendriks and G. Mezey, Gaskell/Royal College of Psychiatrists, London.

122 Kaplan T. (1998) 'Marital conflict by proxy after father kills mother: the family therapist as an expert witness in court', *Family Process*, 37(4): 479–94.

123 Kaplan, T., Harris-Hendriks, J., Black, D. and Blizzard, B. (1994) 'Children who survive after one parent has killed the other: a research study', in *Children and Violence*, edited by C. Chiland and J.G. Young, Jason Aronson, Northvale, NJ.

124 Kempe, C.H. and Helfer, R.E. (1971) *The Battered Child*, 3rd edn, University of Chicago Press, Chicago.

125 Kendall, P.C. (1991) *Child and Adolescent Therapy: Cognitive-behavioural procedures*, Guildford Press, New York.

126 Kilpatrick, K.L. and Williams, L.M. (1997) 'Post-traumatic stress disorder in child witnesses to domestic violence', *American Journal of Orthopsychiatry*, 67(4): 639–44.

127 Klein, R.G. (1991) 'Parent–child agreement in clinical assessment of anxiety and other psychopathology: a review', *Journal of Anxiety Disorders*, 5: 187–98.

128 Kolvin, I., Garside, R.F., Nicol, A.R., Macmillan, A., Wolstenholme, F. and Leith, I.M. (1981) *Help Starts Here: The maladjusted child in the ordinary school*, Tavistock, London.

129 Kranzler, E.M., Shaffer, D., Wasserman, G. and Davies, M. (1990) 'Early childhood bereavement', *Journal of the American Academy of Child and Adolescent Psychiatry*, 29: 513–20.

130 Langmeier, J. and Matejcek, Z. (1973) *Psychological Deprivation in Childhood*, Halstead Press, New York.

131 Lansdown, R. and Benjamin, G. (1985) 'The development of the concept of death in children aged 5–9 years', *Child Care, Health and Development*, 11: 13–20.

132 Layzer, J.I., Goodson, B.D. and Delange, C. (1985) 'Children in shelters', *Response*, 9(2): 2–5.

133 Lieberman, S. (1978) 'Nineteen cases of morbid grief', *British Journal of Psychiatry*, 132: 159–63.

134 MacAskill, C. (1985) *Against the Odds: Adopting mentally handicapped children*, British Agencies for Adoption and Fostering, London.

135 Macksoud, M. S. (1996) 'The war experience and psychosocial development of children in Lebanon', *Child Development*, 67(1): 70–88.

136 MacLeod, L. (1980) *Wife Battering in Canada: The vicious circle*, Ministry of Supply and Services, Ottawa.

137 Madge, N. (1982) *Families at Risk: Studies in deprivation and disadvantage*, Heinemann, London.

138 Main, M. (1995) 'Attachment: overview, with implications for clinical work', in *Attachment Theory: Social, developmental and clinical perspectives*, edited by S. Goldberg, R. Muir and J. Kerr, Analytic Press, Hillsdale, NJ.

139 Main, M. and Hesse, E. (1990) 'Parents' unresolved traumatic experiences are related to infant disorganised attachment status: is frightened and/or frightening behavior the linking mechanism?', in *Attachment in the Pre-school Years*, edited by M.T. Greenberg, D. Cicchetti and E.M. Cummings, University of Chicago Press, Chicago.

140 Main, M., Tomasini, L. and Tolan, W. (1979) 'Differences among mothers of infants judged to differ in security', *Developmental Psychology*, 15: 472–3.

141 Main, M. and Weston, D. (1982) 'Avoidance of the attachment figure in infancy: descriptions and interpretations', in *The Place of Attachment in Human Behaviour*, edited by C.M. Parkes and J. Stevenson-Hinde, Tavistock, London.

142 Malluccio, A., Fein, E. and Olmstead, K.A. (1986) *Permanency Planning for Children*, Tavistock, London.

143 Malmquist, C. (1986) 'Children who witness parental murder: post-traumatic aspects', *Journal of the American Academy of Child and Adolescent Psychiatry*, 25(3): 320–5.

144 Mawson, D., Marks, I.M., Ramm, L. and Stern, R.S. (1981) 'Guided mourning for morbid grief: a controlled study', *British Journal of Psychiatry*, 138: 185–93.

145 McDermott, K. and King, R.D. (1992) 'Prison rule 102: "stand by your man": the impact of penal policy on the families of prisoners', in *Prisoners' Children: What are the issues?* edited by R. Shaw, Routledge, London.

146 McFarlane, A.C. (1987) 'Posttraumatic phenomena in a longitudinal study of children following a natural disaster', *Journal of the American Academy of Child and Adolescent Psychiatry*, 26: 764–9.

147 McFarlane, A.C. (1989) 'The treatment of PTSD', *British Journal of Medical Psychology*, 62: 81–90.

148 McFarlane, A.C. (1989) 'The aetiology of post-traumatic morbidity: predisposing, precipitating and perpetuating factors', *British Journal of Psychiatry*, 154: 221–8.

149 Mezey, G. and Bewley, S. (1997) 'Domestic violence and pregnancy', *British Medical Journal*, 314: 1259.

150 Mitchell, J.T. (1983) 'When disaster strikes: critical incident stress debriefing', *Journal of Emergency Medical Services*, 8: 36–9.

151 Morgan, J. and Zedner, L. (1992) *Child Victims*, Clarendon Press, Oxford.

152 Morrison Tonkins, S. and Lambert, M. (1996) 'A treatment outcome study of bereavement groups for children', *Child and Adolescent Social Work Journal*, 13(1): 3–21.

153 Mowat, R. (1966) *Morbid Jealousy and Murder. International Library of Criminology, Delinquency and Deviant Social Behaviour. No. 11*, Tavistock, London.

154 Mullen, P. (1990) 'Morbid jealousy and the delusion of infidelity', in *Principles and Practice of Forensic Psychiatry*, edited by R. Bluglass and P. Bowden, Churchill Livingstone, London.

155 Mullen, P. and Maack, L. (1990) 'Jealousy, pathological jealousy and aggression', in *Principles and Practice of Forensic Psychiatry*, edited by R. Bluglass and P. Bowden, Churchill Livingstone, London.

156 Mullender, A. (1996) *Re-thinking Domestic Violence*, Routledge, London.

157 Murch, M. and Hooper, D. (1992) *The Lineaments of Family Justice*, Centre for Socio-legal Studies, University of Bristol.

158 Nader, K., Pynoos, R., Fairbanks, L. and Frederick, C. (1990) 'Children's PTSD reactions one year after a sniper attack at their school', *American Journal of Psychiatry*, 147: 1526–30.

159 Napier, M. (1990) 'The attitude of the courts to posttraumatic stress disorder', *Personal and Medical Injuries Law Letter*, 5(4): 28–31.

160 Napier, M. (1990) 'Posttraumatic stress disorder: the Zeebrugge arbitrations', *Personal and Medical Injuries Law Letter*, 5(5): 37–40.

161 Newman, M. (1997) 'Psychopharmacology', in *Psychological Trauma: A developmental approach*, edited by D. Black, M. Newman, J. Harris-Hendriks, and G. Mezey, Gaskell/Royal College of Psychiatrists, London.

162 Newman, M., Black, D. and Harris-Hendriks, J. (1997) 'Victims of disaster: effects on siblings', *Child Psychology and Psychiatry Review*, 2(4): 140–9.

163 Newman, M., Otvos, B. and Harris-Hendriks, J. (1998) 'Evaluating the risk to children', in *Dangerous Care*, edited by R. Dent, The Bridge Child Care Development Service, London.

164 O'Hara, M. (1995) 'Children and domestic violence', *Highlight*, November 139, National Children's Bureau/Barnardo's.

165 Pagelow, M. (1984) *Family Violence*, Praeger, New York.

166 Parkes, C.M. (1980) 'Bereavement counselling: does it work?' *British Medical Journal*, 281: 3–6.

167 Parkes, C.M. (1985) 'Bereavement', *British Journal of Psychiatry*, 146: 11–17.

168 Parkes, C.M. (1986) *Bereavement: Studies of grief in adult life*, 2nd edn, Penguin, Harmondsworth.

169 Parkes, C.M., Laungani, P., and Young, B. (eds) (1997) *Death and Bereavement Across Cultures*, Routledge, London.

170 Parry Jones, W. (1991) 'Post-disaster morbidity in children and adolescents', unpublished.

171 Parry Jones, W. (1992) 'The impact of disasters on children and adolescents', *Young Minds Newsletter*, 10: 10–12.

172 Pigot, Judge (1989) *Report of the Advisory Group on Video Evidence*, HMSO, London.

173 Press Council (1992) *Code of Practice*, Press Complaints Commission, London.

174 Prins, H. (1990) 'Dangerousness: a review', in *Principles and Practice of Forensic Psychiatry*, edited by R. Bluglass and P. Bowden, Churchill Livingstone, London.

175 Pruett, K. (1979) 'Home treatment of two infants who witnessed their mother's murder', *Journal of the American Academy of Child and Adolescent Psychiatry*, 18: 647–57.

176 Pynoos, R.S. (1992) 'Grief and trauma in children and adolescents', *Bereavement Care*, 11(1): 2–10.

177 Pynoos, R.S. (1996) 'Exposure to catastrophic violence and disaster in childhood', in *Severe Stress and Mental Disturbance in Children*, edited by C. Pfeffer, American Psychiatric Press, Washington, DC.

178 Pynoos, R.S. and Eth, S. (1984) 'The child as witness to homicide', *Journal of Social Issues*, 40: 87–108.

179 Pynoos, R.S. and Eth, S. (1985) 'Children traumatized by witnessing acts of personal violence: homicide, rape or suicide behavior', in *Post-Traumatic Stress Disorder in Children*, edited by S. Eth and R.S. Pynoos, American Psychiatric Association, Washington, DC.

180 Pynoos, R.S. and Eth, S. (1986) 'Witness to violence: the child interview', *Journal of the American Academy of Child and Adolescent Psychiatry*, 25: 306–19.

181 Pynoos, R.S., Frederick, C., Nader, K., Arroyo, W. *et al.* (1987) 'Life threat and post-traumatic stress in school-age children', *Archives of General Psychiatry*, 44: 1057–63.

182 Pynoos, R.S., Nader, K., Frederick, C., Gonda, L. and Stuber, M. (1987) 'Grief reactions in school-age children following a sniper attack at school', *Israel Journal of Psychiatry and Related Sciences*, 24: 53–63.

183 Raine, A., Brennan, P.A., Farrington, D.P. and Mednick, S.A. (1996) *Biosocial Bases of Violence*, Plenum Press, New York and London (published in co-operation with NATO Scientific Affairs Division).

184 Raphael, B. (1982) 'The young child and the death of a parent', in *The Place of Attachment in Human Behaviour*, edited by C.M. Parkes and J. Stevenson-Hinde, Tavistock, London.

185 Raphael, B. (1997) 'The interaction of trauma and grief', in *Psychological Trauma: A developmental approach*, edited by D. Black, M. Newman, J. Harris-Hendriks, and G. Mezey, Gaskell/Royal College of Psychiatrists, London.

186 Raphael, B., Field, J. and Kvelde, H. (1980) 'Childhood bereavement: a prospective study as a possible prelude to future preventive intervention', in *Preventive Psychiatry in an Age of Transition*, edited by E.J. Anthony and C. Chiland, Wiley, New York.

187 Raphael, B., Meldrum, L. and McFarlane, A.C. (1995) 'Does debriefing after psychological trauma work?' *British Medical Journal*, 310: 1479–80.

188 Richman, N. (1997) 'Ethical issues in disasters and other extreme situations', in *Psychological Trauma: A developmental approach*, edited by D. Black, M. Newman, J. Harris-Hendriks, and G. Mezey, Gaskell/Royal College of Psychiatrists, London.

189 Rosenberg, M.S. and Rossman, B.B.R. (1990) 'The child witness to marital violence', in *Treatment of Family Violence*, edited by R.T. Ammerman. and M. Hersen, Wiley, New York.

190 Rosenheim, E. and Reicher, R. (1985) 'Informing children about a parent's terminal illness', *Journal of Child Psychology and Psychiatry*, 26: 995–8.

191 Rowe, J. (1983) *Fostering in the Eighties*, British Agencies for Adoption and Fostering, London.

192 Royal College of Psychiatrists (1975) *Report of the Select Committee on Violence in Marriage*, HMSO, London.

193 Royal College of Psychiatrists (1996) *The Evidence of Children, Council Report CR44*, Royal College of Psychiatrists, London.

194 Rutter, M. (1966) *Children of Sick Parents*, Oxford University Press, Oxford.

195 Rutter, M. (1979) 'Protective factors in children: responses to stress and disadvantage', in *Prevention of Psychopathology: Vol. 3. Promoting Social Competence and Coping in Children*, edited by M.W. Kent and J.E. Rolf, University Press of New England, Hanover, NH.

196 Rutter, M. (1991) 'Services for children with emotional disorders', *Young Minds Newsletter*, 9: 1–5.

197 Rutter, M., Taylor, E. and Hersov, L. (eds) (1994) *Child and Adolescent Psychiatry: Modern approaches*, 3rd edn, Blackwell Scientific, Oxford.

198 Scheeringa, M.S., Zeanah, C.H., Drell, M.J. and Larrieu, J.A. (1995) 'Two approaches to the diagnosis of post-traumatic stress disorder in infancy and early childhood', *Journal of the American Academy of Child and Adolescent Psychiatry*, 34: 191–200.

199 Scott, P.D. (1977) 'Assessing dangerousness in criminals', *British Journal of Psychiatry*, 131: 127–42.

200 Shapiro, F. (1989) 'Efficacy of the eye movement desensitisation procedure in the treatment of traumatic memories', *Journal of Traumatic Stress*, 2: 199–223.

201 Shapiro, F. (1995) *Eye Movement Desensitisation and Reprocessing*, Guildford Press, New York.

202 Shaw, M. (1988) *Family Placement for Children in Care*, British Agencies for Adoption and Fostering, London.

203 Shaw, R. (1987) *Children of Imprisoned Fathers*, Hodder & Stoughton, London.

204 Siegal, D. (1997) 'Memory and trauma', in *Psychological Trauma: A developmental approach*, edited by D. Black, M. Newman, J. Harris-Hendriks, and G. Mezey, Gaskell/Royal College of Psychiatrists, London.

205 Silove, D., Sinnerbrink, I., Field, A., Manicavasagar, V. and Steel, Z. (1997) Anxiety, depression and PTSD in asylum-seekers: associations with pre-migration trauma and post-migration stressors', *British Journal of Psychiatry*, 170: 351–7. Also: Comment, *British Journal of Psychiatry*,171: 394.

206 Silverman, P.R. and Worden, J.W. (1992) 'Children's reactions in the early months after the death of a parent', *American Journal of Orthopsychiatry*, 62: 93–104.

207 Smith, S. (1992) 'Adult domestic violence', *Health Trends*, 24: 97–9.

208 Spencer, J.R. and Flin, R. (1990) *The Evidence of Children*, Blackstone, London.

209 Spitz, R.A. (1946) 'Hospitalisation: a follow-up report', *Psychoanalytical Study of the Child*, 2: 113–17.

210 Steinmetz, S. (1977) *The Cycle of Violence: Assertive, aggressive and abusive family interactions*, Praeger, New York.

211 Steinmetz, S. (1978) 'Violence between family members', *Marriage and Family Review*, 1: 1–16.

212 Steinmetz, S. (1978) 'The battered husband syndrome', *Victimology*, 2: 449–509.

213 Stokes, J. and Crossley, D. (1995) 'Camp Winston', in *Interventions with Bereaved Children*, edited by S. Smith and M. Pennells, Jessica Kingsley, London.

214 Straus, M., Gelles, R. and Steinmetz, S. (1980) *Behind Closed Doors: Violence in the American family*, Anchor Press/Doubleday, New York.

215 Strichartz, A. and Burton, R. (1990) 'Lies and truth. A study of the development of the concept', *Journal of Child Abuse and Neglect*, 7: 177–92.

216 Summerfield, D. (1998) 'The social experience of war and some issues for the humanitarian field', in *Rethinking the Trauma of War*, edited by P.J. Bracken and C. Petty, Free Association Books and Save the Children Fund, London.

217 Szur, R. and Miller, S. (1991) *Extending Horizons: Psychoanalytic psychotherapy with children, adolescents, and families*, Karnac, London.

218 Tanne, J.H. (1992) 'Violence in the US: a health issue', *British Medical Journal*, 304: 203.

219 Tayside Women and Violence Group (1994) 'Hit or miss: an exploratory study of the provision for women subjected to domestic violence in Tayside Region, Dundee', reported in Abrahams, C. (1994) *The Hidden Victims: Children and domestic violence*, NCH: Action for Children, London.

220 Terr, L.C. (1979) 'Children of Chowchilla', *Psychoanalytic Study of the Child*, 34: 547–623.

221 Terr, L.C. (1983) 'Chowchilla revisited: the effects of psychic trauma four years after a school bus kidnapping', *American Journal of Psychiatry*, 140: 1543–50.

222 Terr, L.C. (1991) 'Childhood traumas – an outline and overview', *American Journal of Psychiatry*, 148: 10–20.

223 Terr, L. (1994) *Unchained Memories*, Basic Books, New York.

224 Tizard, B. and Phoenix, A. (1990) 'Black identity and transracial adoption', *New Community*, 15: 427–37.

225 Toufexis, A. (1992) 'Home is where the hurt is. Wife beating among the well-to-do is no longer a secret', *Time*, 130(25): 68.

226 United Nations Children Fund (UNICEF) (1995) *Children of Rwanda*, UNICEF, Kigali.

227 van der Kolk, B. (1987) 'The psychological consequences of overwhelming life experiences', in *Psychological Trauma*, edited by B. van der Kolk, American Psychiatric Press, Washington, DC.

228 van der Kolk, B. (1996) 'Trauma and memory', in *Traumatic Stress: The effects of overwhelming experience on mind, body and society*, edited by B. van der Kolk, A.C. McFarlane and L. Weisaeth, Guildford Press, New York and London: Chapter 12.

229 van der Kolk, B. (1996) 'The body keeps the score: approaches to the psychobiology of PTSD', in *Traumatic Stress: The effects of overwhelming experience on mind, body and society*, edited by B. van der Kolk, A.C. McFarlane and L. Weisaeth, Guildford Press, New York and London: Chapter 10.

230 Van Eerdewegh, M.M., Biere, M.D., Parrilla, R.H. and Clayton P.J. (1982) 'The bereaved child', *British Journal of Psychiatry*, 140: 23–9.

231 Van Eerdewegh, M.M., Clayton, P.J. and Van Eerdewegh, P. (1985) 'The bereaved child: variables influencing early psychopathology', *British Journal of Psychiatry*, 147: 188–94.

232 Vidovic, V. (1991) *The Children's Responses to War and Exile in Croatia*, University of Zagreb, Zagreb, Croatia.

233 Walker, L. (1979) *Battered Women*, Harper & Row, New York.

234 Walsh, E. (ed.) (1998) *Working in the Family Justice System: A guide for professionals*, Jordan, Bristol.

235 Ward, B. and associates (1989) *Good Grief 2*, Cruse, Richmond, Surrey.

236 Weller, E.B., Weller, R.A., Fristad, M.A., Cain, S.E. and Bowes, J.M. (1988) 'Should children attend their parent's funeral?' *Journal of the American Academy of Child and Adolescent Psychiatry*, 27: 559–62.

237 Weller, R.A., Weller, E.B., Fristad, M.A. and Bowes, J.M. (1991) 'Depression in recently bereaved prepubertal children', *American Journal of Psychiatry*, 148: 1536–40.

238 Werner E.E. (1998) *Reluctant Witnesses: Children's voices from the Civil War*, Westview Press, New York.

239 Werner, E.E. and Smith, R.S. (1982) *Vulnerable but Invincible: A study of resilient children*, McGraw Hill, New York.

240 Werner, E.E. and Smith, R.S. (1992) *Overcoming the Odds*, Cornell University Press, Ithaca, N.Y.

241 West, R. (1987) *This Real Night*, Virago, London.

242 Westcott, H. and Jones, J. (1997) *Perspectives on the Memorandum: Policy, practice and research in investigative interviewing*, Arena, Aldershot.

243 White, R. (1998) 'Children and the Law', in *Child Psychiatry and the Law*, 3rd edn, edited by D. Black, J. Harris-Hendriks and S. Wolkind, Gaskell/Royal College of Psychiatrists, London.

244 White, R., Carr, P. and Lowe, N. (1990) *A Guide to the Children Act 1989*, Butterworths, London.

245 Widom, C.S. (1984) 'Child abuse, neglect and adult behaviour: research design and findings on criminality, violence and child abuse', *American Journal of Orthopsychiatry*, 59: 335–67.

246 Widom, C.S. (1989) 'Does violence beget violence? A critical study of the literature', *Psychological Bulletin*, 106: 3–28.

247 Wiklund, N. and Lidberg, L. (1990) 'Alcohol as a causal criminogenic factor: the

Scandinavian experience', in *Principles and Practice of Forensic Psychiatry*, edited by R. Bluglass, and P. Bowden, Churchill Livingstone, London.

248 Wilczynski, A. (1997) *Child Homicide*, Oxford University Press, Oxford.

249 Wilkinson, C. (1988) 'The post-release experience of female prisoners', in *Women and the Penal System*, edited by A. Morris and C. Wilkinson, Institute of Criminology, Cambridge.

250 Wilson S.A., Becker, L.A. and Tinker, R.H. (1995) 'Eye movement desensitisation and reprocessing (EMDR) treatment for psychologically traumatised individuals', *Journal of Consulting and Clinical Psychology*, 63(6): 928–37.

251 Wolfe, D.A., Jaffe, P., Wilson, S.K. and Zak, L. (1985) 'Children of battered women: the relation of child behaviour to family violence and maternal stress', *Journal of Consulting and Clinical Psychology*, 53(5): 657–65.

252 Wolfenstein, M. (1966) 'How is mourning possible?' *Psychoanalytic Study of the Child*, 21: 93–123.

253 Wolff, S. (1989) *Childhood and Human Nature: The development of personality*, Routledge, London.

254 Wolfgang, M. and Strohm, R. (1956) 'The relationship between alcohol and criminal homicide', *Journal of Studies on Alcohol*, 17: 411–25.

255 Wolkind, S.N. (1979) *Medical Aspects of Adoption and Foster Care*, Heinemann, London.

256 Women's Policy Group (1999) *Review of Principles, Policy and Procedures on Mothers and Babies/Children in Prison*, HM Prison Service, London.

257 Woodrow, J. (1992) 'Mothers inside, children outside: what happens to the dependent children of female inmates?' in *Prisoners' Children: What are the issues?* edited by R. Shaw, Routledge, London.

258 Woolf, H. and Tumin, S. (1991) *Prison Disturbances, April 1990. Report of an enquiry*, HMSO, London.

259 World Health Organization (1978) *International Classification of Diseases, Injuries and Causes of Death (ICD-9)*, WHO, Geneva.

260 World Health Organization (1992) *International Classification of Diseases and Related Health Problems (ICD-10)*, WHO, Geneva.

261 Young, B. and Black, D. (1997) 'Bereavement counselling', in *Psychological Trauma: A developmental approach*, edited by D. Black, M. Newman, J. Harris-Hendriks and G. Mezey, Gaskell/Royal College of Psychiatrists, London.

262 Yule, W. and Gold, A. (1993) *Wise Before the Event: Coping with crisis in schools*, Calouste Gulbenkian Foundation, London.

263 Yule, W. and Udwin, O. (1991) 'Screening child survivors for post-traumatic stress disorders – experiences from the *Jupiter* sinking', *British Journal of Clinical Psychology*, 30: 131–8.

264 Yule, W. and Williams, R. (1990) 'Post-traumatic stress reactions in children', *Journal of Traumatic Stress*, 3(2): 279–95.

265 Zeanah, C.H., and Emde, R.N. (1994) 'Attachment disorders in infancy and childhood', in *Child and Adolescent Psychiatry: Modern approaches*, 3rd edn, edited by M. Rutter, E. Taylor and L. Hersov, Blackwell Scientific, Oxford.

266 Zeitlin, H. (1986) *The Natural History of Psychiatric Disorder in Children, Maudsley Monograph 29*, Oxford University Press, Oxford.

267 Zisook, S. (1987) *Biopsychosocial Aspects of Bereavement*, American Psychiatric Press, Washington, DC.

Name index

Abrahams C. 25, 34
Adshead, G. 222
Ainsworth, M.D.S. 13, 14, 211
Alessi, J.J. 27
Argent, H. 240, 241
Arnold, L. E. 114
Arroyo, W. 12
Ayalon, O. 81

Bailey, S. 157
Balbernie, R. 176
Barnett, D. 14
Barrett, M.L. 213
Becker, L.A. 114
Benjamin, G. 39, 118
Bennathan, M. 218, 220
Berney,T.P. 213
Bewley, S. 25, 26
Bhate, S. 213
Biere, M.D. 42, 44
Bifulco, A. 45
Birtchnell, J. 43, 45
Black, D. 3, 11, 14, 16, 21, 27, 41, 44, 45, 46, 47, 89, 101, 108, 109, 114, 152, 159, 181, 222, 244, 253
Blake, William 55
Blehar, M.C. 13, 14, 211
Blizzard, B. 3
Bohman, M. 103
Boker, W. 58
Boston, M. 112–13
Bowden, P. 57, 61
Bowes, J.M. 43, 48
Bowlby, J. 10, 41, 44, 103
Braunwald, K.G. 14
Brennan, P.A. 237
Brinich, P.M. 85
Brown, G.W. 45, 156, 194

Brown, L. 89
Brown, R. 83
Bruck, M. 186
Burton, R. 186
Butler-Sloss, Lady Justice 188

Caddle, D. 152
Cain, S.E. 48
Canterbury, C. 222
Carlen, P. 108
Carlson, V. 14
Carr, P. 178
Catan, L. 152
Cathcart, F. 86
Ceci, S.J. 186
Chimbos, P. 53
Christie, R. 89
Cicchetti, D. 14
Clarke, A.M. 156
Clayton P.J. 42, 44, 98
Cooper, J. 89
Copeland, J.R. 45
Crisp, D. 152
Crossley, D. 46

Dalianis-Karanbatzakis, M. 13, 163
Danieli, Y. 13
Davies, G. 186, 187
Davies, M. 45
de Bernières, L. 163
Delange, C. 22, 27
Dent, R. 10, 25, 34, 59
Dillner, L. 108
Drell, M.J. 15, 16, 243
Dyregrov, A. 13

Eastman, N. 244
Edwards, G. 54

Subject index

abandonment 43, 116, 119, 121
abhorrence 200
'abnormality of mind' 61
absence 44
abuse 14, 133; alcohol 35, 52, 197;
    classical descriptions 34; disclosure of
    25; drug 35, 219; emotional 98;
    physical 22, 24, 37, 53, 109, 196;
    sexual 98, 158; substance 52, 219;
    violence following children into adult
    life 156–7
access visits 77
accident and emergency services 25
'accidents' 52, 71, 72, 85, 86, 114, 161,
    177, 182
accusations 56
aches 28, 70
acting out 83, 139
adaptation 13, 14
adjustment 40
adolescents 43, 95, 109, 110, 113, 130;
    anorexia nervosa 162; early
    psychological interventions 82–4;
    effects of parental death 45; murder
    committed by 157; provocation by 115;
    rebelliousness, sexuality and individua-
    tion 212; referral to mental health
    service 135–6
adoption 28, 67, 71, 103, 121, 122,
    239–41; defined 251; numbers 206;
    witnesses to killing not acknowledged
    176
adult life consequences 154–74
adversities 45, 152
affection 56, 115
aftermath 13, 15, 93–9
age of child 27, 45, 194, 197, 201
aggression 14, 20, 26, 30, 143, 157; boys

prone to 27; differential reinforcement
    of 100; excessive 19; history of 35; in
    therapy 123, 131, 136–7, 138, 139, 140;
    verbal 54
agitation 39, 40
alarm period 9–10
alcohol(ism) 51, 55, 102, 105; abuse 35,
    52, 197; chronic 130; relationship to
    homicide 53–4; young people and 158
alertness 34, 81, 84; hyper- 15, 18
alienation 77, 170
Allen Report (1991) 221, 222
alliances 146, 196
Alzheimer's disease 55
ambivalence 14, 102, 108
American Psychiatric Association 14, 237,
    242, 243, 244
anger 29, 30, 51, 54, 75, 118, 156–7;
    coming to terms with 125; coping with
    146; daughter a focus for 132;
    explosion of 149; foster-mother
    alarmed at own 145; grief exacerbated
    by 85; intense 83; listening to
    expressions of 92; resurgence of 214;
    turned inwards 40; turned to pity 56
anniversaries 40
anorexia nervosa 162
anti-social behaviour 157
anxiety: ability to attribute accurately 44;
    about mother 106; exacerbated 182;
    extreme 212; lower levels of 43;
    making sense of 111; probability of 45;
    severe 157; specific 48
appetite 44
arguments 54, 73; resolving 32; violent
    131, 162
arousal 14, 15, 19, 48; high, symptoms of
    159